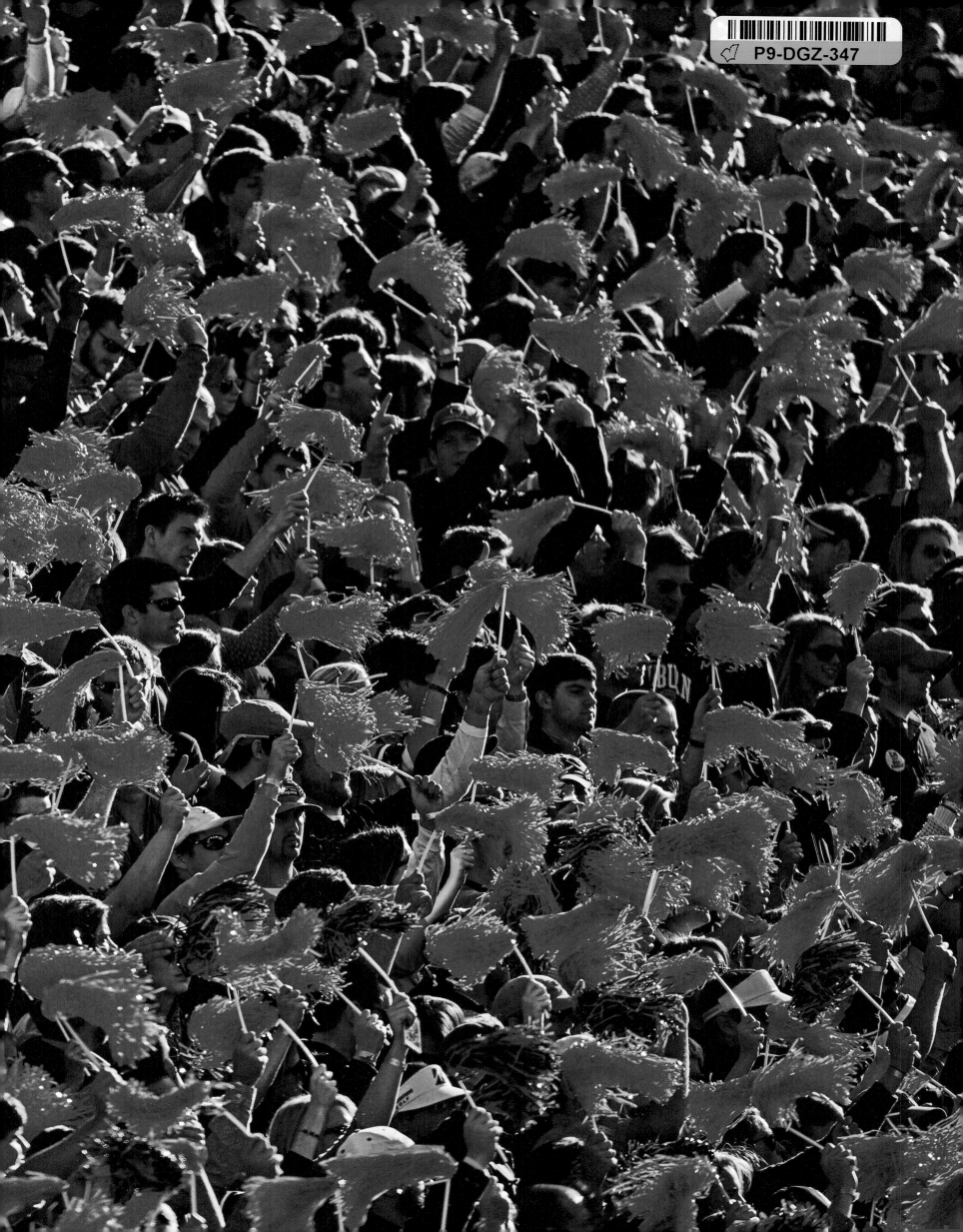

COLLEGE FOOTBALL'S GREATEST

Sports Illustrated

COLLEGE
GREA

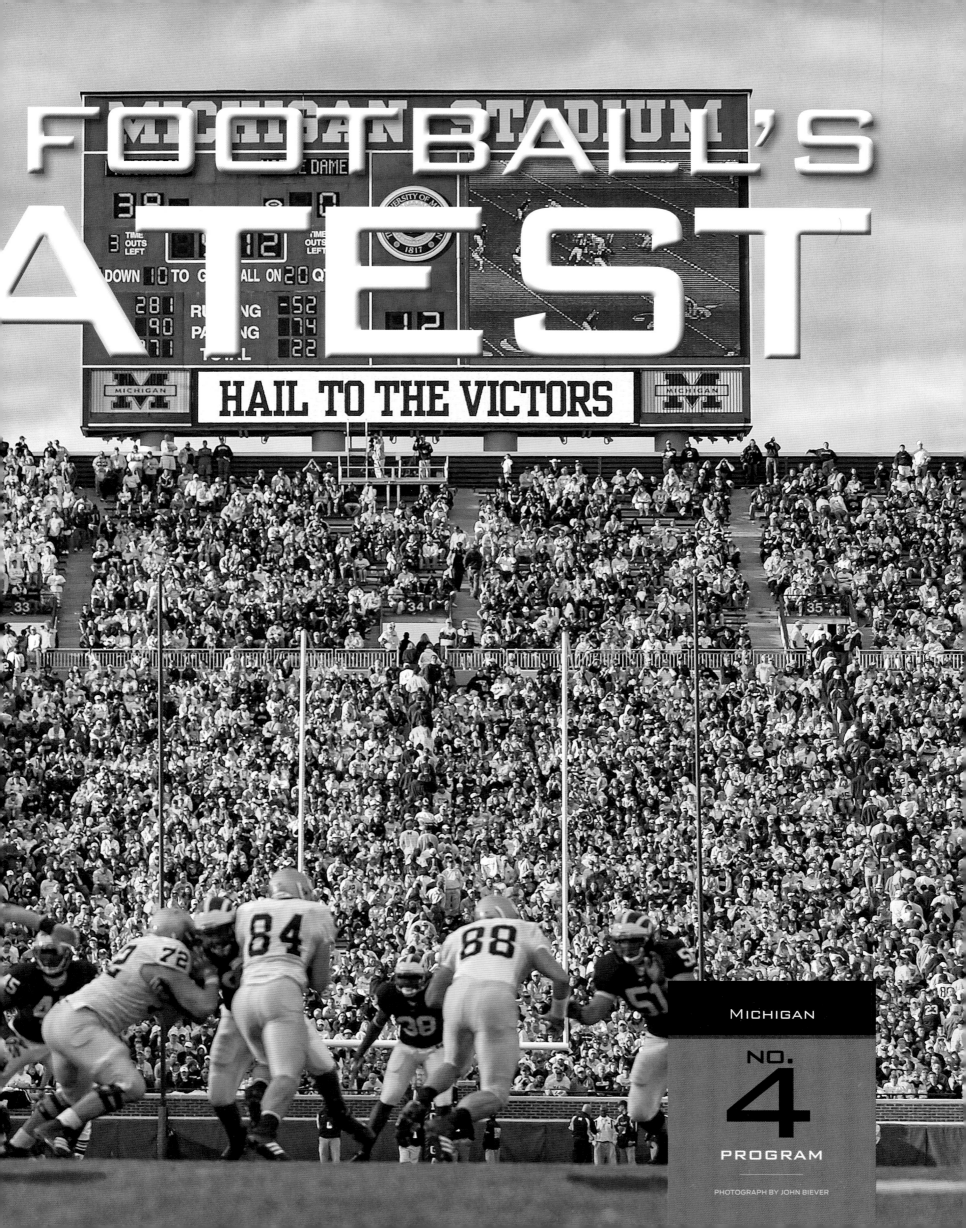

FOOTBALL'S

GREATEST

HAIL TO THE VICTORS

MICHIGAN

NO.

4

PROGRAM

CONTENTS

BILL SYKEN *Editor* / STEVEN HOFFMAN *Creative Director*

CRISTINA SCALET *Photo Editor* / KEVIN KERR *Copy Editor* / JOSH DENKIN *Designer*

STEFANIE KAUFMAN *Project Manager*

WHEN DISAGREEING IS AGREEABLE

BY PHIL TAYLOR

ET US FIRST ACKNOWLEDGE THE DIFFICULTY OF WHAT WE ARE ABOUT TO ATTEMPT. WHAT FOLLOWS IN THESE PAGES IS AN EFFORT TO ANSWER THE UNANSWERABLE, TO COMPARE PLAYERS EVEN WHEN THEY DEFY COMPARISON. ONE OF THEIR FEW CONSTANTS IS THAT THEY ALL EARNED PROMINENT PLACES IN COLLEGE FOOTBALL HISTORY WITH SPECTACULAR CAREERS, BUT NEARLY EVERYTHING ELSE IS A VARIABLE.

ARGUMENTS, FROM WEEKLY POLL STANDINGS TO PLAYOFF SPOTS TO ALL-TIME STATUS, ARE PART OF THE FUN OF COLLEGE FOOTBALL

It's hard to imagine, then, that anyone will look at these lists of the Top 10 players at each position—as well our opinions of the 10 best in several other categories—and agree with every ranking. But debate is one of the linchpins of fandom, particularly in college football, which has always embraced, even depended on, a good argument. What are the Top 25 polls if not a weekly invitation to disagree? This is a sport that has in its not-too-distant past produced co-champions because dueling polls could not arrive at a consensus. Argument has helped make college football great.

Even now, with a four-team playoff allowing the national title to be won on the field instead of by ballot, debates still rage over which teams should be selected as the top four. Consider the final weeks of the 2014 season, when Baylor, Ohio State and TCU were all in contention for the final spot in the four-team playoff field. All three finished that season with one loss, but the selection committee chose the Buckeyes with reasoning that would undoubtedly still start an argu-

ment in Waco or Fort Worth to this day, even though Ohio State was the eventual national champion. The Buckeyes had an edge for that fourth spot, in the eyes of the committee, in part because they won the Big Ten championship outright, while Baylor and TCU were Big 12 co-champs. The Texas schools argued they shouldn't be penalized for playing in a league that didn't have a conference championship game. Round and round the arguments went, as they always do in college football. If there were an objectively "right" answer to be had, the debates would be far less fun.

The same is true of ranking the all-time great players in the sport—the discussion could go on forever. There are any number of obstacles to figuring out a Top 10, but the biggest one is the evolution of the sport itself. The changes in college football, particularly on offense, make it useless to try to draw meaningful comparisons across eras, based on simple statistics. Until the 1990s, the game was played largely on the ground, with the wishbone and other run-oriented formations driving the offensive attack. That's why from 1973 to '88, 13 of the 16 Heisman Trophy winners were running backs. But by 2000, the emphasis switched to the pass, and 13 of the next 16 Heismans went to quarterbacks. Now it's almost impossible for a college team to win big without a sophisticated passing game. Stretch offenses. Five receiver sets. Empty backfields. It has all led to quarterbacks and wide receivers piling up numbers that would have seemed like science fiction a few decades ago.

In 1985, Division I teams threw for an average of 186.1 yards per game. By 2015, that number had risen to 233.2, a 25% increase. It's no coincidence that the NCAA records for most individual yards receiving and passing in a game, season and career have all been set or tied since 1998. We can only wonder, for instance, how many more yards would Boston College's Doug Flutie have generated in a modern-day stretch offense that would have been a perfect fit for his running and throwing skills?

That's not the only problem that comes with evaluating players from different time periods. Consider, for instance, Earl Campbell, the Texas battering ram who pancaked would-be tacklers in the 1970s, and Red Grange, the Galloping Ghost from Illinois who dashed and darted through opponents in the '20s. It isn't just that they had vastly different styles, it's that the bodies of evidence we have to work with in comparing them are anything but equal. With Campbell we have reams of footage to analyze, with slow-motion replays and multiple camera angles. All we have of Grange is a flickering image on old film, making him almost literally a ghost.

Determining which of them was superior requires, among other things, making a judgment about the quality of their competition. The linemen and linebackers Campbell faced were generally bigger and faster than the ones Grange dealt with, which could be seen as a point in Campbell's favor. But Grange became a legend without the benefit of the weight training and nutritional advances that Campbell enjoyed. Advantage, Grange. There are a multitude of what-ifs to consider, educated guesses to make.

Even when players are contemporaries, making compar-

HOW DOES THE QUALITY OF COMPETITION NAVY QUARTERBACK ROGER STAUBACH FACED IN THE 1960S MATCH UP AGAINST WHAT TIM TEBOW DEALT WITH IN THE MODERN SEC? HOW MUCH WEIGHT DO WE GIVE TO THE DIFFERENCE?

isons is a challenge. Think of all the elements to take into account when trying to rank teams during a given season. Simple won-loss records don't reveal enough, because the quality of opponents can vary so widely in college football. Teams with identical records can be vastly different. How did their strength of their schedules compare? What about margin of victory? How did they perform in the most important games? All that only becomes more complicated when you throw in a decade or five of separation. How does the quality of the competition Navy quarterback Roger Staubach faced in the 1960s match up against the opponents Florida's Tim Tebow dealt with in the modern SEC? How much weight do we give to the difference?

Any analysis is helped by data; the more of it, the better the chance of drawing valid conclusions. In baseball, if we want to try to determine where to rank Derek Jeter among the all-time great shortstops, we at least have thousands of at bats and innings to use as a basis for comparisons. Pro basketball provides hundreds of games to analyze over the course of an average career. Even college basketball provides more evidence to work with, compared to college football. A basketball player who stays in school for only one season might play 30 to 35 games. In college football, players come and go in a relative flash. Careers usually last no more than two or three seasons, hardly enough time for players' bodies of work to separate themselves. Larry Fitzgerald only suited up for the Pitt Panthers 26 times.

This removes one of the factors that often used to help determine greatness—longevity. How long was the player able to sustain an elite level of play? Did his athleticism diminish in the later stages of his career, and if so, how well did he adapt to that change? But college football players are never past their prime. There is not enough time to flame out early; nor can they earn points to be earned for consecutive-start streaks, or long-term contributions to the sport.

Not satisfied with the difficulty of ranking players, we decided to tackle a few categories in which there are no objective criteria, matters that are admittedly questions of taste. What is the best rivalry in the sport? Your opinion likely depends on whether you think such confrontations are most compelling when they have a Dixie flavor, like Alabama–Auburn, or when they come with a Northern chill, à la Michigan–Ohio State. The same goes for best game-day experience. Are you a barbecue or bratwurst kind of tailgater? Does a crisp fall afternoon in America's heartland move you, or do you prefer a raucous, sultry night in Death Valley? Reasonable minds can disagree.

In fact, even when there are statistics to analyze and game footage to break down in comparing players, there is always the element of taste, of personal opinion, that creeps in, however subtly, to rankings like these. Your own preferences and background will no doubt affect your opinion of our Top 10s. Do you prefer speedy, graceful cornerbacks who blanket wide receivers, or big, hard-hitting safeties who deliver teeth-rattling hits? The answer may affect how you feel about our slotting of the 10 best defensive backs.

And that is as it should be. Read our rankings and explanations. Sit with them. Ruminate over them. Marvel at our wisdom. Scoff at our foolishness. At some point, perhaps many points, you may want to scream, "What were they thinking?" Do it. There's no sense holding it in.

But know that somewhere, maybe nearby, another reader is reacting the same way—but over completely different choices. A set of rankings that seems crazy to one fan is perfectly rational to another. May the two of you find each other and discuss every page, deep into the night. That's how it should be, because that's college football. Let the debates begin. ■

HOW WE RANKED THEM

These Top 10 lists bring together the expert opinions of seven writers and editors whose knowledge of the game runs deep

FOR THIS BOOK SI WRITERS AND EDITORS WERE polled during the 2015 season and asked to submit Top 10 lists for 15 categories. Votes were tallied with 10 points awarded for a first-place vote, nine points for a second-place vote and so on. Voters were also asked to justify their choices, and those comments appear with each Top 10 selection. In most cases, if one panelist had a player ranked higher than his colleagues, he was asked to speak on that player's behalf.

Panelists were not directed toward any set of nominees or limited by any preset criterion for what constituted all-time excellence. They were simply given categories and asked to select 10 names from the vast history of college football. Panelists were also given the opportunity to create one list on their own, choosing the topic as well as the population of the Top 10. Those personal lists close out the book, along with a compendium of everyone who received a vote in every category. Some names there go back to the early 1900s, which gives a sense of how deep panelists went in their search.

DICK FRIEDMAN *Former SI Senior Editor*

MARK GODICH *SI Senior Editor*

TIM LAYDEN *SI Senior Writer*

AUSTIN MURPHY *SI Senior Writer*

WILLIAM F. REED *Former SI Senior Writer*

ANDY STAPLES *SI Senior Writer*

PETE THAMEL *SI Senior Writer*

HERSCHEL WALKER

NO.
1

RUNNING BACK

PHOTOGRAPH BY HEINZ KLUETMEIER

NO.
3
SINGLE-SEASON
TEAM

PHOTOGRAPH BY NEIL LEIFER

BRIAN BOSWORTH

NO.
2

LINEBACKER

PHOTOGRAPH BY CHUCK SOLOMON

OHIO STATE

NO.
5

GAME-DAY
EXPERIENCE

PHOTOGRAPH BY MATTHEW EMMMONS/
USA TODAY SPORTS

Sports Illustrated

COLLEGE
GRE

FOOTBALL'S
ATEST

10 THE

BEST QUARTERBACKS

IF YOU NEED PROOF THAT COLLEGE FOOTBALL IS A DIFFERENT GAME THAN ITS PRO COUNTERPART, LOOK NO FURTHER THAN THIS LIST OF TOP QUARTERBACKS. ONLY TWO, PEYTON MANNING AND SAMMY BAUGH, ALSO MADE THE TOP 10 IN SI'S NFL'S GREATEST BOOK. BUT FORGET ABOUT GREATNESS: HALF THE PLAYERS HERE WEREN'T ALL THAT GOOD WHEN THEY TRIED THEIR HAND IN THE PROS.

YES, THE LIST INCLUDES PRO FOOTBALL HALL OF FAMERS JOE NAMATH AND ROGER STAUBACH. BUT LOOK AT SOME OF THE OTHERS. FOR A COUPLE OF SEASONS VINCE YOUNG SEEMED AS IF HE MIGHT TRANSFORM FOOTBALL AS A DUAL-THREAT QUARTERBACK, UNTIL HE DIDN'T. MATT LEINART WASHED OUT AFTER SEVEN SEASONS. DANNY WUERFFEL PLAYED SIX SEASONS, THE LAST BEING IN WASHINGTON, WHERE HE AND FORMER COACH STEVE SPURRIER DISCOVERED THEY WERE DEFINITELY NOT IN FLORIDA ANYMORE.

THEN THERE'S TIM TEBOW. HE WAS SO CONVINCING A WINNER IN COLLEGE THAT EVEN AFTER HE WAS TRADED BY THE BRONCOS AND DUMPED BY THE JETS, PATRIOTS AND EAGLES, HE STILL HAD BELIEVERS WHO THOUGHT HE WOULD FLOURISH AS A STARTER. UNLIKELY. BUT THIS WE KNOW: HE WAS A HECK OF A PLAYER AT FLORIDA. NO NFL EXEC CAN EVER TAKE THAT AWAY.

1

TIM TEBOW

" In 2007 Tebow became the first sophomore Heisman winner and played a pivotal role in two BCS title teams ('06 and '08). His legacy will include being the face of the proliferation of the spread offense and redefining collegiate star power. " —PETE THAMEL

▸ 2007, '08 MAXWELL AWARD WINNER
▸ CAREER TOUCHDOWNS: 88 PASSING, 57 RUSHING

AT A TIME when Americans are leaving organized religion in large numbers, Tebow is leading his own personal counterinsurgency. "Every Sunday we have a service for our players and their families," says Gators coach Urban Meyer, who remembers when "three or four kids would show up. Now the room's full." Since Tebow's arrival on campus, and in large part because of him, Florida has launched a series of community-service initiatives. Even as the football program has suffered an embarrassing string of arrests, the number of hours players devote to charitable causes has dramatically increased. "Our community service hours are completely off the charts," says Meyer, who describes his quarterback's influence on the team as "phenomenal."

—*Austin Murphy, SI, July 27, 2009*

Tebow was a triple threat: passer, rusher, leader.

PHOTOGRAPHS BY BOB ROSATO (LEFT) AND JOHN BIEVER

2

ROGER STAUBACH

NAVY 1962–1964

" Roger the Dodger scrambled his way to the Heisman Trophy in 1963, the season he lifted the Middies to a No. 2 ranking. " —DICK FRIEDMAN

▸ LED NCAA IN COMPLETION PERCENTAGE (66.7) IN 1963
▸ 4,253 CAREER YARDS TOTAL OFFENSE

FOR WEEKS the academy has had a ban on Staubach interviews, hiding behind the excuse that a midshipman's routine does not permit them. "More people would like to see Roger Staubach right now than any celebrity," Navy coach Wayne Hardin says, seriously. "If we opened the doors, do you have any idea how many writers and photographers would show up at our practice? A dozen? It would be closer to 5,000." There have been times when not even that many tacklers could have chased Staubach down. With long, powerful strides, Staubach rolls out with deceptive speed. He throws on the run, or backing up. Trapped, he has a startling quickness and a mysterious sense of the profitable direction. And when Staubach gets into trouble he is at his very best. He throws with tacklers tearing off pieces of his jersey or clawing at his legs, or he runs. He can invest every play with unbearable excitement.

—Dan Jenkins, SI, December 2, 1963

Staubach's '63 team was No. 2 in the nation in scoring.

3

Wuerffel still holds the Florida record for passing TDs.

PHOTOGRAPH BY AL TIELEMANS

" No Florida quarterback executed Steve Spurrier's Fun 'n' Gun aerial assault with more precision and panache. For awhile, the Swamp was also known as the Wuerffel House. " —AUSTIN MURPHY

WUERFFEL HAS shown that the level of his game rises at roughly the same rate as his adrenaline. "When things aren't going well, when things are going to hell, everyone looks to Dan," says Bart Edmiston, the Gators' kicker. "He's the calm in the middle of the hurricane."

—*William Nack, SI. October 14, 1996*

▸ 1996 HEISMAN TROPHY WINNER
▸ TWO-TIME NCAA LEADER IN PASSING TOUCHDOWNS

DANNY WUERFFEL

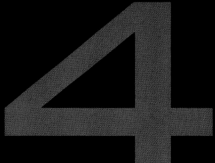

4

TOMMIE
FRAZIER

NEBRASKA 1992–1995

" Though he missed the second half of the 1994 season due to a blood clot in his leg, Frazier returned for the Orange Bowl and rallied the Huskers to victory. He was named MVP of the 1994 and '95 title games. " —MARK GODICH

‣ PLAYED IN THREE NATIONAL
CHAMPIONSHIP GAMES
‣ CAREER TOUCHDOWNS:
43 PASSING, 36 RUSHING

FRAZIER BROUGHT to the game the leadership and relentless toughness that have defined his career. On that memorable 75-yard touchdown run, he broke seven tackles and dragged two Florida defenders several yards before shaking free and rolling down the sideline alone.

—Tim Layden, SI, January 8, 2006

DON'T CALL HIM THOMAS

In an Orange Bowl where he was returning from surgery,
Tommie Frazier answered the taunts of Warren Sapp
with a lethal combination of silence and scoring

BY JOHN ED BRADLEY

OBODY CALLS HIM THOMAS. That's his rule. Tom won't work, either. And make sure you spell Tommie right. Don't go writing it T-O-M-M-Y. You'll make him mad. You'll make him look like he just smelled something dead in the woods.

"Thomas?" a teammate said to him once.

"Hey, I don't answer to that."

"Tom?"

"Sorry. I can't hear you."

T.J. will do, and T. Fraz is all right. But who he is—who he really and truly and don't-you-damn-forget-it is—is Tommie Frazier, quarterback of the Nebraska Cornhuskers.

"Thomas! Hey, Thomas! Where you been?"

It's that noisy Warren Sapp, All-America defensive lineman for the Miami Hurricanes, and, yes, he'll have to be punished. It's early in the fourth quarter of the 1995 Orange Bowl, and Sapp's squad is leading 17–9, what seemed a wide margin until now. Sapp might weigh 285 pounds, and his butt might be so big and charged with life that it resembles a couple of bulldogs fighting in a burlap sack, but now he has infuriated the wrong man.

"Being called Tom or Thomas, that's his Number 1 pet peeve," says running back Damon Benning, Frazier's best friend. "You can change his mood right away by doing that. You can ruin his day. I never understood the significance, but try it on him and see what happens."

"Thomas! Hey, Thomas! Where you been?"

It's a big question, that one, and not the most pleasant for Frazier to have to contemplate here in the Orange Bowl. Frazier was sidelined on Sept. 25 with a blood clot in his right leg and missed the last eight games of the regular season. The clot was dissolved with anticoagulant drugs, but another formed in the same area, and finally surgery was required. To further complicate matters, reserve quarterback Brook Berringer started in Frazier's absence and earned a devoted following among teammates and fans, many of whom have argued that he deserved to lead the Cornhuskers this night in the contest for the national championship.

Frazier won back the starting job in December by outperforming Berringer in bowl practices, but tonight Frazier took the team nowhere on its first possession and he ended the Cornhuskers' second drive by throwing an interception. Since then he's stood on the sideline, waiting for his next shot. Now, early in the fourth quarter, Nebraska is trailing by eight points and coach Tom Osborne is giving him just that, and in cheesy storybook fashion, nothing less than everything is on the line.

"Thomas! Hey, Thomas! Where you been?"

"Where I been?" It's Frazier, piping up at last. "Don't ask me that, don't ask me where I been. Ask me where I'm fixing to go!"

"We're getting it done," Frazier tells his teammates. He's in the huddle, giving each of them a look. "We're scoring now."

When they do just that a couple of plays later, Frazier chooses to cut Sapp a break. He doesn't point a finger or do a dance or repeat their exchange from several minutes earlier. All he does is take the snap and complete a pass for the two-point conversion, tying the score.

Neither does Frazier tell Sapp anything the next time he leads the Cornhuskers on a touchdown drive, this one the game-winner later in the fourth quarter.

As a matter of fact, Tommie Frazier does not speak to Warren Sapp again. He can hear him, though, that obnoxious voice above all others. "He shouldn't have called me Thomas," Frazier says flatly now, his face darkened by the memory. "My name is Tommie."

"It's right there on his birth certificate," says Frazier's mother, Priscilla. "Tommie James Frazier Jr., after his father. "

Frazier learned that he was last year's Orange Bowl MVP in the locker room shortly after the game. His numbers hardly revealed the impact his presence had had on the outcome. He'd completed three of five passes. He'd rushed seven times for 31 yards, 25 of them on a single play. Frazier says, "I was happy to win it, but when I sat down and thought about it, I thought it should have gone to [Nebraska fullback] Cory Schlesinger. Sometimes I think it was a sympathy vote. That bothers me."

The trophy might not have been his to win at all if not for his mother's wise counsel earlier in the year. Frazier was preparing to be operated on when she flew to Lincoln to be by his side. "He was smiling and talking to the coaches and the doctors," she says. "But right away I could read his eyes and tell how much he was hurting. After everyone left the room, I said, 'I can see you're depressed, Tommie. Don't dwell on this.' He said, 'I might as well come back home, Mama, if I can't play ball anymore.'

"I said, 'Number 1, you're here to get your education, and Number 2, to play football, not the other way around. So you concentrate on the schoolwork.' After a while his spirits picked up."

When Frazier went home for spring break, the Nebraska quarterback situation came up only once in conversation. "It'll be just like before the Orange Bowl," Frazier told his mother. "I'll have to win the job back."

"I'm not worried," she replied. "Just go out there and do your best. Remember, Tommie, if you do your best. . . . "

He didn't have to hear the rest. His name is Tommie Frazier, and he's known some things forever. ∎

5

VINCE YOUNG

TEXAS 2003–2005

"Young went 24–1 as a starter in 2004 and '05, playing his best in his biggest game. With the national title on the line in the Rose Bowl, Young accounted for 467 yards of offense and ran for three touchdowns—including the decisive score—against USC." —ANDY STAPLES

> ▸ 2005 MAXWELL AWARD WINNER
> ▸ CAREER TOTALS: 6,040 PASSING YARDS, 3,127 RUSHING YARDS

"IN THE ROSE BOWL against Michigan, Vince Young rushed for 192 yards and four touchdowns, and passed for 180 yards and another score. He brought Texas back from a 31–21 deficit in the last 10 minutes, beginning with his 10-yard touchdown scramble after escaping Wolverines defensive tackle Patrick Massey, who had spun him 360 degrees in the pocket. "How in the world . . . ?" intoned venerable ABC announcer Keith Jackson after Young crossed the goal line. Tampa Bay Buccaneers quarterback Chris Simms, a senior at Texas when Young redshirted as a freshman, watched the Rose Bowl on television, enraptured by the performance of his former understudy. "I knew he had ability," says Simms, "but he's doing things nobody else in college football can do."

—*Tim Layden, SI, August 15, 2005*

Young led Texas to its first NCAA title in 35 years.

PHOTOGRAPH BY JOHN BIEVER

TENNESSEE 1994–1997

Manning became a starter during his freshman year.

PHOTOGRAPH BY JOHN BIEVER

6

PEYTON MANNING

" Manning could have left Knoxville after three years with a degree and the top spot in the NFL draft, but instead stayed for his senior year, won an SEC title and left as the leading passer in conference history. " —TIM LAYDEN

▸ 11,201 CAREER PASSING YARDS, 89 CAREER TDS
▸ 1997 MAXWELL AWARD WINNER

MANNING HAS flabbergasted teammates and coaches with his work ethic. "Peyton lives to be better," says coach Philip Fulmer. "He's like the coach's little son who's 5' 9" and can't break an egg when he throws—except Peyton is 6' 5", with a world of talent."

—Tim Layden, SI, August 26, 1996

7

SAMMY BAUGH

" Slingin' Sam threw for a then-mind-boggling 40 touchdowns for the Horned Frogs. He also was an outstanding defensive back and remains one of the best punters of all time, averaging a nation's-best 43.0 yards in 1935. " —DICK FRIEDMAN

▸ 1936 CONSENSUS ALL-AMERICA
▸ WON SUGAR BOWL AND COTTON BOWL

FOOTBALL WAS better in the '30s because college football was the major league. Pro football consisted largely of second-class citizens waddling around in the baseball parks of blue-collar cities. The pros were pushovers for a Sam Baugh. He led the College All-Stars to victory over the Green Bay Packers.

—*Dan Jenkins, SI, August 31, 1981*

Baugh also played basketball and baseball at TCU.

PHOTOGRAPH BY AP

Despite standing 5' 10", Flutie performed outsized feats.

PHOTOGRAPH BY JERRY WACHTER

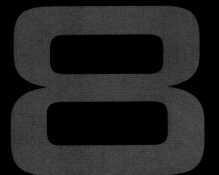

8

DOUG FLUTIE

BOSTON COLLEGE 1981–1984

" Doug Flutie will forever be remembered for his 48-yard heave to Gerard Phelan to propel Boston College to a 47–45 upset of Miami. He also broke the major college passing mark with 10,579 yards. " —PETE THAMEL

▸ 1984 HEISMAN TROPHY WINNER
▸ 67 CAREER TOUCHDOWN PASSES

NOT A SINGLE Division I-A college— save BC—wanted Doug Flutie, and the Eagles didn't want him much. He received the last scholarship the school had to offer in 1981. "We're not hung up on size or anything else around here," says Eagles coach Jack Bicknell. "All I want to know is, 'Can he make the play?' "

—Douglas S. Looney, SI, September 26, 1983

9

MATT LEINART

USC 2002–2005

> " A silky-smooth lefthander, Leinart was at the controls for USC's back-to-back national championships in 2003 and '04 (the latter title was later vacated) and its runner-up finish in '05, throwing for 99 touchdowns. " —TIM LAYDEN

▸ 10,693 CAREER PASSING YARDS
▸ 2004 HEISMAN TROPHY WINNER

PROJECTED AS the possible No. 1 choice in the 2005 draft, he chose loyalty over bucks and came back for his senior year. "I know I could be living in some NFL city right now, maybe being thrown into the mix when I'm not ready," Leinart said in L.A. "Instead, I'm hangin' out with my friends, cherishing my senior year. . . . I'm just like any other college guy." Oh, absolutely, Matt. We all had senior years like yours. Except for needing security to get us around campus; having Lindsay Lohan, Jessica Simpson and Nick Lachey at our birthday parties; doing fashion photo shoots for *GQ* and *Esquire*; appearing on Jimmy Kimmel twice; having our own Internet TV show; hanging out with Maria Sharapova, Wayne Gretzky and Adam Sandler; and being linked to more hot L.A. women than Frederick's of Hollywood.

—Rick Reilly, SI, October 24, 2005

Leinart had three seasons of 3,000-plus passing yards.

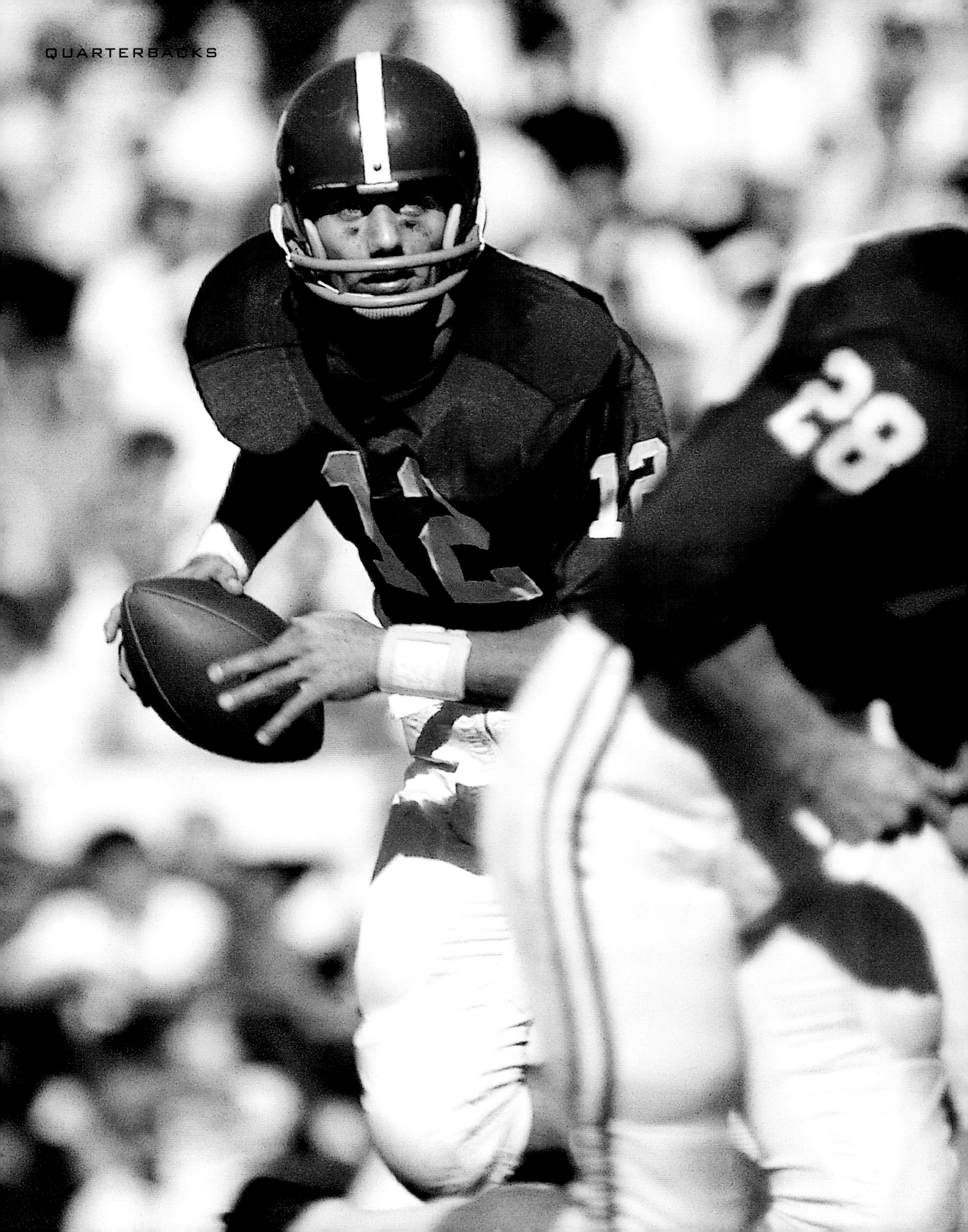
12
12
28

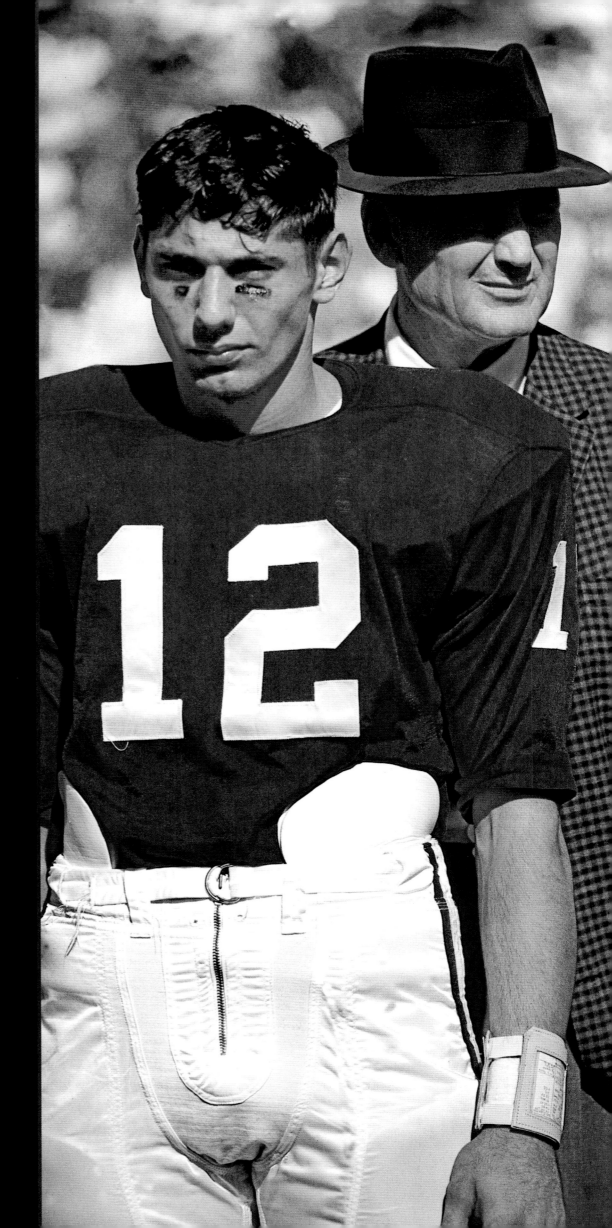

10

JOE NAMATH

ALABAMA 1962–1964

" Hard to believe that a cocky Pennsylvania kid became a folk hero in 1960s Alabama, but that's the unlikely story of Joe Willie Namath, the passing wizard who led Alabama to the 1964 national title. " —WILLIAM F. REED

▸ TIDE WENT 29–4 DURING HIS THREE SEASONS
▸ LED SEC IN PASSING YARDS AND TOUCHDOWNS IN 1962

THAT GEORGIA game was the first fall afternoon anybody outside of Tuscaloosa could marvel at Namath's near balletic jump passes. It was a rout, and Namath basically played just the first half. Of course even if Bear Bryant was somewhat awed by the performance, he wasn't about to yield his own star power. After the game, as the newspaper reporters began to cluster around Namath, Bryant took note and scattered the scrum. "Get away from that popcorn kid," he bellowed. "Go talk to the guys that did the winning." Namath was nearly stung to tears. Linebacker Lee Roy Jordan later explained to Namath that the coach prefers most opinions to come from under his own houndstooth hat. But really, Bryant knew who had done the winning, and it was his popcorn kid.

—*Richard Hoffer, SI Presents, January 17, 2013*

Namath's talents transformed Bear Bryant's offense.

PHOTOGRAPHS BY NEIL LEIFER

THE 10

Best Running Backs

HERE'S TIMING FOR YOU. THE YEAR THE NFL OPENED UP ITS DRAFT TO UNDERCLASSMEN WAS 1990; THE LAST YEAR IN WHICH ONE OF OUR ALL-TIME GREATEST BACKS TOOK THE FIELD WAS TWO YEARS BEFORE, IN '88. BARRY SANDERS WOULD HAVE COMPETED IN '89, HAD HE NOT OBTAINED AN EARLY ENTRY EXCEPTION THE YEAR BEFORE THE FLOODGATES OPENED.

THE ABSENCE OF POST-'88 BACKS ON OUR LIST, THOUGH, HAS MORE TO DO WITH THE INCREASED EMPHASIS ON THE PASSING GAME THAN WITH THE CHANGE IN THE DRAFT. IN FACT, WHILE GREATS SUCH AS ARCHIE GRIFFIN AND TONY DORSETT HAD FOUR-YEAR RÉSUMÉS, MANY OF OUR TOP FINISHERS DID NOT. AMONG THOSE IS HERSCHEL WALKER, WHO SERIOUSLY CONSIDERED CHALLENGING THE DRAFT ELIGIBILITY RULES IN 1982, BEFORE HIS JUNIOR YEAR.

IN MARCH OF 1982 SI RAN A COVER STORY ABOUT THE POSSIBILITY OF WALKER'S SUING TO ENTER THAT APRIL'S NFL DRAFT. A GEORGIA ASSISTANT COACH ARGUED THAT WALKER SHOULD STAY "BECAUSE HE'LL BE PASSING UP THE CHANCE TO BE THE GREATEST COLLEGE PLAYER WHO EVER LIVED." WALKER DID PLAY HIS JUNIOR YEAR, BUT THEN DODGED THE ISSUE OF NFL ELIGIBILITY BY JOINING THE USFL. EVEN WITHOUT A SENIOR YEAR, HE WAS NAMED OUR TOP BACK BY A WIDE MARGIN.

1

HERSCHEL WALKER

GEORGIA 1980–1982

" He was a legend in Georgia before he ever arrived in Athens, but he cemented his status by running over Tennessee's Bill Bates in his first game, and dashing for 1,616 yards as a freshman to help the Bulldogs win a national title. In three seasons, he ran for 5,259 yards and 49 touchdowns. " —ANDY STAPLES

- 1982 HEISMAN TROPHY WINNER
- THREE-TIME CONSENSUS ALL-AMERICA

GIVEN THE intense—some would say fanatic—rivalry that exists between Georgia and Florida in football, Herschel Walker received the ultimate accolade on Saturday. After helping the Bulldogs destroy the Gators 44–0 in Jacksonville, he left the Georgia locker room in the Gator Bowl wearing a white shirt, black tie, black sweater-vest, black socks, neatly pressed black pants, black shoes, red Georgia blazer and a straw hat with an orange-and-green Gator button pinned on it. A Gator button? "A fan gave it to me after the game," Walker explained as a cordon of policemen prepared to lead him out a side door and away from a mob of admirers waiting at the front door. "The guy said that after seeing the game he'd decided to convert."

—*Jack McCallum, SI, November 15, 1982*

Walker was named SEC Player of the Year three times.

PHOTOGRAPH BY RONALD C. MODRA

1

HERSCHEL WALKER

FROM SPORTS ILLUSTRATED
AUGUST 31, 1981

A SINGULAR SENSATION

It took just one season—one game, actually—for the Georgia faithful to realize that Herschel Walker was the kind of football player they had never seen before

BY CURRY KIRKPATRICK

YOU COULD SAY THAT WE become what we are not so much in the sanctuary of the womb or the groves of academe but in that Elysian drive-in joint known as high school. Most everyone went to high school, even a few hockey players. It is there that we were nurtured, our personalities shaped, our bodies structured, our habits and moods and values all having jockeyed for position in the chaotic halls of puberty. High school is enduring. No one is completely delivered from the days of high school.

This is especially true in the case of heroes who learn to be heroes in high school and stay that way. High school nerds can change and turn into real people, but high school heroes aren't permitted the luxury. So why all the hullabaloo over Herschel Junior Walker, 19 and never been hissed? Why such astonishment about his poise, intelligence, charm, graciousness, humility, charisma? Sir John Gielgud once said of Jean Seberg, who came out of little Marshalltown, Iowa, "She had learned to be a star before she became an actress." And so, now, Herschel Walker, the End Zone Stalker.

Walker, the All-America football player, says he runs track better than he plays football. Walker, the world-class sprinter, says he dances better than he sprints. Walker, the jump-splits hoofer, says he spends more time writing poetry than sashaying around the disco floor. But if there is one thing he knows more about than all of this, it is how to be a hero. Herschel Walker, out of little Wrightsville, Ga., learned that before he became anything else.

Time has always been of the essence for heroes. In Wrightsville there was time enough to run for 86 touchdowns and 6,137 yards, 45 and 3,167 of those in his senior year alone, when Johnson County High won the state Class A championship. Current head coach Jimmy Moore remembers the practices: "Track meets," he says. "Run a play—TD. Run a play—TD. I swear Herschel used to let people tackle him so he wouldn't have to run so far."

Where would he go to college? A Clemson man supposedly requested a clandestine meeting with Walker in a graveyard outside of town. Southern Cal coach John Robinson supposedly registered in a hotel, fully prepared to whisk him off to the Pacific Coast; that John Robinson turned out to be a salesman from Huntsville, Ala. Finally, on Easter Sunday, when Walker's decision was relayed to Mike Cavan, the Georgia assistant coach who had virtually lived for six months in Bob Newsome's lakeside cabin while pursuing his quarry, Cavan screamed so wildly his family thought he'd been shot.

Four months later Walker fled his sheltered, teenage kingdom. "It is time to move on and give life a try," he wrote in a poem entitled *It's Almost Gone.* The night before Walker set out on the trail—of whom? Jim Thorpe? Red Grange? Thurgood Marshall?—he took one final drive by the old high school field. He was all alone. The next morning he left for Athens before dawn. He didn't wake his family. It was easier that way.

Is Herschel Walker the first hero ever to ride off into the sunrise? No matter. From his beginnings in the big time, this gentle, poised creature, blessed with such a magnificent body, such immense talent, couldn't seem to escape the circumstances which kept mounting to certify him as mythical. Either that or . . . *this was all planned.*

In the Georgia media guide, first-semester freshmen aren't listed on the depth chart. Under "tailback" last fall there were five other names. During preseason practice Walker moved up to third string, but his timing was off; he wasn't hitting the proper holes and he didn't break one long gainer. Walker showed no consistent power or quickness or assertiveness. There were easy outs, of course. Walker had played in Class A, consisting of the smallest schools in the state. The Georgia varsity was angered by his delay in signing and was ready, gunning to nail him. Defensive lineman Eddie (Meat Cleaver) Weaver: "I just stuck him a couple of serious shots. No whoop-de-do. The man just went down."

As is his wont, Georgia coach Vince Dooley issued daily pessimism pills to any fans who might inquire. The general feeling was that Walker wasn't ready. Privately, Dooley told a friend, "I'm afraid Herschel is just a big, stiff back."

Later, with the full spotlight of the freshman's astonishing season blazing away, an opposing theory gained momentum. It was simply that Walker, the sensitive soul, the pragmatist, the babe from the backwoods who knew the best road, was playing possum.

What happened that first time, that cloudy night of Sept. 6 in Knoxville, and, indeed, what happened on all the rest of Georgia's fairytale Saturdays, furnished no more logical explanation. Walker didn't enter the Tennessee game until the second quarter. He didn't gain his 25th yard until his 11th carry. Then in a span of a little more than seven minutes in the middle of the second half—with the Dogs whimpering and seemingly long gone—Walker took command, carried the ball on eight of 12 plays, gained 53 of Georgia's 91 yards and scored two touchdowns to rally the Dogs from a 15–2 deficit to a 16–15 victory.

The first touchdown run was instantly burned into the souls of Dog fans forever because during the few seconds it took Walker to slant right, cut back and explode 16 yards up the middle, they could see the future—and the future had WALKER MY DOG plastered on bumpers all over the state. As his family, gathered on the front porch in Wrightsville, listened to the game on the radio, Walker beat six different Tennessee defenders, most notably safety Bill Bates, who met him helmet-on and was toppled head-over-fanny backward as easily as if he were an inflatable rubber toy with sand in the base. While Bates was left to wonder if anybody caught the license number, Walker split two more Vols defenders at the goal line and went in standing up.

Dooley would later describe the play as "fantastic, electric. All of a sudden, you just knew. . . . " Center Joe Happe says, "It was stunning. The effect that single run had on our team, I just can't explain it. All of us, we went crazy and played over our heads the rest of the game. [The rest of the season?] There was no way we would lose. Everybody was so psyched."

Ninety-five thousand fans, the largest crowd ever to see a football game in the South, were on their feet not knowing whether to laugh or cry at what they had just witnessed but knowing it was something very special.

There would be other glorious Herschel Walker journeys encompassed in Georgia's perfect 12–0 season. Every week a new wrinkle. For power aficionados there was Walker's 60-yard ramble against Vanderbilt following a play in which he was penalized for a late block. So he got mad and took off, looking for people to blast until he finally, mercifully, found pay dirt. For speed freaks, there was the 76-yard scamper against South Carolina in which three Gamecock defenders had the easy angle to spear Walker over the sideline and into Athens' famous greenery. The trio came up empty. For record-keepers, there was the 65-yarder late in the game with Georgia Tech that broke Tony Dorsett's total yardage mark for freshmen.

Walker closed out the 1980 regular season by rushing for more than 200 yards in three of his last four games. Other numbers were equally staggering. Thirty-five of his 274 carries were for 10 yards or more. Seven of his 15 touchdown runs were for 48 yards or longer. His many records were achieved despite injuries that caused him to miss more than 10 full quarters.

What may be more significant about Walker's extraordinary first year was the effect he had on 99 others, namely the members of the Georgia team whom he turned from a 6–5 crew of stumblebums into national champions partly by showing them how to hang on to his considerable bootstraps. With Walker on their side the Dogs knew they always had a chance against anybody. "I've thought about it a lot," says Happe, "and I guess what Herschel gave us was a sense of image for ourselves. He hardly talked on the field, but his own discipline seemed to diffuse our rambunctiousness. He set a standard of excellence, to try hard all the time, and damn if anybody was going to let up. You knew if you did your job, Herschel would work it out and we'd win. It sounds corny, but I get excited just thinking about him."

Possibly nothing like what happened to Georgia had taken place in college sports since the present junior senator from New Jersey singlehandedly carried a ragtag Princeton basketball team to the NCAA final four in 1965. But Bill Bradley was a senior then. And Bradley failed.

At New Orleans, going for the brass ring against the mighty Fighting Irish, the Georgia offense came up empty; quarterback Buck Belue missed on his first 12 passes, and the Dogs' team yardage—excepting the tailback—amounted to minus 23 yards. On his second carry Walker's left shoulder "subluxated" after a chilling hit from Notre Dame's Bob Crable, and Walker had to leave the game. Georgia trainer Warren Morris said it was the kind of injury that normally knocks a player out for three weeks. On Georgia's next possession Walker went back in. A major part of the Dogs' game plan was to throw screen passes to Walker to counter the Irish rush. No runner had gained 100 yards on Notre Dame all season. But now Walker was ordered not to try to catch a pass, not to stiff-arm and to hold the ball only with his right hand.

Subsequently, half-crippled, Walker ran for 150 yards, scored two touchdowns and led Georgia to a 17–10 victory and its first national championship. ∎

Walker elevated a Bulldogs team that had gone 6–5 the previous season.

MANNY MILLAN

2

ARCHIE GRIFFIN

OHIO STATE 1972–1975

"Griffin remains the only two-time Heisman winner (1974 and '75) in the award's history. In the current era of three-and-done stars and pinball statistics, a repeat winner appears more and more unlikely." —PETE THAMEL

▸ THREE-TIME BIG TEN RUSHING LEADER
▸ CAREER AVERAGE OF 6.0 YARDS PER CARRY

Griffin had a record 31 consecutive 100-yard games.

PHOTOGRAPH BY WALTER IOOSS JR.

GRIFFIN ATTRIBUTES the ricochet effect of his running to a technique he developed as a high school wrestler. When executed to crunching perfection it starts out as a kind of flying shoulder lift and ends up with the defender on his backside and Griffin glancing off for the goal line.

—Ray Kennedy, SI, September 8, 1975

3

BO JACKSON

AUBURN 1982–1985

"Unstoppable and uncatchable, in four seasons No. 34 rambled for 6.6 yards per carry. Bo knew how to find the end zone, scoring 45 career touchdowns. In his senior year, he rushed for 1,786 yards in 11 games on his way to the Heisman Trophy." —DICK FRIEDMAN

- FOUR 200-YARD GAMES IN '85
- HIT .401 AS A JUNIOR FOR AUBURN'S BASEBALL TEAM, ALSO COMPETED FOR THE SCHOOL IN TRACK

IMAGINE AN athlete so gifted that the very abundance of his gifts worked to obscure his greatness. That's a tough concept to latch on to, but consider Jackson's case. "We knew the body was a great talent, but we didn't know he was that great a back in high school," says Auburn coach Pat Dye. And who could tell? At McAdory High in McCalla, Ala., he'd only carry the ball 11 times a game because he was so busy playing every down on defense, returning kicks, kicking off, punting and kicking PATs and field goals. "He didn't pile up the great stats," says McAdory coach Dick Atchison, "because he never came off the field." Jackson says that's not true. "I'd leave the field to put on the kicking shoe," he says. "And I'd leave it to take it off."

—Alexander Wolff, SI, September 5, 1984

Jackson was the definition of an all-around athlete.

4

EARL CAMPBELL

" The Tyler Rose helped guide the Longhorns back to national prominence. "They waited a hundred years for Earl to come along," said Houston coach Bill Yeoman, "and they might have to wait another hundred for another like him to come along." " —MARK GODICH

▸ **1977 HEISMAN TROPHY WINNER**
▸ **1,744 YARDS, 18 TDS IN '77**

AFTER BILLY SIMS of Oklahoma won the 1978 Heisman Trophy, Sooners coach Barry Switzer offered this comparison between Campbell and his own star running back: "Earl Campbell is the greatest player who ever suited up. He's the greatest football player I've ever seen. Billy Sims is human. Campbell isn't."

—Bruce Newman, SI, September 3, 1979

Campbell's drive came from his 34-inch thighs.
PHOTOGRAPH BY RICH CLARKSON

5

O.J. SIMPSON

USC 1967–1968

" Suffice it to say that the Juice, a dazzling combo of speed, power and ankle-breaking moves, is widely considered the greatest tailback in Trojans history. That's a mouthful. His Heisman win was by the most lopsided margin ever. " —AUSTIN MURPHY

- ▸ 1968 HEISMAN TROPHY WINNER
- ▸ TWICE LED THE NCAA IN RUSHING YARDS

A MILD, WARM talkative transfer from City College of San Francisco, Simpson had never really been an endurance runner. Most of his two seasons at CCSF he divided his time between split end and halfback, but still he scored 54 touchdowns, breaking a record set by Ollie Matson. USC coach John McKay was not sure whether Simpson would be a tailback or a flanker or a split end when he recruited him. He found out quickly in spring practice. O.J. attended practice only seven days, partly because he wanted to run on the USC 440-yard relay team and partly because the coaches had learned all they needed to know. "We wanted to see if he could take it inside," said McKay. "We ran him seven straight times in one scrimmage, and that was it. He busted people backward."

—*Dan Jenkins, SI, November 20, 1967*

In '68, Simpson gained a then record 1,709 yards.

PHOTOGRAPH BY NEIL LEIFER

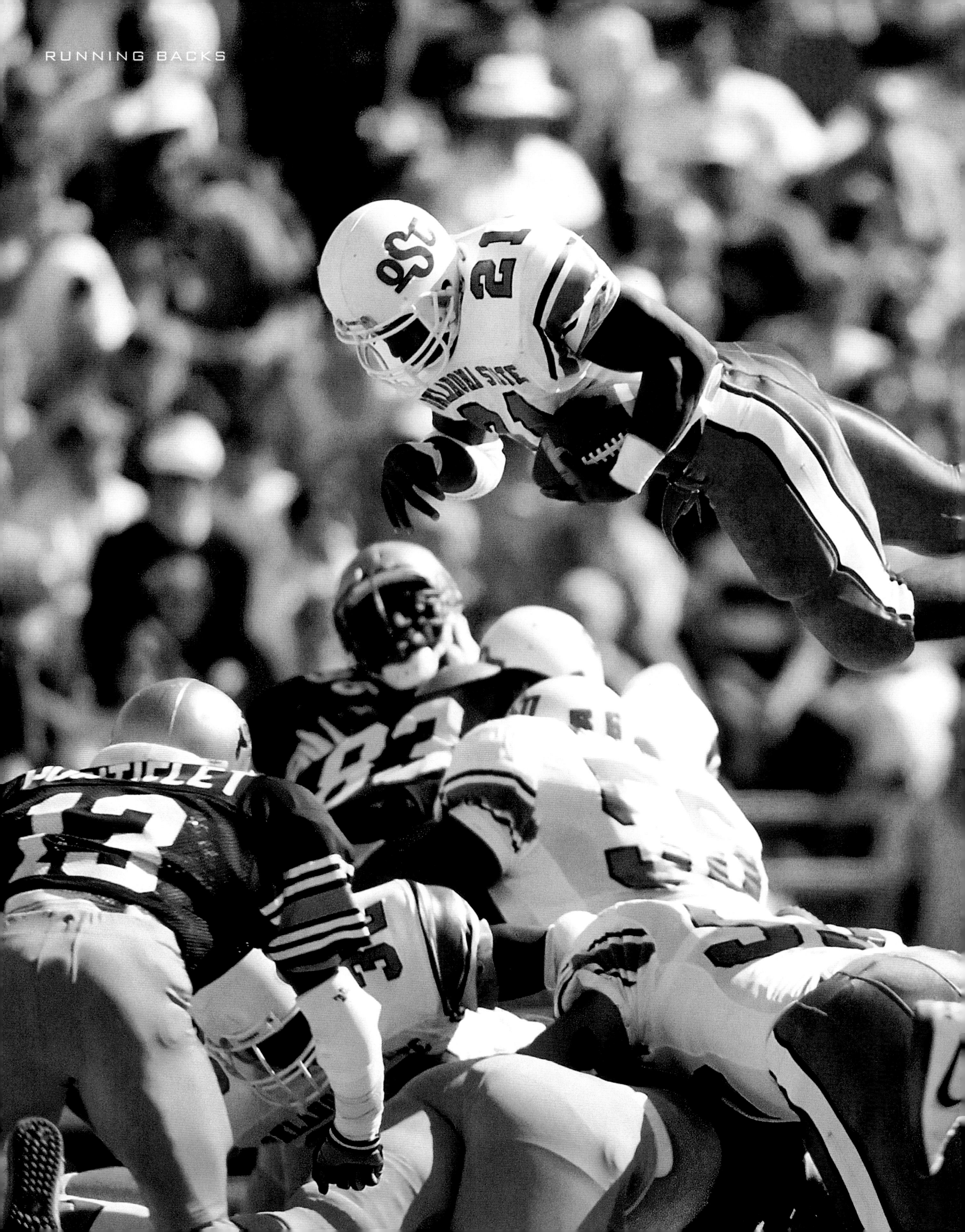

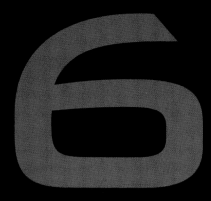

6

BARRY SANDERS

OKLAHOMA STATE 1986–1988

" No one could make tacklers miss like Barry Sanders, who danced through defenses for a record 2,850 yards on 373 carries in his Heisman Trophy season of 1988. " —ANDY STAPLES

▸ 44 TOUCHDOWNS IN 1988
▸ 6.8 CAREER YARDS PER CARRY

SANDERS'S REMARKABLE skills are matched only by his unflagging desire not to be singled out for them. A true junior—he was never redshirted—in his first year as a full-time starter, Sanders had gone from an unheralded replacement for Thurman Thomas, who's now with the Buffalo Bills, to someone whose collegiate highlight film rivals those of O.J. Simpson, Tony Dorsett and Herschel Walker. He's had three 300-yard rushing days, three 200-yard days and six games in which he scored four or more touchdowns. Last week he broke Marcus Allen's single-season rushing mark of 2,342 yards. Sanders isn't the fastest college back in the country, and he's not the biggest. But he combines strength, speed, willpower and an uncanny ability to wriggle, shift and explode into high gear from a dead stop. "He just takes your breath away," says Oklahoma State coach Pat Jones.

—*Rick Telander, SI, December 12, 1988*

Sanders scored at least two TDs in every game in '88.

PHOTOGRAPH BY DAMIAN STROHMEYER

7

TONY DORSETT

PITTSBURGH 1973–1976

" A slippery tailback from the football mecca of Aliquippa, Pa., Dorsett was the first freshman All-America since 1944, and the first major college player to rush for 1,000 yards in four consecutive seasons. He helped Pitt to the '76 national title. " —TIM LAYDEN

- ▸ 1976 HEISMAN TROPHY WINNER
- ▸ 6,256 CAREER RUSHING YARDS

NICE TRY, Penn State. You hoped to stop Tony Dorsett and you thought you could beat Pittsburgh, and even though you didn't come close to accomplishing one or the other, don't feel too bad. No one else this season has stopped Dorsett or his teammates either. As Pitt embarrassed Penn State 24–7, Dorsett concluded his regular-season college career in high gear. By running for 224 yards he wound up with 11 NCAA records, tied three others, set 28 school records and became the first collegian ever to gain more than 6,000 yards. Said Dorsett, "I'm happy." As a result of all this record-smashing (included were most career points, 356, breaking by two Glenn Davis's 1943–46 achievement) Pitt remained undefeated and ranked No. 1 in the nation. Even the skeptics were forced to give Pitt its due.

—Douglas S. Looney, SI, December 6, 1976

Dorsett revived what had been a flagging Pitt program.

PHOTOGRAPH BY MALCOLM EMMONS/USA TODAY SPORTS

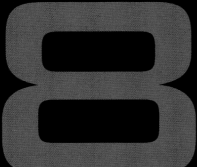

8

SYRACUSE 1954–1956

Brown was named All-America in football and lacrosse.

" Known for his ability to find the hole, shift speeds, and straight-arm tacklers, he made a strong bid to become the first African-American to win the Heisman, but he couldn't get any support outside the East Coast. " —WILLIAM F. REED

▸ CAREER AVERAGE OF 5.8 YARDS PER CARRY
▸ LED NCAA WITH 13 RUSHING TDS (IN EIGHT GAMES) IN '56

BY THE time Brown graduated, Syracuse was eager to recruit black halfback Ernie Davis and then Floyd Little, both of whom wore Brown's number 44. Syracuse won a national title in '59 and now regularly fills the Carrier Dome, and much of that is directly attributable to the heroics of Brown.

—*Steve Rushin, SI, August 16, 1994*

JIM BROWN

9

DOAK WALKER

SMU 1945, 1947–1949

"The Doaker was a do-it-all talent who was instrumental in SMU's moving its home games from a campus site to the Cotton Bowl. A plaque outside the venerable stadium reads, THE HOUSE THAT DOAK BUILT." —MARK GODICH

▸ 1948 HEISMAN TROPHY WINNER
▸ THREE TOP-THREE HEISMAN FINISHES

The 5' 11", 173-pound Walker was swift and slippery.

FOR A WHILE it looked as if TCU had Doak Walker all bottled up. Trap Walker? Fat chance. Putting on his best display of start-and-stop of the season, Walker feinted and sprinted. When TCU finally did find Walker standing still, it was 61 yards downfield—across the goal line.

— *Sports Illustrated, September 19, 1966*

10

RED GRANGE

" The Galloping Ghost rambled to immortality on Oct. 18, 1924, when he scored six TDs against Michigan—four in the first 12 minutes. In 20 games, No. 77 averaged 5.3 yards on the ground with 31 touchdowns. " —DICK FRIEDMAN

▸ THREE-TIME CONSENSUS ALL-AMERICA
▸ SCORED A TD IN 19 OF HIS 20 COLLEGE GAMES

GRANGE PLAYED 57 minutes in a 24–2 defeat of heavily favored Pennsylvania. In ankle-deep mud, he amassed 363 yards and scored on runs of 56, 13 and 20 yards. Laurence Stallings, who had cowritten the war drama *What Price Glory?*, agonized over his portable and finally said, "This story's too big for me. I can't write it."

—*John Underwood, SI, September 4, 1985*

Grantland Rice called Grange "a streak of fire."

PHOTOGRAPH BY BETTMANN/CORBIS

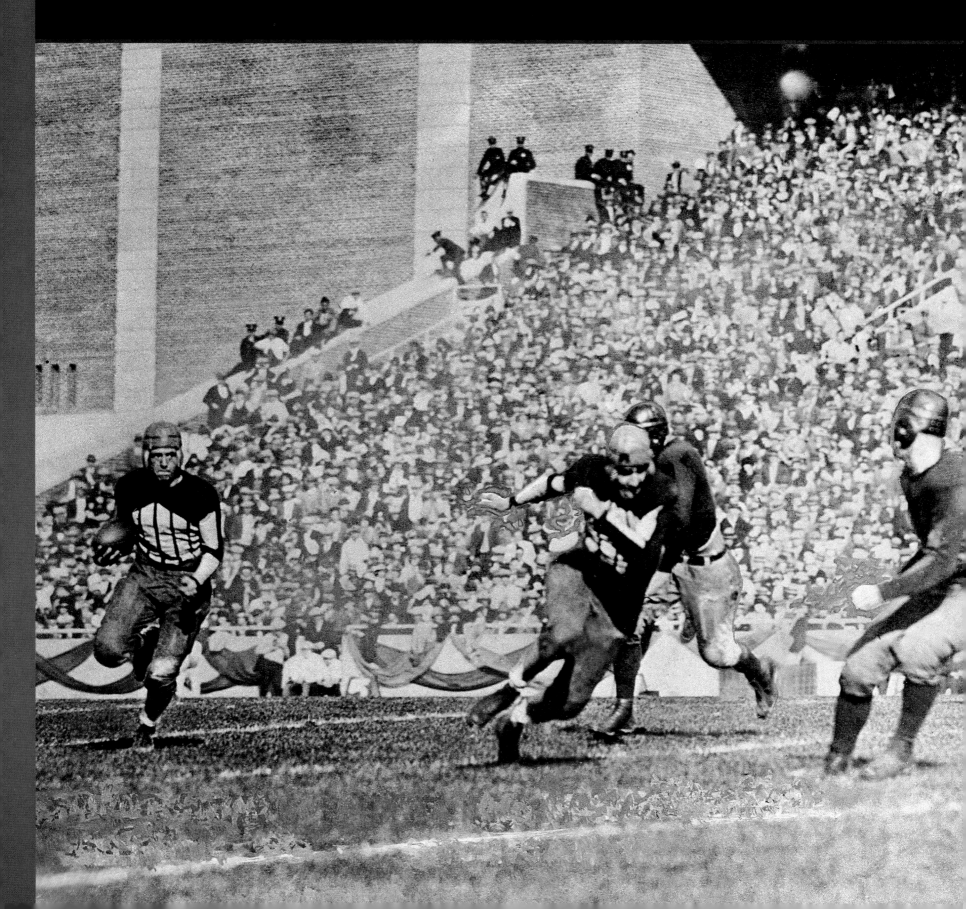

10

THE

BEST WIDE RECEIVERS

THE VOTING FOR THIS CATEGORY PRODUCED A RESULT THAT WAS UNPRECEDENTED, NOT ONLY FOR THIS BOOK BUT ALSO FOR THE FOUR PREVIOUS VOLUMES OF THE "GREATEST" SERIES. A TOP VOTE-GETTER WON A CATEGORY WITHOUT HAVING RECEIVED A FIRST-PLACE VOTE ON ANY PANELIST'S BALLOT.

LARRY FITZGERALD ASCENDED TO THE LEAD POSITION BECAUSE HE WAS ONE OF ONLY TWO RECEIVERS TO BE NAMED ON ALL SEVEN BALLOTS. THE OTHER RECEIVER WHO DID SO, RANDY MOSS, ACTUALLY RECEIVED TWO FIRST-PLACE VOTES, BUT SEVERAL LOW RATINGS. BLAME IT ON THE COMPETITION HE SAW AT MARSHALL.

BUT WHAT HAPPENED IN THE RECEIVERS CATEGORY SAYS LESS ABOUT THE POSITION THAN IT DOES ABOUT THE CHALLENGE OF DETERMINING COLLEGE FOOTBALL'S GREATEST. IN THE PROS, IN WHICH CAREERS RUN LONGER, STATISTICS POINT YOU TO THE OBVIOUS GREATS. IN COLLEGE, IN WHICH MOST PLAYERS START FOR TWO OR THREE YEARS AND COMPETITION CAN VARY GREATLY, STATS ARE LESS DEFINITIVE. IN THE PRO FOOTBALL'S GREATEST EDITION NEARLY EVERYONE HAD JERRY RICE NUMBER 1 (WITH ONE SECOND-PLACE VOTE); IN THIS BOOK THE JERRY RICE OF MISSISSIPPI VALLEY STATE ONLY EARNED ONE TOP VOTE, AND WAS LEFT OFF TWO BALLOTS ENTIRELY.

LARRY FITZGERALD

PITTSBURGH 2002–2003

"As a sophomore at Pitt in 2003, Fitzgerald had a dream season, leading the nation is both receiving yards (1,672) and touchdowns (22) to gain All-America status." —WILLIAM F. REED

▸ PLACED SECOND IN 2003 HEISMAN VOTE
▸ FIRST SOPHOMORE TO WIN BILETNIKOFF AWARD

FITZGERALD IS only modestly fast by the stopwatch, running the 40 in the 4.5-second range (although he promises that the next time he is timed, he will run in the 4.4s). But he has an unreal ability to react to a pass in the air. "It's like the football is a smart bomb and he's a target," says Pitt offensive coordinator J.D. Brookhart. He has the veteran's full arsenal of tricks, like bumping a defender off balance, not with an extended arm (obvious offensive interference), but a strong, coiled forearm (barely noticeable). According to one NFL scout, "Some receivers have physical ability and some guys have common sense [about how to play the game]. He has both." Some of Fitzgerald's physical gifts are simply amazing. During practice, Brookhart fires 15-yard spirals directly at Fitzgerald, who snags the ball one-handed, point-first, without the point reaching the palm of his hand. Try it sometime.

—Tim Layden, SI, December 8, 2003

Fitzgerald had 34 touchdowns in 26 collegiate games.

PHOTOGRAPHS BY SIMON BRUTY (LEFT) AND GEORGE GOJKOVICH/GETTY IMAGES

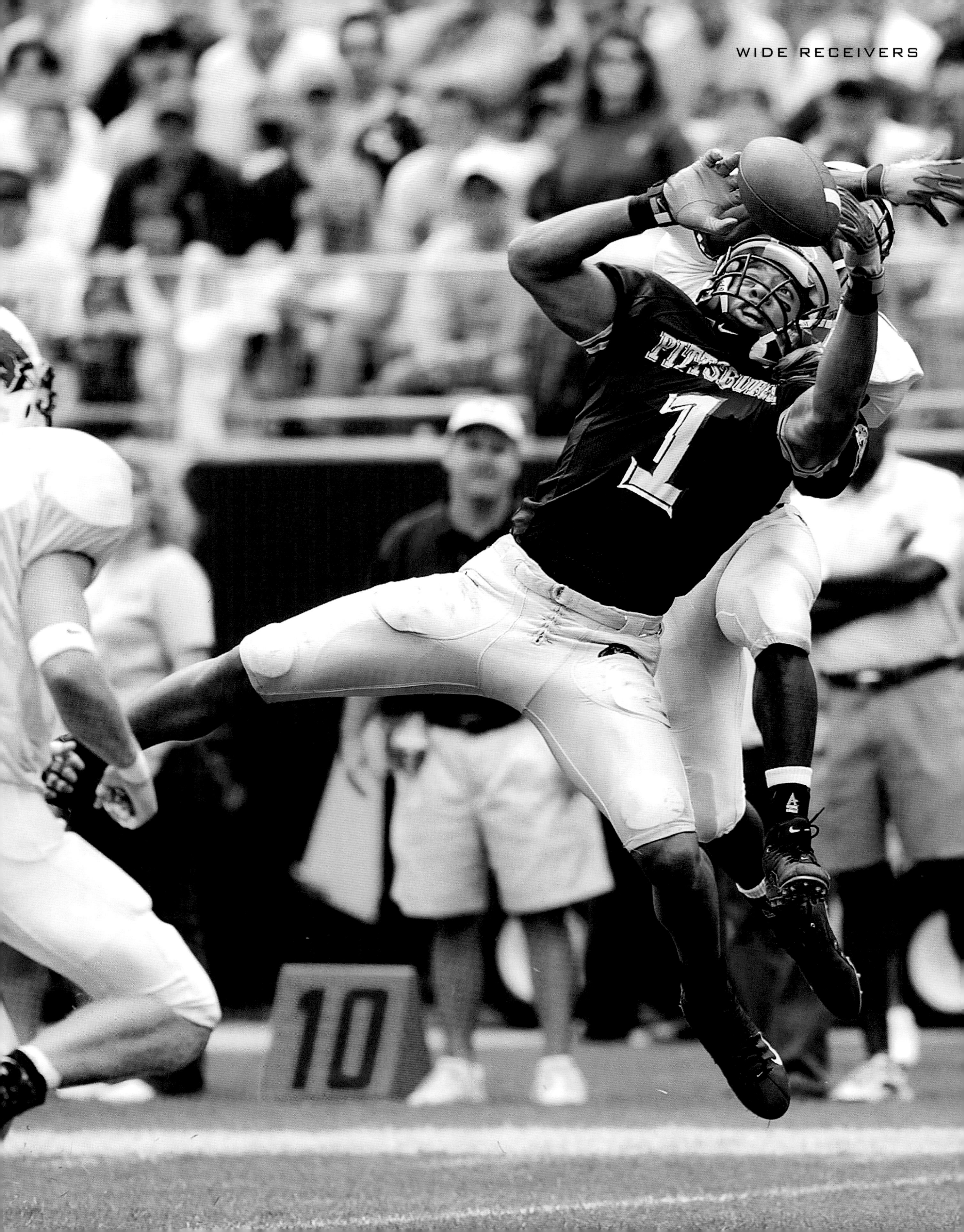
PITTSBURGH
1
10

2

RANDY MOSS

MARSHALL 1996–1997

"After getting booted out of Florida State, where he was a redshirt freshman, Moss wound up torching defenders at Marshall. In '97, his only season in Division I-A, Moss caught 96 passes. In two seasons with the Thundering Herd, Moss racked up 15 100-yard receiving games." —ANDY STAPLES

▸ 1997 BILETNIKOFF AWARD WINNER
▸ IN '97 LED NCAA IN RECEIVING YARDS (1,820) AND TOUCHDOWNS (26)

HE PLAYED at Marshall for two years; by the time he left, he had helped the program make a successful jump from Division I-AA to I-A. "Randy was great with us," says coach Bob Pruett, whose Marshall teams went 15–0 and then 10–3 during the Moss years. "He's the guy who brought the attention. He was the Heisman Trophy candidate. He was the competitor who gave us the edge and helped us get better players. He got it started for Marshall football." Moss's talent and potential were so great that SI, in '99, asked if Moss would "turn out to be the NFL's Michael Jordan?" Instead he has turned out to be the NFL's Allen Iverson, down to the game-breaking ability, controversies, tattoos and cornrows.

—*Karl Taro Greenfeld, SI, May 16, 2005*

The 6' 5" Moss had an advantage on jump balls.

PHOTOGRAPH BY AL TIELEMANS

THERE'S ALWAYS A CATCH

Being bumped from Notre Dame and then Florida State before he caught his first college pass had little effect on the confidence of the supremely athletic Randy Moss

BY S.L. PRICE

EVERYBODY'S WATCHING HIM. Randy Moss can feel the eyes of the lunchtime crowd at the Bob Evans restaurant, the double takes and furtive glances from the men in short sleeves and wide ties. He's got his act down: gray hood over his head, butt slumped in the booth, eyes as lifeless as buttons. Moss is a wide receiver at Marshall University, in Huntington, W.Va., and he figures to be rich before long. He jabs at his toast with a plastic straw.

"If I didn't have this hood on, and they saw us sitting here, people would say an agent picked up Randy Moss and took him to Bob Evans," he says. "That's why I got this hood on. Some people are looking, and some are not. Some know I'm here and you're here, they see a bill and they'll say, 'The agent paid for his food.' Anything can happen."

He shrugs. Moss says he doesn't care about the world's judgments anymore, and it's easy to believe he means it. Certainly no player in college football bears more stains on his name. Two and a half years ago, as a high school senior, Moss stomped a kid in a fight, pleaded guilty to two counts of battery and was sentenced to 30 days in jail and a year's probation. That cost him a scholarship to Notre Dame. He enrolled at Florida State. The following spring he broke probation by smoking marijuana, was kicked out of Florida State and served two more months, in prison. Then last fall, as Moss was on his way to shattering various NCAA and Marshall records, he was charged with domestic battery against the mother of his baby daughter.

Yet Moss is not much interested in image-mending. His first words this morning were that he slept through his communications class. His hair is braided in long rows against his skull, a style he knows will give the wrong impression. "People perceive: Only black thug guys have braids," he says, his voice carrying to a dozen tables. "If I want to grow hair, I'll grow it. If I want to wear lipstick and makeup, I'll do that. God didn't put makeup on this world just for women. They perceive me as a thug? I'm not. I'm a gentleman. I know what I am, my mom knows what I am, most people know what I am. Don't judge me until you know me."

Notre Dame did just that, and Moss will never forgive the school for it. "They didn't take me, because they see me as a thug," he says. "Then Florida State . . . I don't know. You win some, you lose some. That's a loss." Moss pauses, laughs a humorless laugh. "But in the long run I'm going to have the victory. In the long run . . . victorious."

Moss is sure of this because he has sports' trump card: talent. Better, Moss has the kind of breathtaking athletic gifts seen once in a generation. At 6' 5", with a 39-inch vertical leap and 4.25 speed in the 40,

he established himself as West Virginia's greatest high school athlete since Jerry West. Irish coach Lou Holtz declared him one of the best high school football players he'd ever seen. Moss was twice named West Virginia's Player of the Year—in basketball. "He does things you've never seen anyone else do," says Jim Fout, Moss's basketball coach at DuPont High in the town of Belle. Moss also ran track for a while. As a sophomore he was the state champ in the 100 and 200 meters.

Nearly every college wanted him, troubled or not. During Moss's trial for the stomping incident, Kanawha County prosecutor Bill Forbes received a half-dozen calls from football coaches around the country assuring him they could make Moss a better citizen if he was released to their care. Florida State coach Bobby Bowden ultimately got Moss and quickly understood his colleagues' hunger. Early in the fall of 1995, during an impromptu late-night footrace among the Seminoles' fastest players, Moss came in second. When he went through practice the following spring as a redshirt freshman, the defense couldn't stop him from scoring. "He was as good as Deion Sanders," Bowden says. "Deion's my measuring stick for athletic ability, and this kid was just a bigger Deion."

Marshall took Moss in last summer after his chances elsewhere had dwindled to nothing, and he was instantly recognized as the best player on the practice field. He then strolled through Marshall's Southern Conference schedule like a grown man dropped into Pop Warner games. His teammates called him the Freak. In the Division I-AA title game, a 49–29 rout of Montana, Moss caught four touchdown passes to tie the single-season college record of 28 set by Jerry Rice in 1984 as a senior.

Before coming to Marshall last year, football coach Bobby Pruett spent two years as defensive coordinator at Florida watching dominant Gators wideouts such as Ike Hilliard and Reidel Anthony, who went seventh and 16th, respectively, in the first round of the 1997 NFL draft. Neither, Pruett says, has Moss's weaponry. "He's the best athlete I've ever been around," Pruett says.

Already Moss is being touted as a Top 5 pick in next year's draft. "There's no doubt where he'd be placed: very, very high," says Atlanta Falcons scout Boyd Dowler. "Joey Galloway, J.J. Stokes, Keyshawn Johnson—I don't recall anybody who's had his combination of exceptional athletic ability in all these areas. Keyshawn is bigger than Randy, but he's not as talented, not as fast and not as quick."

That kind of praise doesn't impress Moss anymore. "The way I look at it," he says, "God's got a magic wand, and he taps just a few on the head." That he can say this, straight-faced, isn't nearly as disconcerting as the fact that he says it here, in Huntington, in a place about as far from the universe of blue-chip cockiness as you can get. ∎

3

TIM BROWN

" Arguably the most electrifying playmaker ever to thrill a crowd in South Bend, Brown amassed 5,024 all-purpose yards and won games single-handedly. He was the second wide receiver ever to win the Heisman. " —AUSTIN MURPHY

▸ 1987 HEISMAN TROPHY WINNER
▸ SIX CAREER RETURN TOUCHDOWNS

"BROWN LOOKED like Superman. He touched the ball just nine times and gained 173 all-purpose yards. He ran for 80 more yards that were wiped out because of penalties. Not bad for a guy who played only one full quarter after having the nail on his ring finger torn off. Coach Lou Holtz's assessment: "He's the most exciting player I've ever seen."

—*E.M. Swift, SI, November 9, 1987*

Brown was a threat on runs, receptions and returns.

PHOTOGRAPH BY JOHN BIEVER

4

JERRY RICE

MISSISSIPPI VALLEY STATE
1981–1984

" In coach Archie (the Gunslinger) Cooley's hurry-up scheme, Rice put Mississippi Valley State on the map, hauling in 214 passes in his final two college seasons. " —AUSTIN MURPHY

▸ 112 RECEPTIONS, 1,845 YARDS, 27 TDS IN 1984 ▸ 24 RECEPTIONS IN ONE GAME, 17 RECEPTIONS IN TWO OTHERS

JERRY RICE'S hands are big, thick, rough, the kind that convey power even in a gentle introductory clasp. And when people describe one of Rice's catches, they usually finish the simulation with a kind of space age *schhoooop* that cuts off as the imaginary pigskin is sucked neatly into form-fitting fingers. Gloster Richardson, Rice's receiving coach at Mississippi Valley State, lived by his hands for 10 years in the AFL and NFL. They are adorned with two Super Bowl rings from victories in 1970 and '72 with Kansas City and Dallas, respectively. Richardson's admiration for the dexterity in Rice's battle-scarred mitts is almost loving. "They're just beautiful," says Richardson, playing a Rice highlight film in his head. "Real soft, real quiet. Always right on time. He doesn't need to use his body to catch the ball. His hands are just a gift."

—Jaime Diaz, SI, November 14, 1983

Rice caught 50 touchdowns as a Delta Devil.

PHOTOGRAPH BY MANNY MILLAN

The speedy Rodgers made big plays in big games.

PHOTOGRAPH BY RICH CLARKSON/CLARKSON CREATIVE

NEBRASKA 1970-1972

" This gamebreaker thrilled Lincoln throngs with his pass catching and punt returns. The '72 Heisman winner took a then-record seven punts to the house for the Cornhuskers. " —DICK FRIEDMAN

▸ 27 CAREER RECEIVING TDS, 16 CAREER RUSHING TDS

▸ SCORED FOUR TDS, PASSED FOR ANOTHER VS. NOTRE DAME IN 1973 ORANGE BOWL

JOHNNY RODGERS

IN THE Orange Bowl Rodgers took a punt on a sudden bounce 77 yards from the Alabama goal, with red jerseys engulfing him. A swerve to the right, quickly, a turn upfield, a couple of blocks, an alley, and it was burn, baby, burn, right past the Crimson Tide bench.

—Dan Jenkins, SI, January 10, 1972

6

ANTHONY CARTER

MICHIGAN 1979–1982

" Playing in an era when the running game still dominated and for a coach (Bo Schembechler) who believed strongly in power football, A.C., as he was known, caught 161 passes for 37 touchdowns, the latter still the second-most in Wolverines history. " —TIM LAYDEN

‣ TWO-TIME CONSENSUS
ALL-AMERICA
‣ 1982 BIG TEN PLAYER
OF THE YEAR

"IF YOU want a single-word capsulization of Carter," says UCLA coach Terry Donahue, "you spell it p-h-e-n-o-m-e-n-a-l. In caps." Adds Purdue's Leon Burtnett, "We've tried double and triple coverage, and he still catches passes." How? Carter gives a cute shrug. "Maybe it's this hook I have on my finger," he says smiling, holding up a meanly misshapen index finger on his left hand, the result of a high school injury. How does any superior receiver catch balls lesser men can't handle? Carter's hands are of normal size by human—forget football—standards. The ball may come speeding at him like a bullet, yet there is no sense of impact when it meets his hands, nor is there any extraneous movement in his transition from receiver to ballcarrier. It is a physical puzzle that would confound Einstein.

—John Papanek, SI, November 22, 1982

Carter averaged 19.1 yards per catch for his career.

PHOTOGRAPH BY CARL SKALAK

7

FLORIDA STATE 1962–1964

FRED BILETNIKOFF

"The son of Russian immigrants, Biletnikoff played both ways as a junior, leading the Seminoles in both receptions and interceptions. It's no wonder that today the receiver voted the nation's best at the position receives a trophy named for Biletnikoff." —WILLIAM F. REED

- ▸ 1964 CONSENSUS ALL-AMERICA
- ▸ SEVEN 100-YARD RECEIVING GAMES

KEEN OBSERVATION of the opponent is one of the keys to his success. "Too many receivers don't watch closely," Biletnikoff says. "They'll watch what the cornerback does and let it go at that. I take all four guys on my side of the field into consideration. How do they rotate up? How quickly do the linebackers get into the zone, and how deep?"

—*Robert F. Jones, SI, December 13, 1976*

Biletnikoff was FSU's first unanimous All-America.

PHOTOGRAPH BY FLORIDA STATE UNIVERSITY/COLLEGIATE IMAGES/GETTY IMAGES

MICHIGAN 1989–1991

Howard twice led the Big Ten in yards receiving.

PHOTOGRAPH BY JOHN BIEVER

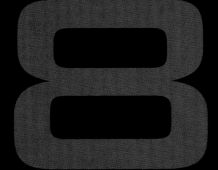

DESMOND HOWARD

" The last receiver to win the Heisman, Howard dazzled with all-around dominance. His diving fourth-down catch in a victory over Notre Dame is one of the iconic moments in Michigan football history. " —PETE THAMEL

▸ 1991 HEISMAN TROPHY WINNER
▸ LED NCAA WITH 19 RECEIVING TDS IN '91

DURING ORIENTATION Howard went with the defensive backs, thinking he might have a better chance of playing at that position. Coach Gary Moeller found Howard sitting with the safeties and tried him at receiver to see if he could catch at all. "We stood there and said, 'Yeah, he can catch the ball,'" Moeller recalls.

—*Sally Jenkins, SI, December 9, 1991*

Johnson seemed to major in aerial acrobatics.

PHOTOGRAPH BY BOB ROSATO

9

" After three seasons Johnson left Georgia Tech as the school's leader in career receiving yards, TD receptions and 100-yard games, and was second in receptions. " —MARK GODICH

▸ 2006 BILETNIKOFF AWARD WINNER
▸ 2006 CONSENSUS ALL-AMERICA

CALVIN JOHNSON

JOHNSON WREAKED havoc against Virginia, catching TD passes of 58 and 66 yards on consecutive pass plays. Next up was Virginia Tech, whose coach, Frank Beamer, deadpanned, "We don't have any defensive backs who are 6' 5", 235." Johnson isn't looking to humiliate anyone; it just works out that way.

—Austin Murphy, SI, October 23, 2006

10

MICHAEL CRABTREE

TEXAS TECH 2007–2008

" Crabtree was the perfect fit in coach Mike Leach's incendiary "Air Raid" passing game offense that helped transform college football in the 2000s. A former high school quarterback, Crabtree caught 231 passes for 41 touchdowns in just two seasons. " —TIM LAYDEN

▸ TWO-TIME BILETNIKOFF AWARD WINNER
▸ NCAA LEADER IN RECEPTIONS, RECEIVING YARDS AND TDS IN 2007

ON THE final play from scrimmage in the best game of the season, it was just plain unfair. There is little doubt that Curtis Brown, a sophomore cornerback making his second start, has a bright future at Texas. But with eight seconds left, with the Longhorns defending a one-point lead over the nation's No. 1 passing team, Brown found himself staring across the line at Michael Crabtree. It must have been a lonely feeling. Afterward the Longhorns' coaches insisted that Brown had not been left on an island with Crabtree, that Tech's best player had been double-covered. Red Raiders quarterback Graham Harrell saw it differently. "They tried to man up Crab!" he shouted on the field after the game, meaning Texas had Crabtree single-covered. "There's not anyone in the country can man up Crab!"

—Austin Murphy, SI, November 10, 2008

Crabtree made the catch that felled Texas in '08.

PHOTOGRAPH BY DARREN CARROLL

THE 10

BEST TIGHT ENDS

MANY OF THE STATISTICS YOU WILL SEE IN THIS SECTION ARE NOT ESPECIALLY IMPRESSIVE TO THE MODERN EYE. OUR TOP TIGHT END, KEITH JACKSON, HAD ONLY 65 RECEPTIONS IN HIS FOUR YEARS AT OKLAHOMA. OTHER GREATS HAD EVEN SMALLER NUMBERS. CONSIDER THE CAREER RECEPTIONS TOTAL OF JOHN MACKEY (27 TOTAL CATCHES), OR, HOLY COW, DAVE CASPER (21). IN THE 2015 SEASON 48 MAJOR-COLLEGE TIGHT ENDS HAD MORE RECEPTIONS THAN THAT, LED BY NORTH CAROLINA STATE'S JAYLEN SAMUELS, WITH 63.

DOES THIS MEAN THAT JAYLEN SAMUELS AND FRIENDS ARE ON TRACK TO ALL-TIME GREATNESS? YOU NEVER KNOW, AND SAMUELS IS ONLY A SOPHOMORE. THE REAL STORY BEHIND THE NUMBERS, THOUGH, IS THE TRANSFORMATION OF THE TIGHT END POSITION. WHEREAS ONCE HE WAS ONCE MORE LIKE AN OFFENSIVE LINEMAN, NOW THE TIGHT END IS PART OF THE RECEIVING CORPS.

MANY OF THE MEN WHO MADE THIS LIST ARE HERE BECAUSE THEY DROVE THAT TRANSFORMATION. MACKEY, DESPITE HIS PALTRY NUMBER OF CATCHES, WAS A DEEP THREAT FOR SYRACUSE, AND THAT HELPED CHANGE THE WAY TIGHT ENDS WERE USED. MIKE DITKA ALSO PUSHED THE EVOLUTION, AS DID OZZIE NEWSOME. AT TIGHT END, THE NUMBERS MATTER LESS THAN THE STORY BEHIND THEM.

1

KEITH JACKSON

OKLAHOMA 1984–1987

" Over his career Jackson caught 62 passes for 1,470 yards; his 71-yard TD grab from Jamelle Holieway in the Orange Bowl helped deliver Oklahoma the 1985 national title. " —PETE THAMEL

▸ TWO-TIME CONSENSUS ALL-AMERICA
▸ VOTED OU'S OFFENSIVE PLAYER OF THE CENTURY

WITH LESS than two minutes remaining, underdog Nebraska was ahead 17–10. Then Sooners coach Barry Switzer flipped through the playbook of his mind and decided, as he said later, "Ah, the hell with it. Let's just out ath-a-lete 'em." At Oklahoma, that usually means get the ball into the immense hands of the 6' 3", 241-pound Jackson. The balletic tight end overpowered cornerback Brian Davis to snare a 17-yard pass in the end zone to tie the game at 17–17 with 1:22 left. A minute later, Jackson outfinessed defensive end Broderick Thomas on a twisting, one-handed, juggling catch along the sideline for a 41-yard gain. That spectacular grab set up Tim Lashar's 31-yard winning field goal. "I guess it came down to the biggest, strongest and fastest person just playing his game," said Jackson who, with only 14 receptions all year, is still considered the most gifted tight end in the country.

—Jaime Diaz, SI, December 1, 1986

Jackson shone despite playing in a run-heavy offense.

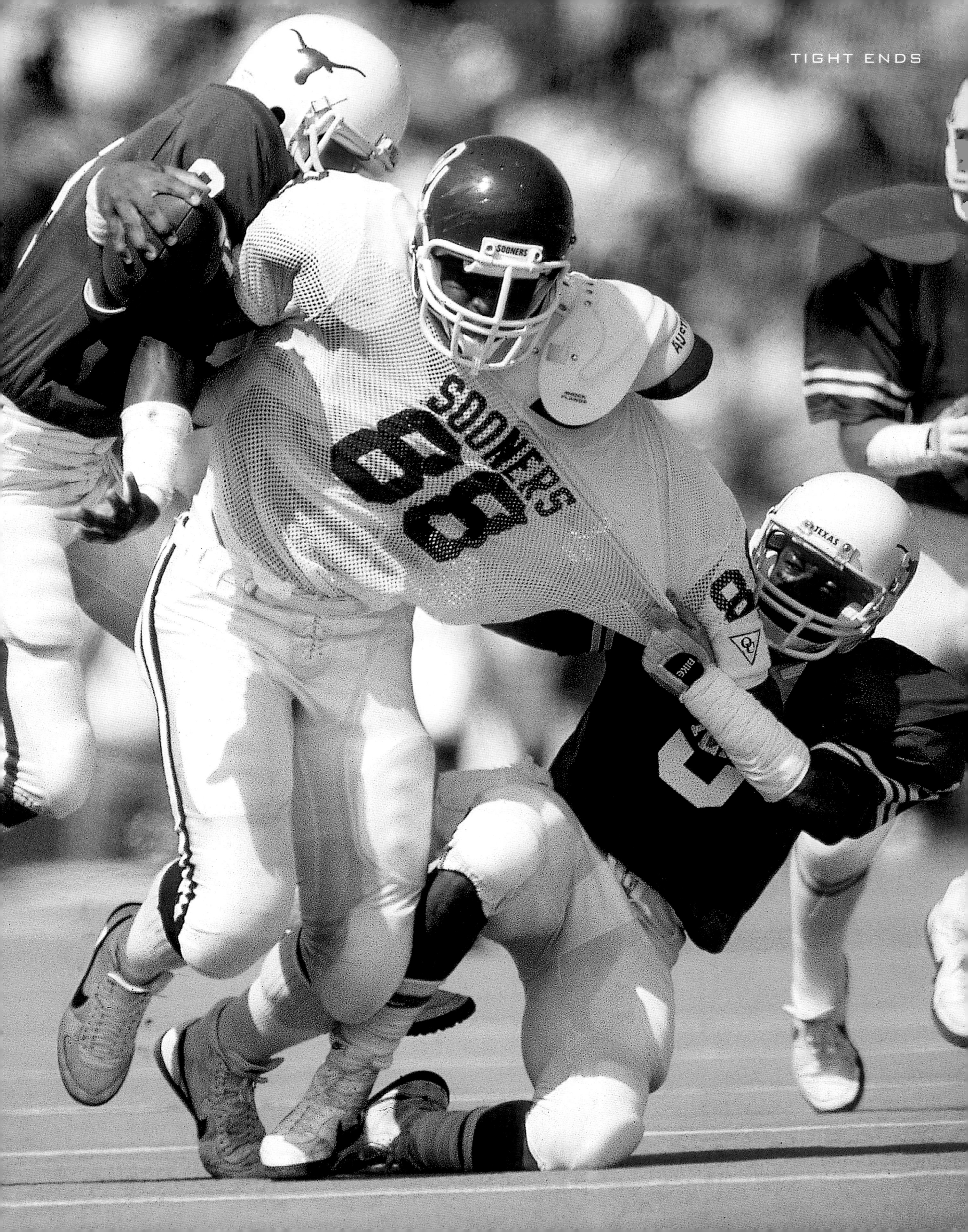
SOONERS
SOONERS
88
TEXAS

2

MIKE DITKA

PITTSBURGH 1958–1960

" The fiery Ditka stamped himself as a forerunner of the modern tight end. Iron Mike was the Panthers' leading receiver in all three of his collegiate seasons, a superb punter and a rugged presence on defense. " —DICK FRIEDMAN

▸ 1960 CONSENSUS ALL-AMERICA ▸ 45 CAREER CATCHES FOR 730 YARDS, SEVEN TOUCHDOWNS

"I WASN'T always the best, but nobody worked harder," says Ditka. "One-on-one. You and me. Let's see who's tougher. I lived for competition. Every game was a personal affront. Everything in my life was based on beating the other guy." At Pitt sometimes it didn't matter if the other guy was on his side. Ditka was a manic practice player who once charged blindly into a solid steel blocking sled, knocking both himself and the sled cold. It got so the Panthers coaches couldn't scrimmage Ditka during the week; he played every Wednesday as if it were Saturday. In Ditka's senior year, Pittsburgh went 4-3-3 with two of the losses by one point and three home games ending in brawls; the Panthers were seven points away from 9–1, 19 away from a perfect season. Ditka became so frustrated that year that he once punched out two teammates in a huddle.

—*Curry Kirkpatrick, SI, December 16, 1985*

Ditka also played baseball and basketball at Pitt.

PHOTOGRAPH BY WALTER STEIN/AP

KELLEN WINSLOW

MISSOURI 1976–1978

" Tight ends were used primarily for blocking in the 1970s, but Winslow helped prove they could be productive receivers as well. In three seasons he caught 71 passes for 1,089 yards and 10 touchdowns. " —ANDY STAPLES

▸ 1978 CONSENSUS ALL-AMERICA
▸ TWO-TIME ALL-BIG EIGHT
SELECTION

WINSLOW DETESTS the dumb jock image that goes with his size and profession, mainly because it clashes with the egghead image he pursued at East St. Louis (Ill.) High. A star member of the chess club, he played no sports until his senior year (except for baseball as a sophomore), curried his teachers' favor, lived for geography and history classes and cut a social swath so narrow that "nobody even knew I existed." At Missouri, he kept up the bookwork by majoring in counseling psychology. But if Winslow was, in his own words, "a nice quiet kid, a nerd" in high school, he was also a classic late bloomer. Cornelius Perry, Winslow's phys-ed teacher and the East St. Louis football coach, made it his project to get Winslow into pads. "He was a natural athlete, that was easy to see," says Perry, "but he lacked confidence. I had to make him see that there were better things ahead."

—*Rick Telander, SI, September 1, 1982*

Winslow twice led the Big Eight in receiving touchdowns.

CALIFORNIA 1994–1996

Gonzalez averaged 15.9 yards per catch in '96.

PHOTOGRAPH BY RVR PHOTOS/USA TODAY SPORTS

❝ Before he was an NFL All-Pro, Gonzalez showed his rare skills in the college game. A forward on the Cal basketball team, he used his athleticism to beat overmatched linebackers and defensive backs. ❞ —MARK GODICH

▸ 1996 SPORTING NEWS AND FOOTBALL NEWS ALL-AMERICA
▸ 89 CAREER RECEPTIONS FOR 1,302 YARDS

"I WAS AWFUL at football when I was a little kid," Gonzalez says. "I didn't have the aggressiveness. I was big, but I was just a puddin'—everybody pushed me around." At the end of eighth grade, things changed, in part because he found basketball. Basketball gave him confidence.

—*Leigh Montville, SI, December 27, 1999–January 3, 2000*

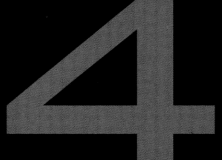

4

TONY GONZALEZ

5

JOHN MACKEY

" College football's top tight end annually receives the John Mackey Award, named for the player who redefined the position. The 225-pounder ran a 4.6 40, making him a deep threat who gained 17.8 yards per catch. " —DICK FRIEDMAN

‣ 27 CAREER CATCHES FOR 481 YARDS, FIVE TDS
‣ RUSHED 58 TIMES FOR 259 YARDS, FIVE TOUCHDOWNS

IN ONE drill he will catch sideline passes while endeavoring to keep his feet inbounds. In another he will [make receptions] while he has any number of neighborhood kids clinging to his arms, legs or shoulders. "If you practice these things," Mackey says, "then they won't bother you when they suddenly come up in a game."
—*Gwilym S. Brown, SI, August 30, 1971*

Mackey's 321 receiving yards in '61 were a school record.

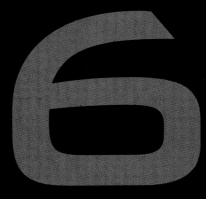

6

OZZIE NEWSOME

ALABAMA 1974–1977

❝ Newsome was recognized as Alabama's best receiver since the immortal Don Hutson in the 1930s, catching 102 passes in four seasons for 2,070 yards. He was named tight end and Hutson wide receiver on Alabama's All-Centennial Team. ❞ —WILLIAM F. REED

▸ 1977 CONSENSUS ALL-AMERICA
▸ AVERAGED 20.3 YARDS PER CATCH FOR HIS CAREER

THE TIDE'S 13–6 victory in the Sugar Bowl did not come easily, but a win against Penn State never does. Bear Bryant was the first to take off his houndstooth hat to the Nittany Lions, and he did it before the game, revealing a seldom-seen bald spot and his superstitious nature. He may have credited his upbringing for not wearing his familiar hat indoors [at the Superdome} but the real reason was he wanted a change of luck. The luckiest charm of all, though, was the Alabama passing game, the best of any wishbone team in the country. Bryant told quarterback Richard Todd to send Ozzie Newsome long, and Newsome faked out freshman defensive back Bill Crummy for a 56-yard gain. Two plays later Todd pitched to Mike Stock, who sped outside Willie Shelby's block for 13 yards and the touchdown.

—*Larry Keith, SI, January 12, 1976*

Newsome alternated between tight end and receiver.

PHOTOGRAPH BY BETTMANN/CORBIS

7

CHARLES YOUNG

"The 6' 4", 228-pound Young was too fast for linebackers to cover and too big for defensive backs to handle. He caught 68 passes for 1,090 yards and 10 touchdowns in his career and helped the Trojans win the 1972 national title." —TIM LAYDEN

▸ 1972 CONSENSUS ALL-AMERICA
▸ LEADING RECEIVER ON '72 TITLE TEAM

"IF I CAN find the gymnasium, I'll show you some fantastic athletes," coach John McKay said. "We've never before had a former basketball star at tight end [Charles Young], a shot-putter at fullback [Sam Cunningham], a flanker who can long-jump [Lynn Swann] and a linebacker who can high-jump 6' 6" [Ray Rodriguez]."

—*Dan Jenkins, SI, November 27, 1972*

Young was nicknamed Tree.
PHOTOGRAPH BY JAMES FLORES/GETTY IMAGES

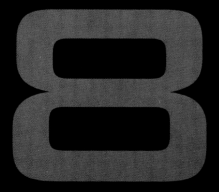

Casper helped the Irish top No. 1 Alabama in 1973.

PHOTOGRAPH BY RICH CLARKSON

8

DAVE CASPER

" So talented was Casper that Ara Parseghian started him at offensive and defensive tackle, and for one game at wide receiver. Casper's transcendent play in the '73 Sugar Bowl sealed an undefeated season and national title for the Irish. " —AUSTIN MURPHY

▸ 1973 CONSENSUS ALL-AMERICA
▸ HONORABLE MENTION
ALL-AMERICA AT TACKLE

THE MOST versatile, and probably the best, athlete on the squad, Dave Casper is tough to ruffle. Last year the coaches told him his hair was too long, so he shaved his head. "They thought I was gung ho," he says. "I shaved it because if I can't wear my hair the way I want, I don't want any."

—Pat Putnam, SI, October 8, 1973

9

JASON
WITTEN

" Witten would blossom in the NFL, but his combination of size and speed at Tennessee helped plant the seed for the flex tight end era. When Witten outran Michigan's entire secondary in the 2002 Citrus Bowl, it was clear he was something special. " —ANDY STAPLES

▸ 2002 ALL-SEC FIRST TEAM
▸ 39 CATCHES FOR 493 YARDS, FIVE TDS IN '02

WITTEN ARRIVED in Knoxville as a defensive end, another reminder of why the tight end spot was long a repository for stiffs. "Everybody would like to have a guy who's 6' 5", 260 and runs a 4.65," says Curt Cignetti, who coaches tight ends for North Carolina State. "But most of them are going to play defense."

—Austin Murphy, SI, December 2, 2002

Witten only became a full-time starter as a senior.

PHOTOGRAPH BY COLLEGIATE IMAGES/GETTY IMAGES

BYU 1981–1983

After BYU, Hudson had only a brief pro career.

10

GORDON HUDSON

" The most productive tight end in college football history, Hudson holds NCAA records at his position for most catches per game (5.4), yards in a single game (259) and career yards per game (75.3). " —PETE THAMEL

▸ TWO-TIME CONSENSUS ALL-AMERICA
▸ 178 CAREER RECEPTIONS, 22 TOUCHDOWNS

WITH BYU leading 40–12 in the fourth quarter, Steve Young was still in the game. "Why run up the score?" asked San Diego State coach Doug Scovil afterward. The final score was 47–12 as Young threw for 446 yards and Gordon Hudson caught four passes to break the NCAA career reception record for tight ends.

—Brooks Clark, SI, October 31, 1983

THE BEST CONNECTION

A strong bond with quarterback Steve Young helped Gordon Hudson define the standard for pass-catching tight ends in an offense that was ahead of its time

BY JACK MCCALLUM

HAVE YOU HEARD THE STORY about the Brigham Young quarterback? Yes, you probably have. You've probably heard many of them. But sit back because here's another. It might be the best yet.

In the pocket he looks like Kenny Stabler, dancing on little cat feet and aiming quick darts over the middle, and he runs like Tony Dorsett once he's out of it. His father was so tough that when he played for the Cougars in the 1950s, he was called Grit. His great-great-great-grandfather was Brigham Young. *The* Brigham Young.

How good is he? "[BYU coach] LaVell Edwards may not admit this," says Gil Brandt, the Dallas Cowboys' vice president of player personnel, "but I think he's the best they've had there. And he's the most accurate passer I've ever seen. Period." Exclamation point.

The quarterback's best friend, meanwhile, has caught more passes for more yards than any tight end in college history. He also holds the tight-end record for most yards in a single game. Says Washington Redskins general manager Bobby Beathard, "He may not be the big blocking type you're looking for, but as a receiver he's got it all."

Their names are Steve Young and Gordon Hudson, respectively. No quarterback–tight end combo in recent years has worked so well for so long, not Mark Herrmann and Dave Young at Purdue (who combined for 67 completions in 1980), not Todd Dillon and Darren Long at Long Beach State (68 in '82), not even Jim McMahon and Clay Brown at BYU (48 in '80). When Young and Hudson finish their college careers after the Holiday Bowl in December, in all likelihood they will have combined for more than 130 receptions in two years, making them arguably the best college quarterback–tight end tandem in history.

Tall (6' 4") and rangy, with unstylishly short hair, Hudson could be on a Latter-Day Saints recruiting poster. He married his high school sweetheart, the former Mindy Carr, in July 1982, and they live in an apartment off campus. Though serious about his role as young husband and soon-to-be father, Hudson is a lot looser about other things, such as his studies. "I just tend to get by on my natural smarts," says Hudson, who will probably graduate a semester late with a degree in physical education. "I'm not proud of it; that's just the way it is." As part of BYU's homecoming festivities before the New Mexico game Hudson finished first in a campus jalapeño pepper–eating contest by consuming 13.

Young, who was best man at Hudson's wedding, is only a shade over six feet and carries a well-muscled 198 pounds. A more polite athlete than Young has yet to appear on the interview horizon, but he's by no means a vanilla personality. He's popular with the other players and has a quick wit, particularly when he's jousting with Hudson. No pair of teammates, in fact, has ever forged more achievement out of more bickering. Women, studies, sports, attitudes—you name it, they fight over it. "A nice conversation between us is an argument," says Young. When they roomed together as sophomores, they even fought over who would answer the phone. "We'd sit there yelling at each other until the damn thing stopped ringing," says Young.

In truth, though, the verbal gymnastics only mask their mutual affection. "We can get in a knockdown, drag-out argument and forget about it as soon as one of us convinces the other," says Hudson.

"Usually. I'm the one who lets myself be convinced," says Young. "He's a hundred times more stubborn than me. But he's right. We can forget about it. There's no tension between us at all afterward."

Which is fortunate, because much of BYU's success has been carved out of off-the-field discussions between Young and Hudson. Hudson talks about feeling "connected" to Young during a game, almost as if "a line" existed between him and his quarterback. That feeling didn't just happen. "We do a lot of mental work together," says Hudson. "We'll go over what I should do if he scrambles a certain way. If I feel a guy will be on my inside, for example, I'll tell Steve that I'll do an inside pressure step, fake outside, then go back inside. Most everybody else would just stay outside. See, we don't do the usual thing."

Rarely does any BYU receiver "do the usual thing." Many of the patterns run by Hudson and the wide receivers are "option routes," that is, they have to read the defense before making their move. One basic pattern can be run three or four different ways, and Hudson, in particular, has become a master at making the right decision. "Gordie is unusual in his total knowledge of our offense," says receivers coach Norm Chow, who calls the plays on game days. "As a staff we are more than willing to listen to his suggestions."

The give-and-take on the Cougars' practice field is unusual in college ball. During a recent workout, for example, quarterbacks coach Mike Holmgren asked Chow what pattern should be run against a certain type of man-to-man. Young and Hudson were working on a new quick route to the outside. Hudson caught the ball but told Young, "A little too fast. Slow it down just a count." They probably argued about it later, but Young slowed it down.

What's eye-catching about BYU's passing drills is how infrequently the ball touches the ground when Young is throwing. That's what captured Brandt's attention when he watched a Cougars practice last year. "Young simply refuses to throw a bad pass," says Brandt. "That's not the case everywhere you go. Even some good quarterbacks throw it all over the place once in a while. Not Young. Can Hudson catch a bad ball? I don't know. He's never had to do it." ∎

THE 10

BEST OFFENSIVE LINEMEN

NEARLY EVERY PLAYER WHO MAKES OUR TOP 10 AT THIS POSITION IS EITHER IN THE PRO FOOTBALL HALL OF FAME OR IS ON THE ROAD TO MEMBERSHIP. JOE THOMAS, THE ONLY ACTIVE PLAYER ON THE LIST, HAS BEEN A PRO BOWL PLAYER FOR EVERY SEASON OF HIS NFL CAREER. WE SEE A HIGHER CORRELATION BETWEEN COLLEGE AND PRO SUCCESS AT OFFENSIVE LINE THAN AT ANY OTHER POSITION IN THIS BOOK.

ONE OR POSSIBLY TWO THINGS ARE GOING ON HERE. IT MAY SIMPLY BE POSSIBLE THAT OFFENSIVE LINE EXCELLENCE TRANSLATES BETTER FROM COLLEGE TO THE NFL BETTER THAN IT DOES AT ANY OTHER POSITION.

THE OTHER IS THAT THE COMET IS BEING JUDGED IN PART BY ITS TAIL—MEANING THAT PRO SUCCESS IS INFLUENCING RATING OF A COLLEGE CAREER. IF ANY POSITION IS PRONE TO THIS IT IS THE OFFENSIVE LINE, WHICH GENERATES NO STATISTICS AND IS THUS THE MOST CHALLENGING TO ASSESS. SO NFL GREATNESS CAN VALIDATE AN UNDERGRADUATE IMPRESSION. CONSIDER IOWA'S ROBERT GALLERY. IN 2003 HE WON THE OUTLAND TROPHY, GIVEN TO THE NATION'S BEST LINEMAN, BUT THE NO. 2 OVERALL PICK OF THE OAKLAND RAIDERS IN '04 WAS ENOUGH OF A BUST THAT HIS HAWKEYE GLORY HAS BEEN WASHED AWAY. HE DID NOT APPEAR ON A SINGLE BALLOT FOR THIS BOOK.

1

JOHN HANNAH

ALABAMA 1970–1972

" Alabama coach Paul (Bear) Bryant once called Hannah "the finest offensive lineman I've ever been around." The 6' 2", 265 pound tackle was a punishing technician. " —TIM LAYDEN

▸ 1972 CONSENSUS ALL-AMERICA
▸ MEMBER OF BOTH THE COLLEGE AND PRO FOOTBALL HALL OF FAMES

THE ABILITY to explode into an opponent and drive him five yards back was what first attracted the recruiters to Albertville, Ala., where Hannah grew up and played his final year of high school ball. It's the first thing you look for, if you're building a running game. Hannah says he always had that ability, but it was his first coach at Baylor School for Boys in Chattanooga, Major Luke Worsham, who taught him how to zero in on a target, to aim for the numbers with his helmet, to keep his eyes open and his tail low. Next came the quick feet. Forget about pass blocking if you can't dance. Worsham helped there too. "For all his size and explosiveness and straight-ahead speed," Patriots GM Jack Kilroy says, "John has something none of the others ever had, and that's phenomenal, repeat, phenomenal lateral agility and balance, the same as defensive backs."

—*Paul Zimmerman, SI, August 3, 1981*

Hannah also competed in wrestling and track at Bama.

2

ORLANDO PACE

OHIO STATE 1994–1996

" Pace mauled Big Ten opponents before becoming the No. 1 overall pick in the 1997 draft. He's the only two-time Lombardi Award winner, earned consensus first-team All-America honors twice and ushered the pancake block into the mainstream. " —PETE THAMEL

- 1996 OUTLAND TROPHY WINNER
- NO SACKS ALLOWED IN HIS FINAL TWO SEASONS

IN THE EARLY 1990s, two-way players were as rare as wooden goalposts. The situation has changed dramatically, however, in the last two seasons. A year ago at least 12 players saw time on offense and defense in the same game; this year at least 23 have gone both ways. Two factors account for the two-way trend: smaller rosters and the compelling talent of a few players. The NCAA-imposed 85-scholarship limit, which took effect in '94, has forced coaches to be creative in filling the holes left by injuries and suspensions. Most two-way players are getting their additional minutes because they're too good to sit for half the game. Ohio State uses the devastating, 6' 6", 320-pound Orlando Pace in its short-yardage and goal line defenses because, just as on offense, he is difficult to move or get past.

—Tim Layden, SI, November 18, 1996

Pace finished fourth in the 1996 Heisman vote.

THE (BUCK)EYE OF THE STORM

Orlando Pace pushed around defensive linemen so completely that by his junior season he had become a star from what is usually an anonymous position

BY TIM LAYDEN

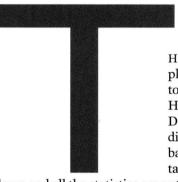

HE BEST COLLEGE FOOTBALL player in the country didn't score any touchdowns last Saturday afternoon. He didn't rush for hundreds of yards. Didn't throw the ball, didn't catch it, didn't kick it. He didn't sack any quarterbacks or intercept any passes. When the tape of his most recent game is broken down and all the statistics are put on paper and disk, the log of his performance will read more like the menu at Denny's than the résumé of a Heisman Trophy candidate: seven pancakes. The best college football player in the country stands 6' 6" (at least) and weighs 320 pounds (at least), with the girth of a grizzly bear and the feet of a ballerina. His job is to move people, and this is sweetly appropriate because, more than any other player, offensive tackle Orlando Pace has moved Ohio State into the race for the national championship.

More than 10 months have passed since the Buckeyes' brilliant 1995 season was trashed in a 31–23 loss to Michigan in Ann Arbor, a defeat that kept the Buckeyes out of the Rose Bowl and still haunts them. From that team Ohio State lost four splendid offensive players to the NFL: Heisman Trophy–winning tailback Eddie George, wideout Terry Glenn, tight end Rickey Dudley (all taken in the first round) and quarterback Bobby Hoying (third round). Yet Ohio State has rushed back into the Top 5 in the polls. It has done so with laughably easy wins over Rice and Pittsburgh (combined score: 142–7) and a 29–16 defeat of Notre Dame in South Bend. Their biggest star, literally and figuratively, is the 20-year-old Pace, who last season became the first sophomore to win the Lombardi Award, given to the nation's best lineman.

It is late afternoon, six days before the Notre Dame game. The Buckeyes are nearing the end of their practice on a grass field outside the Woody Hayes Athletic Center, and they are straining through torturous 200-yard sprints. Four waves of players are running from one goal line to the other, stopping for a beat, then running back. Pace is unmistakable among the linemen. He is the broadest and tallest of them, with such a wide chest and neck that his round head seems to sit on his round shoulders like a snowman's. He sprints with stunning economy. There is no thud with each stride; Pace simply rolls along, gliding over the turf like a much smaller man. By the last of a dozen killer runs, Pace is leading his group, eating earth in soft, giant bites.

"The guy is unbelievable," says Jim Lachey, a former Ohio State and three-time Pro Bowl offensive lineman who covers the Buckeyes for a Columbus radio station. "I mean, he's got the whole package: great feet, great hands, long arms. I try to tell people that you just don't see guys who are this big and this good. He could be in the NFL right now, and he'd easily be among the top 10 or 15 left tackles. Right now."

Pace's impact on the Ohio State offense has been palpable. "We've become obviously lefthanded," says offensive coordinator Joe Hollis. "We try to self-scout, to watch for our tendencies, but if you're a pitcher and you've got a 98-mile-per-hour fastball, you're going to throw it, even if the batter expects it."

To wit: Leading Notre Dame 15–7 late in the second quarter, Ohio State ran a touchdown-scoring toss-sweep to junior Pepe Pearson from the Irish's one-yard line, with Pace leading the play. It is rare to give the ball off so deep in the backfield, so close to the goal line. Coach John Cooper laughed at the retelling after the game. "Toss-sweep from the one," he said mocking his own team's call. "We can do that because of Orlando Pace."

This utter reliance on Pace took hold a year ago, when George was running for 1,927 yards en route to the Heisman. The signature game was against Illinois, when George carried for 314 yards on 36 carries and Pace dominated All-America linebackers Simeon Rice and Kevin Hardy. "Simeon was a good challenge for me in my first year," says Pace. "Not too much of a challenge last year."

George, now with the Houston Oilers, says, "When situations were crucial, we always ran to his side. Every time I ran behind him was a guaranteed five yards, because he'd push his man that far backward. He's the best I've ever seen."

Short-term goals remain, a checklist that expires in January. "Rose Bowl," says Pace. "Win the Lombardi again, win the Outland Trophy [awarded to the nation's best interior lineman]." He pauses, and decides not to say the word Heisman, not to press the absurd. Then he continues. "To be the best college football player in the country."

Three buses waited outside Notre Dame stadium for Pace to finish a postgame television appearance. Coaches and players had been spilling from the dressing room for more than 30 minutes, stopping to assess their performances, often laying credit at Pace's feet.

"A couple of times out there, I knew Orlando was pulling across to block," said center Juan Porter. "Now I know he's going to crush his guy every time, which he did, so I'm just thinking I have to clear out or he'll crush me too."

The cool, satisfied laughter of victory was in the air. Pearson and Pace—the running back and his escort—returned from the interview in a security van. As the big man walked toward the bus, he stopped to embrace his mother. A man shoved a ticket stub in front of Orlando, asking for an autograph. Pace borrowed a reporter's pen and at that same moment he laughed out loud, throwing his head back. "Nice to be recognized," he said. Then he signed his name on the ticket in neat, flowing script. ∎

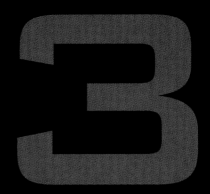

3

ANTHONY MUÑOZ

USC 1976–1979

"A sublime blend of agility and brute force, Muñoz served up so many pancake blocks his nickname should have been IHOP." —AUSTIN MURPHY

▸ PLAYED ON 1978 NATIONAL CHAMPIONSHIP TEAM
▸ PITCHED FOR THE TROJANS' NCAA-CHAMPION BASEBALL TEAM IN 1978

WHEN THE helmet of a Texas Tech player struck Muñoz's left knee in the opening game of his senior season, he required major reconstructive surgery. His coaches and teammates thought that if he didn't petition the Pac-10 for another year of eligibility, his college career was over. "I'm going to play again this year," Muñoz announced one day within earshot of John Robinson, Southern Cal's coach. Robinson laughed and said, "Sure, we'll use you at wide receiver." Robinson didn't mean to be cruel, but Muñoz went home and cried. "You don't ever tell Anthony he can't do something," says Muñoz's wife, DeDe. Desperate to fulfill every Trojan's dream of participating in the Rose Bowl—Muñoz made it back for the game. He spent the day blowing away Buckeyes and threw the key block that sprung tailback Charles White for the winning touchdown against Ohio State.

—*Jay Greenberg, SI, September 10, 1990*

Muñoz's teams made it to three Rose Bowls.

4

DAVE RIMINGTON

"The 290-pound center was the linchpin of the Cornhuskers' crunching running attack. Since 2000, the Rimington Trophy has been presented annually to the nation's most outstanding center." —DICK FRIEDMAN

> ONLY TWO-TIME WINNER OF THE OUTLAND TROPHY
> 1982 BIG EIGHT OFFENSIVE PLAYER OF THE YEAR

NEBRASKA MOVED the football against Oklahoma behind an offensive line centered by Rimington. Mike Rozier went slashing left and right off Rimington's haunches and looping wide on options for 96 yards in the first two quarters. "It wasn't too hard with Rimington and our offensive line blocking for me, even with my bad ankle," Rozier said.

—*John Papanek, SI, December 6, 1982*

Rimington's No. 50 jersey was retired after his senior year.

PHOTOGRAPH BY MANNY MILLAN

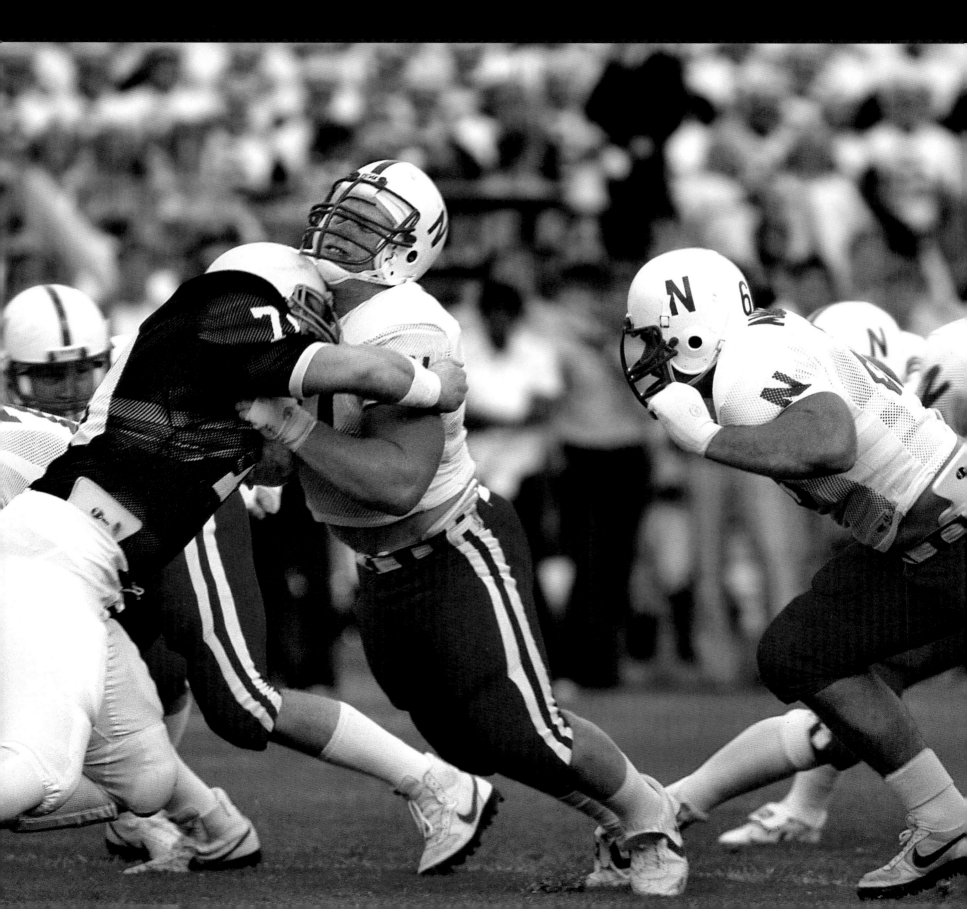

5
BILL FRALIC

" Fralic was such an intimidating blocker that before his senior year, the Pitt sports information department invented the "pancakes" statistic for each time the big lineman put a defender on his back. " —WILLIAM F. REED

▸ TWO-TIME CONSENSUS ALL-AMERICA
▸ TWICE PLACED IN TOP 10 OF HEISMAN VOTE

FRALIC WAS issued a body designed by God instead of one of God's assistants. "But you see quite a few bodies like that," says Joe Moore, Pitt's offensive line coach nonpareil. "The secret is that he has the mentality of a 180-pound guard who's busting his ass all the time just to survive. He has that inner toughness."

—*Douglas S. Looney, SI, September 10, 1984*

Fralic brought an attacking mentality to his position.

PHOTOGRAPH BY GEORGE GOJKOVICH/GETTY IMAGES

Ogden was unassuming off the field, dominating on it.

PHOTOGRAPH BY AL BELLO/GETTY IMAGES

6

" Ogden allowed only one sack in his final two seasons at UCLA, and his massive size (6' 9", 340 pounds) allowed him to punish defenders on running plays. " —ANDY STAPLES

OGDEN, WHO was too big to play Pop Warner, has slimmed down to the point where he looks almost lean. His strength and ability to accelerate, much of which he has learned from track, have helped make him a lineman who is quick enough to pull and lead sweeps, which is unusual for a tackle.

—*Michael Silver, SI, April 22, 1996*

▸ 1995 OUTLAND TROPHY WINNER
▸ ALSO COMPETED FOR THE BRUINS IN THE SHOT PUT

JONATHAN OGDEN

OFFENSIVE LINEMEN

RON YARY

USC 1965–1967

Yary came to USC from Cerritos Junior College.

❝ How's this for versatile? After being voted first-team all-conference as a defensive tackle in 1965, Yary moved across the line of scrimmage. He was a two-time All-America at tackle and a key cog on the Trojans' 1967 national-title team. ❞ —MARK GODICH

▸ 1967 OUTLAND TROPHY WINNER
▸ TOP PICK OF 1968 NFL DRAFT

"RON IS as good as I've seen," said Southern Cal coach John McKay. Yary, who weighs 225 pounds and stands a shade over 6' 6", hardly fits the image of the compact USC lineman. "He has better movement than a boy his size should show," McKay continued. "He is fast and hard to move out, he's so strong."

—Sports Illustrated, September 20, 1965

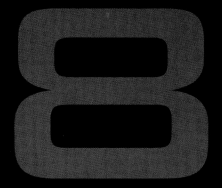

8

JOE THOMAS

" The most physically gifted offensive lineman in Wisconsin—and, arguably, Big Ten—history, Thomas quietly dominated the conference for four years, leading the Badgers to a school-record dozen wins as a senior. " —AUSTIN MURPHY

▸ 2006 OUTLAND TROPHY WINNER
▸ 39 STARTS AT TACKLE

"THE FIRST game last season," Thomas says, "I give up a sack. I was embarrassed. I was determined not to give up a sack the rest of the year, and I didn't. The left tackle and cornerback positions are different. You can play well 69 of 70 plays, but if you give up a sack or a big reception, you're not doing your job. You need to be perfect."

—*Peter King, SI, April 23, 2007*

Thomas has always been extraordinarily consistent.

PHOTOGRAPH BY J.C. RIDLEY

OHIO STATE 1954–1956

Parker led the Buckeyes' run-oriented attack.

PHOTOGRAPH BY THE SPORTING NEWS/GETTY IMAGES

" As a sophomore in 1954, Parker starred at guard and middle linebacker for the undefeated Buckeyes. He played only offensive line his final two seasons, and Woody Hayes called Parker the greatest offensive lineman he ever coached. " —ANDY STAPLES

THE KEYNOTE offensive linemen all had speed, they all had high intelligence. And none of them was especially interested in lifting weights. "I always felt that wrestling helped me more than weightlifting," Parker says. "I was always more interested in agility than strength."

—Paul Zimmerman, SI, August 3, 1981

▸ 1956 OUTLAND TROPHY WINNER
▸ '56 OHIO STATE TEAM MVP

JIM
PARKER

CHUCK BEDNARIK

" A center and a linebacker who was one of the most rugged two-way players ever, Bednarik won the 1948 Maxwell Award. Since '95, the Bednarik Award has been awarded to the best defensive player in the country. " —MARK GODICH

▸ TWO-TIME CONSENSUS ALL-AMERICA
▸ PLACED THIRD IN 1948 HEISMAN VOTE

BEDNARIK TOOK his high school coach's advice and as a result became the least likely Ivy Leaguer that the University of Pennsylvania has ever seen, a hard case who had every opponent he put a dent in screaming for the Quakers to live up to their nickname and deemphasize football.

—*John Schulian, SI, September 6, 1993*

Bednarik was taken No. 1 by the Eagles in the '49 draft.

10

THE

BEST DEFENSIVE LINEMEN

THE VOTE IN THIS SECTION PRODUCED JUST TWO PLAYERS WHO WERE NAMED ON EVERY BALLOT. ONE WAS OUR TOP FINISHER, LEE ROY SELMON, WHO RECEIVED TWO NUMBER 1 VOTES AND A PAIR OF 2S. THE OTHER WAS BUBBA SMITH, WHO WAS RATED NO HIGHER THAN THIRD ON ANY BALLOT. BUT HE IMPRESSED MORE THOROUGHLY ACROSS THE PANEL THAN THE OTHERS WHO COLLECTED FIRST- AND SECOND-PLACE VOTES.

IT COULDN'T HAVE HURT THAT SMITH HAD THE MOST MEMORABLE SLOGAN OF ANY LINEMAN—AND PERHAPS ANY PLAYER—IN COLLEGE FOOTBALL. MICHIGAN STATE STUDENTS WORE BUTTONS THAT READ, "KILL, BUBBA, KILL" AND THEN URGED HIM TO DO EXACTLY THAT. THIS WAS THE '60S, WELL BEFORE FANS AND PLAYERS HAD BECOME EDUCATED ABOUT HOW DEADLY THE GAME COULD BE.

THE TWO-TIME CONSENSUS ALL-AMERICA FOR THE TITLE-WINNING SPARTANS TEAMS ALSO REINFORCED HIS IMAGE WITH A GREAT PRO CAREER AND WITH HIS ACTING AS A TOUGH GUY IN FILMS AND COMMERCIALS. IN THE 1970S AND '80S SMITH PEDDLED MILLER LITE, AND AT THE END OF A POPULAR AD HE DECLARED, "I ALSO LOVE THE EASY-OPENING CANS" AS HE TORE THE TOP OFF HIS BEVERAGE CONTAINER. IT WAS AN IMAGE TO REMEMBER.

1

LEE ROY SELMON

OKLAHOMA 1972–1975

" He joined brothers Lucious and Dewey at Oklahoma and blossomed into a two-time consensus All-America who anchored the Sooners' defense in their national championship seasons of 1974 and '75. " —WILLIAM F. REED

▸ 1975 OUTLAND TROPHY WINNER
▸ TOP PICK IN THE '76 NFL DRAFT

THE SELMONS are not hard to see, being the logistic middle of the Oklahoma line. Before a play they stand there, three abreast, looking like an alliance of shoguns on the wall of a besieged (but impregnable) city. Brother Lucious, the 5' 11", 236-pound middle guard, is flanked by 6' 1", 249-pound brother Dewey on the left and 6' 2", 252-pound brother LeRoy on the right. Lucious is a senior, Dewey and LeRoy sophomores. Coach Barry Switzer found himself caught up in the continuing contretemps of comparison. Lucious, he said, was the more experienced, the steadying hand and maybe the stronger. But then, Dewey had the closest thing to a mean streak one could find among the Selmons. Clearly the most aggressive. And yet, here was LeRoy, a growing boy already bigger than the others. And faster, too. "When he finds out nobody can block him. . . . " Switzer whistled softly.

—*John Underwood, SI, November 12, 1973*

Despite his bulk Selmon boasted exceptional balance.

PHOTOGRAPHS BY RICH CLARKSON

Green won the Maxwell and Walter Camp awards.

PHOTOGRAPH BY GEORGE GOJKOVICH/GETTY IMAGES

2

" The 6' 2", 225-pound Green was a nonstop whirling dervish for the Panthers, often sprinting across the field to make tackles on plays run directly away from him. " —TIM LAYDEN

▸ THREE-TIME CONSENSUS
ALL-AMERICA
▸ PLACED SECOND IN
1980 HEISMAN VOTE BEHIND
GEORGE ROGERS

HUGH GREEN

GREEN IS easily the best defender on the nation's best defense, and he has an obvious zest for his job. "On defense, all we want to do is hit, get up and then hit harder the next time," he says. "Offense is more for the witty and brainy types. Me, if I don't crush somebody on a play, I'm disappointed."

—*Mike DelNagro, SI, December 1, 1980*

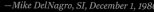

THE LIGHT IS GREEN

As a 13-year-old orphan, Hugh Green once ran away from home, but after dedicating himself to football, the merciless Panther had opposing offenses seeking shelter

BY DOUGLAS S. LOONEY

N COLLEGE FOOTBALL—UNLIKE THE SITUATION in the pros—a single dominating defensive player is enormously important because he controls strategy on both sides of the line. "In the pros they have this secret technique for neutralizing a great defensive player," says a top collegiate coach. "You may have heard of it. It's called holding."

John Marshall, a former assistant at Southern Cal who now is the special teams coach at Green Bay, says, "The value of an outstanding individual in the college game has to do with the level of talent. In college the players not only aren't as good, but the truly good ones are spread out." Oklahoma defensive coordinator Rex Norris says, "A great college defensive player dominates everybody he plays against. In the pros, there's a balance of superplayers."

Thus, in college football a team not only weakens its own offense by double- or even triple-teaming a player like Hugh Green, but its own defensive game plan must also take into consideration the fact that there can be no slipups; the offense can't be expected to compensate for defensive lapses. The result is often overcautious defense. In short, rivals are forced to alter their entire style of play.

What exactly does Green do? Ray Zingler, Pitt's defensive end coach, says, "He does two things. First, he'll rip your head off, then he'll cut your heart out." Oklahoma State coach Jimmy Johnson, a former Pitt assistant, says Green "has the agility of a 170-pounder. He is never off his feet, just like a cat." A very mean cat, albeit a very cooperative one. Says Johnson, "You can build your entire defense around him. Heck, you can build your entire team around him. If Hugh Green is on your team, you're automatically one of the finest in the country."

Green, who is 21, grew up fatherless in Natchez, Miss., and his mother died when he was six. He was taken in by his aunt, Lucy Berry, and her husband, Eltee. Eltee, a masonry worker, says, "Hugh always thought I was rough and mean on him. I wasn't mean. But I was rough because I wanted to get it in him that whatever you do, you do it right."

Back then, a big time for Green consisted of rolling a tire down the street with a stick during the day and sitting on the bluffs overlooking the Mississippi at night. He used to spend a lot of time under the bridge that leads to Vidalia, fishing for perch and catfish, but even that was not exactly a thrill-a-minute activity. When he was 13, Hugh ran away from home. He slept overnight in a parked bus in Natchez. The next morning a policeman spotted him sitting in a tree near the river, sulking. "How old are you?" the cop shouted up to the youngster. Said Green, "Thirty-five." That witticism got him thrown into jail. A kindly judge later said to Hugh, who was obviously well-built even then, "You ever tried football? That would be better for you than running away." Green took his advice.

The first team Hugh played for was a junior high squad that went 0–4 in a curtailed season. In high school Green thought so many players at North Natchez were better than he that he quit football. But the empty afternoons got to him, and so did Eltee Berry's philosophy. So Green tried again. Since then, he has never considered quitting.

Recruiters traditionally have not fancied Natchez as a breeding ground for football talent. Thus, Green was lightly recruited. Mississippi State was the only major school to show serious interest, and Green signed a letter of intent in the winter of 1976. Pitt had hired Sherrill after Johnny Majors, then leading the Panthers to a national championship, announced he'd be leaving for Tennessee. Sherrill was raised on a chicken ranch in Biloxi and therefore pays particular attention to prospects from Mississippi. He had his eye on a tailback from Pascagoula named Rooster Jones, who had scored 52 touchdowns. While studying films of Jones, which included a game with North Natchez, Sherrill and his assistants kept noticing a Natchez kid who seemed to be playing in the Pascagoula backfield. It was Green, doing his thing. Ultimately, Jones, who also had signed with Mississippi State, defected to Pittsburgh and urged Green to check the school out.

"I went," says Green. "And after one day I called home and said, 'I hate it, it's ugly. Have you ever seen black snow?' Next day I called home and said, 'I love it, it's gorgeous. You should see this pretty snow.' "

As it was, Mississippi State had pretty much ignored Green after getting his signature on a letter of intent, and Hugh, a gentle but emotional person off the field, doesn't deny he was flattered by the attention from the North. "I hate to admit it," he says, "but I think I went to Pitt because I wanted to get on national TV and say, 'Hi, Mom.' "

Although Sherrill and others deny it, the truth is that Green was a come-along with Jones, who has turned out to be a good but not lights-out kind of player. Says Rooster now, "Hugh has hit me a lot but never the way he wants to. And I wouldn't want him to. Man, if he has a weakness, it's only in his dreams, because when he gets on the field, he's all real."

The Pitt coaches began to suspect they had something special when, the summer before he reported, Green asked to look at films. "The great ones, like [1976 Pitt Heisman winner] Tony Dorsett and Green, are all alike," says Sherrill. "They sit in the front row at team meetings, look you in the eye and ask you questions."

But Sherrill normally doesn't start freshmen. So in Green's first game, against Notre Dame, Hugh was forced to watch from the bench—until the second play. Green was first-string for the rest of the season and went on to be a second-team All America. The only time Green is benched now is in Pitt's practice sessions. "I guess this is unfair to Hugh," says defensive coordinator Serafino Fazio, "but there's no need to embarrass our own players." ∎

MICHIGAN STATE 1964–1966

Smith's Spartans were the consensus champs in '65.

PHOTOGRAPH BY JAMES DRAKE

BUBBA SMITH

" The chant of "Kill, Bubba, Kill" echoed throughout Spartan Stadium as the 6' 8" Smith prowled along the line of scrimmage. A two-time consensus All-America, Smith was the first pick in the 1967 NFL draft. " —MARK GODICH

▸ MEMBER OF THE NCAA'S TOP RUSHING DEFENSE IN '65
▸ MSU AVERAGED 6.9 POINTS ALLOWED IN '65, 9.9 IN '66

WHEN NOTRE DAME quarterback Terry Hanratty, a sensational sophomore, slid off right tackle on a keeper, Bubba Smith whomped him in the left shoulder and separated it. He caught him just right, as they were falling. It looked as if Hanratty had been smacked by a giant swinging green door.

—Dan Jenkins, SI, November 28, 1966

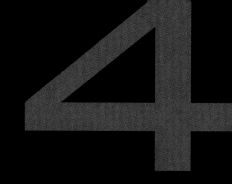

4

REGGIE WHITE

TENNESSEE 1980–1983

" The future Minister of Defense mastered his quarterback-terrorizing techniques in Knoxville. As a senior in 1983, the Lombardi Award finalist had 100 tackles, 72 of which were unassisted, and a school-record 15 sacks. " —DICK FRIEDMAN

▸ 1983 SEC PLAYER OF THE YEAR
▸ 32 CAREER SACKS

DALE HAUPT, the Philadelphia Eagles' defensive line coach, remembers seeing White play at Tennessee in the early 1980s, before White signed with the Memphis Showboats for a two-year stint in the USFL. "What you really noticed was his strength and explosion," says Haupt. "He was just bull rushing guys backward."

—Paul Zimmerman, SI. November 27, 1989

White's senior-year eruption presaged pro greatness.
PHOTOGRAPH BY BILL LUSTER

5

BRUCE SMITH

"The best player ever to strap it on in Blacksburg (sorry, Mike Vick) was nicknamed "The Sack Man." Duh. A one-man wrecking crew, his 71 career tackles for loss totaled a staggering minus-504 yards." —AUSTIN MURPHY

▸ 1984 OUTLAND TROPHY WINNER
▸ LED NATION WITH 22 SACKS IN 1983

THIS IS Bruce Smith. Forty-six collegiate sacks. Feet so fast they blur in photos. The fellow whose huge frame features a big butt, no waist and no neck but who says, "I look in the mirror and say, 'Oh, my, this body of mine do look good.' " The thoroughly rowdy player has been described as playing like the lead boulder in an avalanche.

—*Douglas S. Looney, SI, October 7, 1985*

Smith had 71 career tackles for loss for the Hokies.

SHEFFIELD
1

93

NEBRASKA 2006–2009

In 2010 Suh pledged to donate $2.6 million to Nebraska.

PHOTOGRAPH BY KARL ANDERSON/ICON SPORTSWIRE

6

❝ Suh affected every play when he was on the field. As a senior he led Nebraska in tackles (85), tackles for loss (24), quarterback hurries (26) and sacks (12). Those are astounding numbers for a nosetackle. ❞ —ANDY STAPLES

▸2009 OUTLAND TROPHY AND LOMBARDI AWARD WINNER
▸ '09 AP NATIONAL COLLEGE PLAYER OF THE YEAR

NDAMUKONG SUH

SUH NEARLY single-handedly took down Texas, with 12 tackles (seven for losses, including 4½ sacks), despite being double-teamed on almost every down. Said Texas coach Mack Brown, "I wanted to find him after the game and wish him good luck in the NFL. Because I don't want to see him anymore."

—*Albert Chen, SI, December 14, 2009*

7

TED HENDRICKS

MIAMI 1966–1968

"The Mad Stork, at 6' 7" and 220 pounds, finished fifth in the 1968 Heisman race and was the first Hurricane player in the College Football Hall of Fame. Since 2002, the Ted Hendricks Award has been presented to the top defensive end in the country." —MARK GODICH

▸ TWO-TIME CONSENSUS
ALL-AMERICA
▸ 327 CAREER TACKLES

HENDRICKS'S STRING-BEAN contours were so unusual for a football player that the pros made 11 defensive picks before Baltimore took him in the second round of the 1969 draft. During his college career, Miami coaches spoke wishfully of the pounds Hendricks was expected to add during the off-season by lifting weights, but the weightlifting program was a myth, and his weight stayed the same. The Hurricanes were a team of nicknames on the Mad motif. Guard Nelson Salemi was the Mad Dog. Oscar Gonzalez, the 165-pound punt returner, was the Mad Dwarf. Jimmy Dye, the little defensive back, was the Mad Fly. Hendricks became the Mad Stork. After Hendricks's senior year, Miami coach Charlie Tate said, "No one who ever played defensive end on the college level ever played it any better."

—Paul Zimmerman, SI, October 17, 1983

The agile Hendricks lived in the opponents' backfield.

PHOTOGRAPH BY JAMES DRAKE

NOTRE DAME 1946–1949

SI's panel also gave Hart votes as a Top 10 tight end.

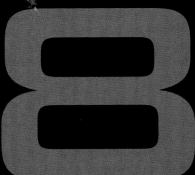

8

LEON HART

" Hart was a dominant two-way player who helped the Fighting Irish go 36-0-2 during his four seasons. His 1949 Heisman Trophy made him just the second-ever lineman to win the award. " —PETE THAMEL

‣ TWO-TIME CONSENSUS ALL-AMERICA
‣ 1949 AP MALE ATHLETE OF THE YEAR

"I PRODUCED a film, *The Golden Age of Notre Dame Football*" Hart says. "It was wonderful to see the way the game was played. The precise timing of the blocking, the way the holes opened up. It wasn't just running to daylight, behind a whole lot of pushing and shoving. It was beautiful football."

—*Paul Zimmerman, SI, November 24, 1997*

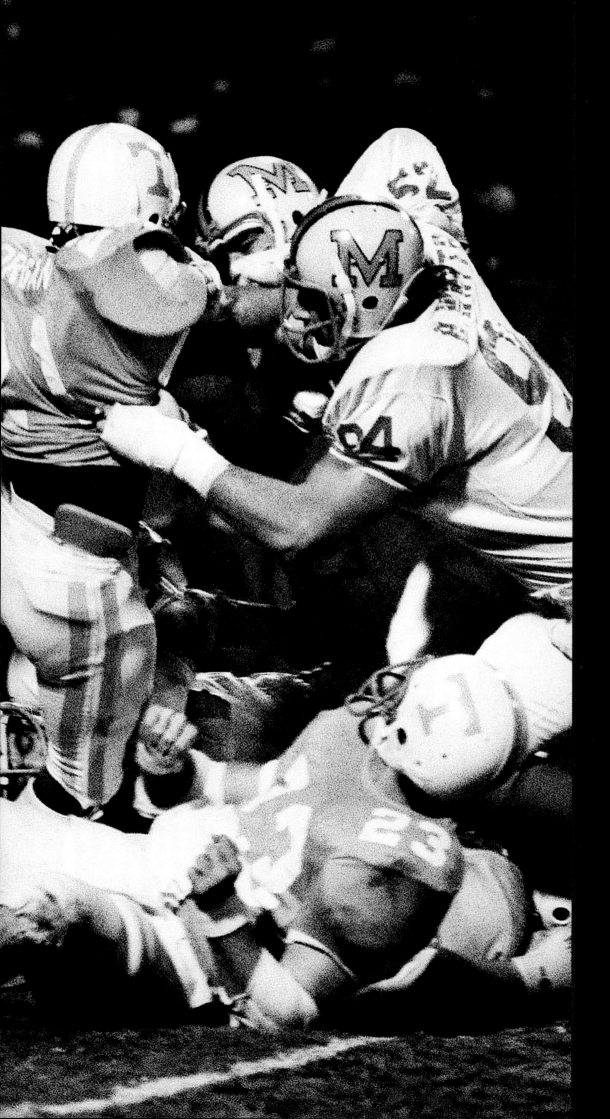

9

RANDY WHITE

MARYLAND 1972–1974

> " He arrived at Maryland in 1971 as a 212-pound fullback and left as the most dominant defensive player in the nation. White carried the once-doormat Terps to two Top 20 rankings, with five shutouts in the fall of '74. " —TIM LAYDEN

▸ 1974 OUTLAND TROPHY AND LOMBARDI AWARD WINNER
▸ 24 TACKLES FOR LOSS IN '74

AS A SENIOR White was a shoo-in for the Outland Trophy. Among his credentials was the fact that the season before, when Maryland played Penn State, he tackled John Cappelletti—the eventual Heisman winner—10 times, twice for big losses. Syracuse coach Frank Maloney tried to neutralize White by using two offensive tackles directly in front of him, instead of a tackle and a smaller guard. When the tackles still couldn't block White, Maloney inserted a third, with no more success. Maloney called White "the greatest lineman I've ever seen." Such compliments apparently went unnoticed by White. At the end of his junior season, he was ordered to coach Jerry Claiborne's office. While waiting outside, he asked one assistant, then another, "What's wrong? What'd I do?" Finally, Claiborne summoned him inside. "Congratulations," he said. "You made the All-America team."

—John Underwood, SI, October 22, 1984

White brought a running back's speed to the position.

PHOTOGRAPH BY AP

10

MERLIN OLSEN

"Although better known as a Rams All-Pro and for his TV career as an analyst and actor, Olsen remains, by far, the greatest player in Utah State history. As a senior, Olsen anchored a defense that allowed opponents a nation-best 50.8 yards rushing." —WILLIAM F. REED

‣ 1961 OUTLAND TROPHY WINNER
‣ 1961 CONSENSUS ALL-AMERICA

THE OLSENS are Mormons, and the Mormons have an absolute penchant for odd names. So the name Merlin figures. At first, folks thought that it was a melding of his parents' names, Merle and Lynn, but not so. Lynn had simply liked the name ever since she'd read King Arthur. Don't laugh; it could have been Gawain Olsen.

—*Bob Ottum, SI, January 19, 1981*

Olsen was also a three-time academic All-American.

10

THE

BEST LINEBACKERS

THE PASSAGES FROM SPORTS ILLUSTRATED THAT ACCOMPANY THE PHOTOGRAPHS IN THIS BOOK ARE GENERALLY LAUDATORY BECAUSE THEY ARE MEANT TO HELP ILLUSTRATE WHAT MADE THE PLAYER A TOP 10 SELECTION. FOR ONE PLAYER IN THIS SECTION, FINDING WORDS OF PRAISE REQUIRED WADING THROUGH MUCH NEGATIVE REPORTAGE. THAT'S THE WAY IT WAS WITH BRIAN BOSWORTH. THE GOOD OFTEN CAME WITH A HELPING OF BAD.

IF YOU MISSED THE HEYDAY OF THE BOZ IN THE MID-'80S, SUFFICE IT TO SAY THAT HE CARRIED HIMSELF LIKE A ROCK STAR. HIS PROFILE WAS SUCH THAT AFTER HIS THREE-YEAR PROFESSIONAL CAREER CAME TO AN END, HE WAS ABLE TO STAR IN A MOVIE, PLAYING THE VIOLENT RENEGADE COP IN THE 1991 FILM *STONE COLD*.

BOSWORTH APPEARED SOLO ON SI'S COVER IN 1987, AN HONOR THAT IS QUITE RARE FOR A COLLEGE DEFENSIVE PLAYER. IT IS UNLIKELY HE WAS CELEBRATING THE MOMENT, THOUGH. THE COVER LINE READ "THE BOZ FLUNKS OUT," AND THE STORY DETAILED HOW HE WAS AMONG AT LEAST 21 PLAYERS BANNED FROM THE COLLEGE POSTSEASON AFTER TESTING POSITIVE FOR ANALBOLIC STEROIDS. IN THE STORY, HE WAS UNAPOLOGETIC. "STEROIDS AREN'T DESTROYING SOCIETY," HE CLAIMED. WITH HIS BLOND MOHAWK AND BULGING MUSCLES, HE WAS THE IMAGE OF BRASH, DEFIANT YOUTH.

1

DICK BUTKUS

ILLINOIS 1962–1964

" Exceedingly mobile and even more hostile, the 243-pound Butkus demolished Big Ten offenses and led the Illini to a 1964 Rose Bowl win. Since '85, the Butkus Award has been presented annually to the nation's top linebacker. " —DICK FRIEDMAN

▸ TWO-TIME CONSENSUS ALL-AMERICA
▸ PLACED THIRD IN 1964 HEISMAN VOTE

IF EVERY college football team had a linebacker like Dick Butkus, all fullbacks would soon be three feet tall and sing soprano. Dick Butkus is a special kind of brute whose particular talent is mashing runners into curious shapes. There are a lot of reasons why Butkus is the most destructive defensive player in collegiate football, one who personally made 145 tackles and caused 10 fumbles last season. The first reason is his size. Butkus is 6' 3" and weighs 243 pounds, which means that he is the biggest college linebacker on the list of good ones who are just as tough and willing, but they cannot hit as hard because they simply are not as big. Butkus not only hits, he crushes and squeezes opponents with thick arms that also are extremely long. At any starting point on his build, he is big, well-proportioned, and getting bigger.

—Dan Jenkins, SI, October 12, 1964

Butkus also played center and fullback for the Illini.

PHOTOGRAPHS BY LEE BALTERMAN (LEFT) AND JAMES DRAKE

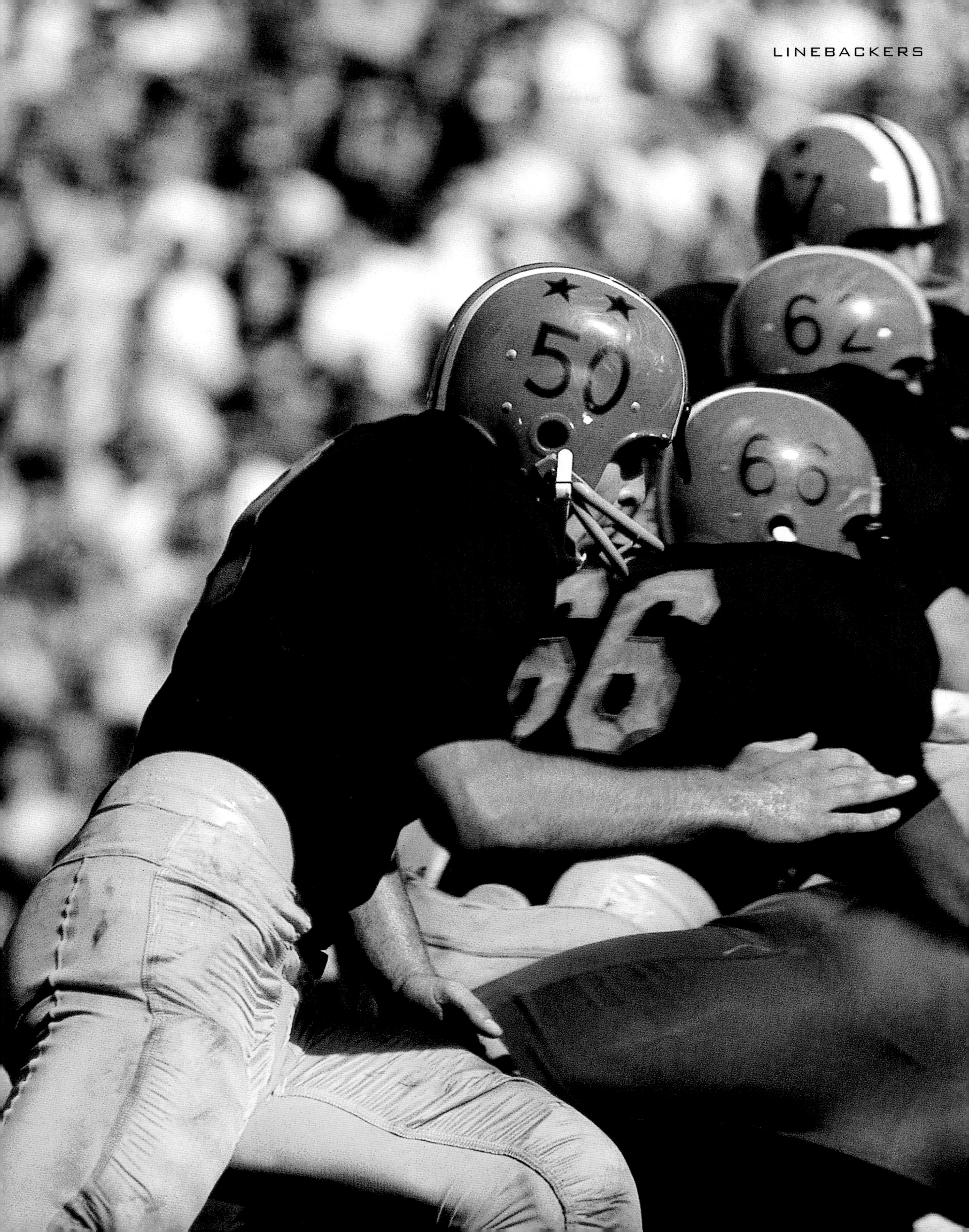
50
62
66
66

BRIAN BOSWORTH

OKLAHOMA 1984–1986

" Forget, if you can, his heavy metal 'do; forget Bo Jackson's bulldozing him in the pros. The Boz won the first two Butkus Awards, had 395 tackles in three seasons and led OU to the 1985 national title. " —AUSTIN MURPHY

▸ TWO-TIME CONSENSUS
ALL-AMERICA
▸ PLACED FOURTH IN 1986
HEISMAN VOTE

THE STAGE for second-half hysteria was set in the first 30 minutes, when Texas went up 10–0. Their touchdown came after Oklahoma punter Mike Winchester let the snap slide through his hands. Given the soggy conditions, the Longhorns' halftime lead looked enormous. In a stunning span of six minutes, 50 seconds in the third quarter, Oklahoma flickered with a spark it hasn't shown since the glory days of the '70s. It all started when Texas tailback Terry Orr was crushed by Brian Bosworth. Orr fumbled, and strong safety Keith Stanberry recovered on the Texas six. Bosworth had spent the week spouting off about how much he hates Texas, Burnt Orange and Austin. All of his published remarks ended up in Austin, posted for the Longhorns to read and ponder. Coach Switzer now calls Bosworth, a freshman from Dallas, Mr. Bulletin Board.

—Douglas S. Looney, SI, October 22, 1984

The Boz was a magnetic presence on and off the field.

PHOTOGRAPH BY JOHN BIEVER

Nobis gave all-out effort on every snap.

PHOTOGRAPH BY ART SHAY

TEXAS 1963–1965

3

TOMMY NOBIS

" Nobis was a two-way player who also excelled as a guard. Then SMU coach Hayden Fry called Nobis "a once-in-a-lifetime player." " —MARK GODICH

▸ 1965 OUTLAND TROPHY AND MAXWELL AWARD WINNER ▸ HAD BOWL WINS OVER ROGER STAUBACH (NAVY) AND JOE NAMATH (ALABAMA)

LAST YEAR, playing both ways, Tommy Nobis bulled and quicked his way to more than 20 individual tackles—most of them near the scrimmage line—in each game against Army, Oklahoma, Arkansas, SMU and Baylor, and nearly every Texas writer ran out of exclamation points.

—Dan Jenkins, SI, October 18, 1965

4

DERRICK THOMAS

ALABAMA 1985–1988

" Thomas won the 1988 Butkus Award after piling up 27 sacks as a senior. Against Penn State that year, the linebacker/defensive end hybrid had a school-record nine hurries, three sacks and a safety. " —ANDY STAPLES

- 1988 CONSENSUS ALL-AMERICA
- NAMED SEC'S TOP ATHLETE IN 1988–89 ACROSS ALL SPORTS

IN HIS sophomore year he played behind All-America outside linebacker Cornelius Bennett, now with the Atlanta Falcons, who set a school single-season record with 10 sacks. Thomas was told he would never be as good as Bennett, but in 1987, he had 18 sacks. He topped himself with his astounding senior year. "He rushes the passer just like a great dribbler in basketball," says San Diego Chargers running backs coach Sylvester Croom, who was the linebackers coach at Alabama during Thomas's first two years with the Crimson Tide. Croom says Thomas's best move is the football equivalent of the crossover dribble: He lines up in a three-point stance and takes two quick steps to the outside, then cuts back to the inside. He repeats this sequence until the blocker is forced to commit himself to an outside stance, then Thomas blows past him to the inside.

—Michael Silver, SI Presents, Fall 1996

Thomas had 10 career forced fumbles for the Tide.

Johnstown (Pa.)'s Ham went from PSU to Pittsburgh.

PHOTOGRAPH BY JAMES PURRING

5

JACK HAM

" Among the first players to establish Penn State as "Linebacker U.," Ham was a leader on consecutive unbeaten Nittany Lions' teams in 1968 and '69. His four blocked punts still stand as a school record. " —TIM LAYDEN

‣ 1970 CONSENSUS ALL-AMERICA
‣ 91 TACKLES, FOUR INTERCEPTIONS IN '70

ON THE draft-room blackboard, Steelers owner Art Rooney Jr. wrote under Round 2: "Jack Ham." One of the coaches walked to the board and wrote, "Phil Villapiano." Rooney yelled, "I don't go in and tell you guys what plays to call. You don't tell me what to put on the blackboard."

—*Peter King, SI, January 22, 1990*

NORTH CAROLINA 1977–1980

Taylor attacked with a sudden ferocity.

6

LAWRENCE TAYLOR

" He began his North Carolina career on the defensive line, but when the Tar Heels coaching staff had him take his hand off the ground, that was the first step in Taylor's becoming football's most feared pass rusher. " —ANDY STAPLES

▸ 1980 CONSENSUS ALL-AMERICA
▸ 16 SACKS IN '80

"THERE IS nothing better in life than a violent head-on collision," Taylor says. "Look, football is supposed to be a rough game, and not everybody is supposed to be able to play. So if I knock a guy silly, he'll be wondering where I am and what I'm going to do to him the next time he runs my way."

—Douglas S. Looney, SI, October 27, 1980

TRUE-BLUE TEAMMATES

Lawrence Taylor's friendship with Tar Heel defensive back Steve Streater endured while one's star soared in the NFL and the other was left paralyzed from a car crash

BY JILL LIEBER

WHEN THEY WERE younger, just a couple of big-talking, know-it-all jocks, Steve Streater and Lawrence Taylor would strut across the University of North Carolina campus in caps and faded blue jeans. They hung out in the student union game room, taking on the world in eight ball. They fished for bream at Dr. Biggers's pond on the edge of Chapel Hill. They played a mean game of cards.

"We beat everybody in the dorm," Streater says. "We just knew each other so well that we sensed the cards each other was holding."

For three years they were inseparable. Roommates with the same dream. Until April 30, 1981.

Streater, a defensive back, had just signed a free-agent contract with the Redskins. Driving home from the airport in the rain that same night, he lost control of his new sports car on a slippery road, and the crash left him paralyzed from the chest down.

Taylor, the No. 1 draft choice of the New York Giants, was attending rookie minicamp when he heard about the accident. Within hours he was at Streater's bedside.

"I looked up and saw the fear in Lawrence's face," Streater recalls. "He began beating on the walls, beating on the door, and he screamed, 'Steve, get up from there! This isn't you! Steve, you must get up!'"

Taylor was crying uncontrollably. "Have you ever seen a 6' 4", 240-pound man fall apart?" Streater asks. "Lawrence Taylor, so strong, so invincible. He could do anything. He'd soar 10 feet in the air to block punts, leap over piles, tackle three people at once.

"For the first time I told Lawrence I loved him. He stopped crying, and he told me I'd pull through, that with his help, someday I'd walk again."

Later, Taylor broke down again, this time in the arms of his fiancée, Linda Cooley. "Why couldn't I have been driving?" he cried. "Why couldn't it have been me in that car instead?"

That night Lawrence told Linda he wanted to quit football.

Taylor had begun in football only at 13. When he was nine, Lawrence begged to play for the Williamsburg City League football team, but his mother feared he would be hurt. Instead, he played baseball and was an all-star four summers in a row as a catcher/designated hitter. Finally, when he was 13, Taylor got his wish to play football in a local kids league.

Then in the fall of Lawrence's sophomore year at Lafayette High, Mel Jones, the assistant football coach, noticed Taylor "standing outside the commons . . . with that baby face . . . doing nothing."

"Son, are you playing football?" Jones asked Taylor.

"Yes, sir, for the city league," Taylor replied. "We play games in places like Pottstown, Pennsylvania, and each member gets a trophy."

"Son, I have some trophies at home. What size do you want?" Jones said. "I've never seen a young man yet get a college scholarship playing city league."

A few weeks later, Jones pestered Taylor again. "Get off my back," Taylor moaned. "I'll play for you."

For a time the University of Richmond was the only school seriously interested in Taylor. Jones even had to try to persuade a recruiter from Norfolk State to say hello to Taylor. Jones said the recruiter wouldn't do it.

Taylor was determined to go to college. The Friday night discussions with his parents had made an impression. Mrs. Taylor would ask her sons what they wanted in life, and on a pad of paper she would calculate how far they could go on a minimum wage.

"Can you get what you want from this?" she would ask. "A nice house? A nice car? Clothes? Put money in the bank?"

"No," Lawrence would answer, fearful of working next to his father in the shipyards. "I need to go to college."

The North Carolina recruiters came across Taylor on film late in the spring and thought he was worth a scholarship. For the first three years at Chapel Hill he played on special teams and bounced from nose-guard to inside linebacker to outside linebacker. He had a reputation as an undisciplined player and an irresponsible student. Some of that changed, thanks to linebackers coach Mel Foels, who joined the Tar Heels before Taylor's senior season. Foels, now an assistant coach at Tennessee, hounded Taylor. Be on time for meetings. Go to class. Take charge. Apparently his strategy worked. Taylor was a consensus All-America that year and the second player taken in the 1981 NFL draft, and was named the league MVP in '86.

Streater visits the Taylors' six-bedroom home in Upper Saddle River, N.J., a couple of times each year. His physical condition is not a problem; LT takes him everywhere. Sometimes he picks up his friend and carries him through restaurants. Two years ago he bought him a $3,000 motorized scooter.

"Lawrence made me feel life again," Streater says. "He made me laugh. He never gave up on me."

Streater is now the director of Students Against Driving Drunk in the North Carolina state department of administration. Although he will probably never walk again, his comeback showed Taylor that a life could be turned around, with a little help. "I know I couldn't have come through it as well," Taylor said. ∎

7

MIKE SINGLETARY

" Those eyes! Legend has it that Singletary cracked 16 helmets at Baylor. Deemed too small and too slow, he amassed a staggering 232 tackles as a sophomore in 1978. " —MARK GODICH

▸ TWO-TIME CONSENSUS ALL-AMERICA
▸ HOLDS BAYLOR'S TOP THREE SINGLE-SEASON TACKLE MARKS

AGAINST GEORGIA in 1978, Singletary knocked over two pulling linemen who were leading a sweep and then flattened the ballcarrier, knocking the man out of the game. It was an astonishing hit, made extraordinary by the fact that Singletary had lost his helmet in mid-play and had stopped the runner bareheaded.

—Rick Telander, SI, January 27, 1986

Singletary's competitive spirit shone on his face.

PHOTOGRAPH BY ANDY HAYT

OHIO STATE 1984–1987

Spielman owns the OSU career record for solo tackles.

PHOTOGRAPH BY ANTHONY NESTE

8

"A paragon of intensity and production, Spielman's 29 tackles—29!—against Michigan in '86 are tied for most in a single game in school history. If statistics quantified grit, he'd hold that Ohio State record as well." —PETE THAMEL

‣ 1987 LOMBARDI AWARD WINNER
‣ TWO-TIME CONSENSUS ALL-AMERICA

HIS FIRST year as a Buckeye, Spielman didn't play in the first half of Ohio State's opener against Oregon State. He spent the half shouting "Play me! This is why you recruited me!" Spielman went in, made 10 tackles, deflected a pass and forced the fumble that enabled Ohio State to win. He was ready.

—*Austin Murphy, SI, August 31, 1987*

CHRIS
SPIELMAN

ALABAMA 1960–1962

Bryant said that Jordan "never had a bad day."

PHOTOGRAPH BY BETTMANN/CORBIS

" If not Bear Bryant's all-time favorite player, Jordan has to be in the conversation. Undersized but quick, Jordan starred at center and linebacker for Bryant's 1961 national championship team. " —WILLIAM F. REED

ON THE list of the eight greatest individual bowl performances, include Lee Roy Jordan's in the 1963 Orange Bowl. Some math: Oklahoma ran 60 plays from scrimmage. Four were incomplete passes and zero were for scores, meaning a Sooner was tackled 56 times. Jordan had 31 of them.

—*Mark Bechtel, SI, December 31, 2012*

▸ WON BOWL MVP AWARDS IN BOTH 1960 AND '63
▸ ALSO EXCELLED AT CENTER

9

LEE ROY JORDAN

10

LUKE KUECHLY

"A sensational, cerebral quarterback on D, Kuechly racked up 158, 183, and 191 tackles in his three seasons at BC. As NFL quarterbacks have discovered, he's also excellent in pass coverage." —AUSTIN MURPHY

▸ WON NAGURSKI, BUTKUS, LOMBARDI AWARDS IN '11
▸ NCAA CAREER RECORD 14.0 TACKLES PER GAME

"BC LOST TO USC in the Emerald Bowl. Afterward, Kuechly took a while to get back to the locker room. Defensive coordinator Bill McGovern asked where he'd been: "He's embarrassed. He says, 'I had to stay out there for something.' He's holding his helmet behind his back. Inside the helmet is his trophy for being the game's defensive MVP."

—*Austin Murphy, SI, November 4, 2013*

Kuechly had 33 consecutive games with 10-plus tackles.

PHOTOGRAPH BY ANTHONY NESMITH/CAL SPORT MEDIA

10 THE

BEST DEFENSIVE BACKS

FOOTBALL PLAYERS, WHEN COMPARING THEIR COLLEGE AND PRO EXPERIENCES, WILL SAY THAT THE REAL DIFFERENCE ABOUT BEING IN THE NFL IS THAT YOU'RE WORKING A FULL-TIME JOB. THAT'S ALL YOU DO. IN COLLEGE, ON THE OTHER HAND, ATHLETES HAVE CLASSES TO ATTEND AND MORE OF AN OFF-SEASON. COLLEGE IS A MORE DIVERSE EXPERIENCE, SOMETIMES GREATLY SO.

IT SEEMS ESPECIALLY TRUE OF DEFENSIVE BACKS, OR AT LEAST THOSE THAT MADE OUR TOP 10. CHARLES WOODSON IS THE MOST PROMINENT EXAMPLE OF AN ATHLETE WHO MADE A MARK ON OFFENSE TOO. THEN THERE ARE PLAYERS WHO BRANCHED OUT INTO OTHER SPORTS ENTIRELY. KENNY EASLEY PLAYED JV BASKETBALL AT UCLA. ROD WOODSON WAS AN ACCOMPLISHED HURDLER AT PURDUE, AND IN HIS FINAL FOOTBALL GAME STARTED AT RUNNING BACK AS WELL AS CORNERBACK (AND GAINED 93 YARDS ON 15 CARRIES, WITH THREE CATCHES FOR 67 YARDS).

THEN THERE'S DEION SANDERS, THE RARE THREE-SPORT ATHLETE. HE RAN TRACK AT FLORIDA STATE, AND HE ALSO PLAYED BASEBALL WELL ENOUGH TO STAR IN THE MAJORS FOR NINE SEASONS, WHEN HE WASN'T WINNING SUPER BOWLS IN DALLAS AND SAN FRANCISCO. SANDERS WAS THE RARE PERSON WHO COULD KEEP THAT COLLEGE LIFESTYLE GOING LONG AFTER HE LEFT CAMPUS.

1

CHARLES WOODSON

MICHIGAN 1995–1997

" Against Ohio State in 1997, Woodson made an end zone interception, returned a punt 78 yards for a touchdown and, as a wide receiver, hauled in a key 37-yard reception. The tour de force helped earn him the only Heisman won by a primarily defensive player. " —DICK FRIEDMAN

▸ WON THORPE, NAGURSKI AND BEDNARIK AWARDS IN 1997
▸ 18 CAREER INTERCEPTIONS

WHAT DISTINGUISHES Woodson is that he does something no other player has done to such great effect since two-platoon football took hold more than three decades ago: Because of his ability to overwhelm on defense and his threat to score on offense, he demands that the other team find him on every snap. It's no longer true that only a quarterback controls every play—Woodson has seen to that. Even before this season, Woodson had earned the reputation as being unbeatable in man-to-man coverage. The best part of all is that Woodson hasn't coasted on his talent. "When we finish practice, and he's done his two periods of offense and tried not to let anybody catch a single pass on him on defense, he's spent," says Michigan coach Lloyd Carr. "But he has gotten better since he walked in here. Some guys get bored, get in a comfort zone. Not Charles."

—*Tim Layden, SI, November 24, 1997*

Woodson led Michigan to the 1997 national title.

DEION SANDERS

FLORIDA STATE 1985–1988

❝ One of the best athletes in college football history, Sanders embodied the swagger and showmanship that marked the Seminoles' dominance in the late 1980s. A four-year starter and shutdown cornerback, Sanders intercepted 17 passes in his career and was also a lethal punt returner. ❞ —TIM LAYDEN

- ▸ TWO-TIME CONSENSUS ALL-AMERICA
- ▸ 1988 JIM THORPE AWARD WINNER

SANDERS SET records for on-field trash talk. Regularly he critiqued opposing players' routes: "Boy, you keep runnin' that sloppy stuff, you goin' to Arena Football." He showed up for the game against traditional rival Florida, at Tallahassee, last year in a tuxedo and a white stretch limo. Florida receivers, he once said, "must think I'm God." He and Gator Ricky Nattiel—now a wide receiver for the Denver Broncos—engaged in a bitter competition that carried over in to the pros. Preparing for a punt return on the road at Clemson, he pointed and shouted over to the Tigers bench, "This one's going back!" Then he toasted the defense, whirling 76 yards for the touchdown, after which he struck a long pose for the end zone fans and screamed, "How you like me now?"

—*Curry Kirkpatrick, SI, November 13, 1989*

Sanders had the skills to back up his big talk.

PHOTOGRAPH BY FOCUS ON SPORT/GETTY IMAGES

Lott's Trojans had a 28-game unbeaten streak.

PHOTOGRAPH BY HEINZ KLUETMEIER

3

RONNIE LOTT

" A heralded high school running back, Lott was moved to safety upon arriving at USC. Though only 200 pounds, he was known for his physical style of play. In 1980 Lott intercepted a nation-leading eight passes. " —MARK GODICH

▸ NAMED DEFENSIVE PLAYER OF PAC-12'S FIRST 100 YEARS
▸ 1980 CONSENSUS ALL-AMERICA

RONNIE HAD difficulty channeling the aggressiveness he had developed playing games on pavement. During one recess Lott clobbered a fifth-grade teacher with a kickball while making a tag and was ordered to write and illustrate a booklet on sportsmanship, which his mother still has.

—*Jill Lieber, SI, January 23, 1989*

OHIO STATE 1968–1970

Tatum often made trouble in the opponent's backfield.

PHOTOGRAPH BY WALTER IOOSS JR.

" Known as "The Assassin" for his NFL hits, Tatum came to OSU as a tailback but switched to defensive back in the spring of his freshman year on the advice of a Woody Hayes assistant named Lou Holtz. " —PETE THAMEL

JACK TATUM

▸ TWO-TIME CONSENSUS ALL-AMERICA
▸ 1970 NATIONAL DEFENSIVE PLAYER OF THE YEAR

THE DEFENSE belongs to Jack Tatum down on the field and assistant coach Lou McCullough up in the booth. This is a destruction outfit that encourages ballcarriers and receivers to slip down and crawl under the grass before the redshirts arrive, one that limits opponents to just over a touchdown per Saturday.

—Dan Jenkins, SI, November 24, 1969

5

KENNY EASLEY

UCLA 1977–1980

" Easley was the total, menacing package: a headhunting ballhawk with amazing range. His reputation for monster hits gave many a wideout alligator arms. " —AUSTIN MURPHY

▸ THREE-TIME CONSENSUS ALL-AMERICA
▸ ONLY DEFENSIVE PLAYER TO EARN FIRST-TEAM ALL PAC-10 HONORS FOUR TIMES

AS A QUARTERBACK at Oscar Smith High School in Chesapeake, Va., Easley became the first player in the state to both run and pass for 1,000 yards in a season. He also played JV basketball for UCLA and his coach said the only other player who could cover the floor the way Easley did was [college player of the year] Marques Johnson.

—*Rick Telander, SI, November 12, 1984*

Easley's 19 career interceptions remain a UCLA record.

PHOTOGRAPH BY LENNOX MCLENDON/AP

6
CHAMP BAILEY

" At Georgia, Bailey did everything but groom UGA, the Bulldogs mascot. The lockdown cornerback won the 1998 Bronko Nagurski Trophy given to the nation's best defensive player. " —WILLIAM F. REED

▸ 1998 CONSENUS ALL-AMERICA
▸ THREE 100-YARD GAMES AS WR, THREE INTERCEPTIONS AS CB IN '98

IN 1998 HE was on the field for 957 plays—offense, defense and special teams combined—and put up impressive numbers: 47 catches for 744 yards and five touchdowns, 16 carries for 84 yards, 52 tackles, three interceptions, a 21.8-yard average on kickoff returns and a 12.3 on punt returns.

—*Josh Elliott, SI, August 20, 2001*

Georgia found ways to get the ball into Bailey's hands.
PHOTOGRAPH BY BOB ROSATO

Gray intercepted seven passes his senior season.

PHOTOGRAPH COURTESY OF TEXAS ATHLETICS

7

JERRY GRAY

TEXAS 1981–1984

"The first in a long line of outstanding defensive backs at Texas, Gray was a two-time Southwest Conference Defensive Player of the Year, winning the honor in both his junior and senior seasons." —MARK GODICH

▸ TWO-TIME CONSENSUS ALL-AMERICA
▸ 16 CAREER INTERCEPTIONS AND 20 PASSES BROKEN UP

SORRY, GUYS. Here are the players who deserve the Heisman at least as much as Bo Jackson but have no chance of getting it because they're not offensive backs: 1) Pitt tackle Bill Fralic. The best pure player in college this year; 2) Texas safety Jerry Gray. Puts on a clinic every Saturday afternoon.

—*Douglas S. Looney, SI, September 5, 1984*

ED REED

MIAMI 1998–2001

"Reed was the heart and soul of Miami's 2001 national title team. He came to Miami when the Hurricanes were suffering through NCAA sanctions, and he helped lead them back to a championship level." —ANDY STAPLES

▸ TWO-TIME CONSENSUS ALL-AMERICA
▸ 21 CAREER INTERCEPTIONS, FOUR RETURNED FOR TDS

AS A SENIOR at Destrehan (La.) High he had 83 tackles and seven interceptions and was recruited by Miami, LSU and Tulane. He chose the Hurricanes, where he helped them win the 2001 national title and graduated with a degree in liberal arts. By his senior year he had established himself as one of Miami's leaders, on and off the field. Each weekday morning before the season he would direct his teammates through their conditioning drills. At night he would join his friends and teammates at one of the area's many clubs, usually to make sure they avoided trouble. After he was selected by Baltimore in the 2002 draft, Reed gravitated to fellow Miami alum Ray Lewis. The two players watched game tapes for hours at Lewis's home, and they trained together in the off-season. Some teammates jokingly called Reed "Ray Jr.," but he didn't mind.

—*Jeffri Chadiha, SI, September 5, 2005*

Reed averaged 18.5 yards per interception return.

CHAMPIONSHIP MATERIAL

Ed Reed may not have been the most athletic member of the Miami secondary, but his focus and his field sense helped the safety elevate his team to rare heights

BY KELLEY KING

ITH LOCKER-ROOM benches as his pulpit, Miami senior free safety Ed Reed has delivered his share of emotional speeches this season. However, it was in a 1976 Oldsmobile Cutlass that Ed's father and namesake delivered a memorable message eight years ago that has motivated his son throughout an extraordinary career at Miami. "We were on our way to our house [in St. Rose, La.], and my dad was talking about his work," recalls Ed Jr., whose 45-year-old father's hands are still stippled with burn marks from 25 years of 12-hour shifts as a welder at a shipyard outside New Orleans. "'Son,' he said, 'you don't want my job.' He told me that if I worked hard at school and at football, I had the ability to have all the opportunities he missed out on."

Heeding that advice, Ed Jr. passed up a chance to become a first-round choice in last spring's NFL draft to become the first member of his family to graduate from college. Since then he has become the leader of arguably the best defensive unit in college football, cemented his status as an even higher first-round pick in next spring's draft and played a major role in putting top-ranked and unbeaten Miami in the national championship game. "This season has been great," says Reed. "This is what I have been working so hard for, to help my teammates and the coaches win a national championship. I have no regrets."

When attempting to explain Reed's preeminence among their defensive backs, Miami coaches and players often begin with what Reed is not. He's not the fastest member of the starting secondary. (That would be junior Phil Buchanon, a cornerback who runs the 40 in 4.2 seconds, compared with Reed's 4.5.) He's not the most prolific tackler in that group. (That would be senior strong safety James Lewis, who has 59 tackles to Reed's 44.) He's not the best leaper. (Senior cornerback Mike Rumph has a 39½-inch vertical jump to Reed's 37.) Rather, it's Reed's uncanny field sense that makes him "the complete player," says defensive backs coach Mark Stoops. "He's such a reliable safety that he inspires everyone in front of him to play with confidence."

Having played the previous three years in Miami secondaries that were ranked no higher than 70th in pass defense at the conclusion of the regular season, Reed entered spring drills determined to make the defensive backfield better as a whole. "I started to challenge Mike, Phil, James and the rest of them," says Reed, who also added seven pounds of muscle through 5:30 a.m. weightlifting sessions over the summer, "and I expected them to be critical right back."

Not long after defensive coordinator Randy Shannon mandated 10 push-ups from every player who dropped an interception in practice, Reed took the challenge to the next level. After a pass brushed his fingertips in a game against West Virginia, he started the next day's practice with a set of self-imposed push-ups. Since then Miami defensive backs have taken to pointing to the ground whenever a teammate is beaten—or "juiced," as they call it—in practice. It's not uncommon to see a defensive back reflexively drop and do 10 between snaps during a game.

The most impressive thing about Reed, says first-year coach Larry Coker, is his ability to back up his inspirational words with indelible plays. Following a lackadaisical first half against Troy State on Nov. 6, in which Miami built a 17–7 lead, Reed challenged his teammates to elevate their play. He then sparked a 21-point third quarter by returning an interception 27 yards for a touchdown.

Midway through the next week's grudge match against Florida State, which Miami led 21–13 at intermission, Reed made a motivational prop out of the right shoulder he had dislocated while breaking up a pass in the second quarter. "Stop asking me if I'm hurt!" he hollered at his teammates, his eyes tearing up. "Of course I'm hurt! I'm in pain! But I'm really hurt that we're not taking care of business out there!" He proceeded to pick off two passes in the second half of the 49–27 victory.

Reed missed the preseason drills before his freshman year because of a sprained right ankle sustained in a pickup basketball game, and he ended up redshirting. The following season, with Miami still shackled by NCAA scholarship reductions levied in 1995, secondary coach Chuck Pagano gave Reed a shot at becoming the first-string strong safety. Reed earned the job, but in the third game of his sophomore season he had the most humbling experience of his athletic career. With the Hurricanes ahead 23–20 and 1:41 remaining in a home game against underdog Penn State, Rumph, then a true freshman, let Nittany Lions receiver Chafie Fields get past him for a 79-yard game-winning touchdown reception. Rumph and Reed, who failed to back up Rumph on the play, were benched the next week. It would be the only game in Reed's four years that he didn't start. "I was angry at first that I was being made an example of," Reed says, "but the incident made me work harder."

After making eight interceptions and 80 tackles and being named a consensus All-America as a junior last year, Reed was projected as a potential first-round NFL draft pick but decided that a chance to earn his degree and a shot at the national title was worth more than one year's salary, of perhaps as much as $1.5 million. "Good Lord, my family could have used the money," he says, "but I didn't want to leave without helping Miami win a championship."

"I'm incredibly proud of how far we've come together," said Reed. "These guys will always be like family to me." ∎

9

ROD WOODSON

PURDUE 1983–1986

"Woodson used his nose for the ball and outsized athleticism to blanket the field—and to flip it. He intercepted 11 passes (returning three for touchdowns), recovered seven fumbles and once held the Purdue record for combined return yards (2,014)." —DICK FRIEDMAN

▸ 1986 CONSENSUS ALL-AMERICA
▸ ALSO TWO-TIME ALL-AMERICA IN HURDLES

Woodson was a three-time All-Big Ten selection.

PHOTOGRAPH BY TONY TOMSIC

HE APPROACHED hurdling with a football mentality, running through the hurdles instead of clearing them cleanly. "In practice, blood was always streaming down his legs," says Purdue track coach Mike Poehlein. "Most hurdlers would call for medical attention, but Rod wouldn't stop until practice was over."

—Jill Lieber, SI, September 7, 1992

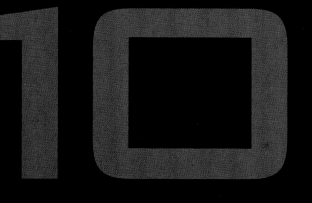

10

TROY POLAMALU

USC 1999–2002

" Polamalu finished his career with six interceptions, 13 deflections and four blocked punts. His knack for big plays and quiet leadership helped usher in USC's decade of dominance under Pete Carroll. " —PETE THAMEL

▸ 2002 CONSENSUS ALL-AMERICA
▸ 29 CAREER TACKLES FOR LOSS, THREE INTERCEPTION RETURNS FOR TOUCHDOWNS

SUCCESS IN football was also part of his heritage. His brother, Kaio Aumua, played at Texas–El Paso; his cousin Nicky Sualua was a tailback for the Cincinnati Bengals and the Dallas Cowboys; and Troy's uncle Kennedy Pola played fullback at USC from 1982 to '85. Polamalu maintained the family tradition at USC, where he was one of three finalists for the 2002 Thorpe Award. It was at USC too, that he had his last haircut—in 2000, when as a sophomore he was told to do so by a coach. Polamalu's mane is now so long that it obscures the name on the back of his jersey, revealing only the first and last letters, but he has no plans to cut it again unless his wife, Theodora, insists. "It's a part of you," he says. "It just feels like an appendage. I guess I'd save a lot of money on shampoo and conditioner, rubber bands . . . . "

—*Nunyo Demasio, SI, November 14, 2005*

Polamalu made his name with big plays and big hair.

PHOTOGRAPH BY STEPHEN DUNN/GETTY IMAGES

10

BEST COACHES

IN THE FOURTH QUARTER OF THE 2016 NATIONAL CHAMPIONSHIP GAME, NICK SABAN CALLED A PLAY THAT, AS HE NOTED AFTERWARD, HE WOULD HAVE BEEN KILLED FOR HAD IT GONE WRONG. HE WENT FOR AN ONSIDE KICK AGAINST CLEMSON, AND IT WAS EXECUTED SO PERFECTLY THAT ALABAMA'S MARLON HUMPHREY CAUGHT THE BALL ON THE FLY. THE CRIMSON TIDE SOON SCORED A TOUCHDOWN AND TOOK A LEAD IT WOULD NEVER RELINQUISH.

THE DARING CALL IS THE KIND THAT NOT ONLY WINS A TITLE BUT ALSO BUILDS A LEGEND. AND A LEGEND HELPS IF YOU WANT TO BE REMEMBERED AS AN ALL-TIME GREAT COACH. OUR PANEL'S TOP COACH BEGAN BUILDING HIS BEFORE HE EVER STEPPED ON THE FOOTBALL FIELD, WHEN HE WAS A YOUNG MAN ATTENDING A CARNIVAL AND HE AGREED TO WRESTLE AGAINST A BEAR.

PAUL (BEAR) BRYANT HAS HIS CHAMPIONSHIPS TOO, BUT THE MAN IN THE HOUNDSTOOTH HAT ALSO HAD AURA. HIS STATURE IS SUCH THAT IT IS WAS SHOCKING THAT AFTER SABAN'S CALL SOME WERE SUGGESTING THAT HE COULD OVERTAKE THE BEAR AS THE GREATEST COACH EVER. THE REAL WINNERS OF SUCH A COMPETITION ARE ALABAMA FANS. BRYANT AND SABAN ARE THE ONLY INDIVIDUALS FROM THE SAME SCHOOL TO FINISH ONE-TWO IN ANY CATEGORY IN THIS BOOK.

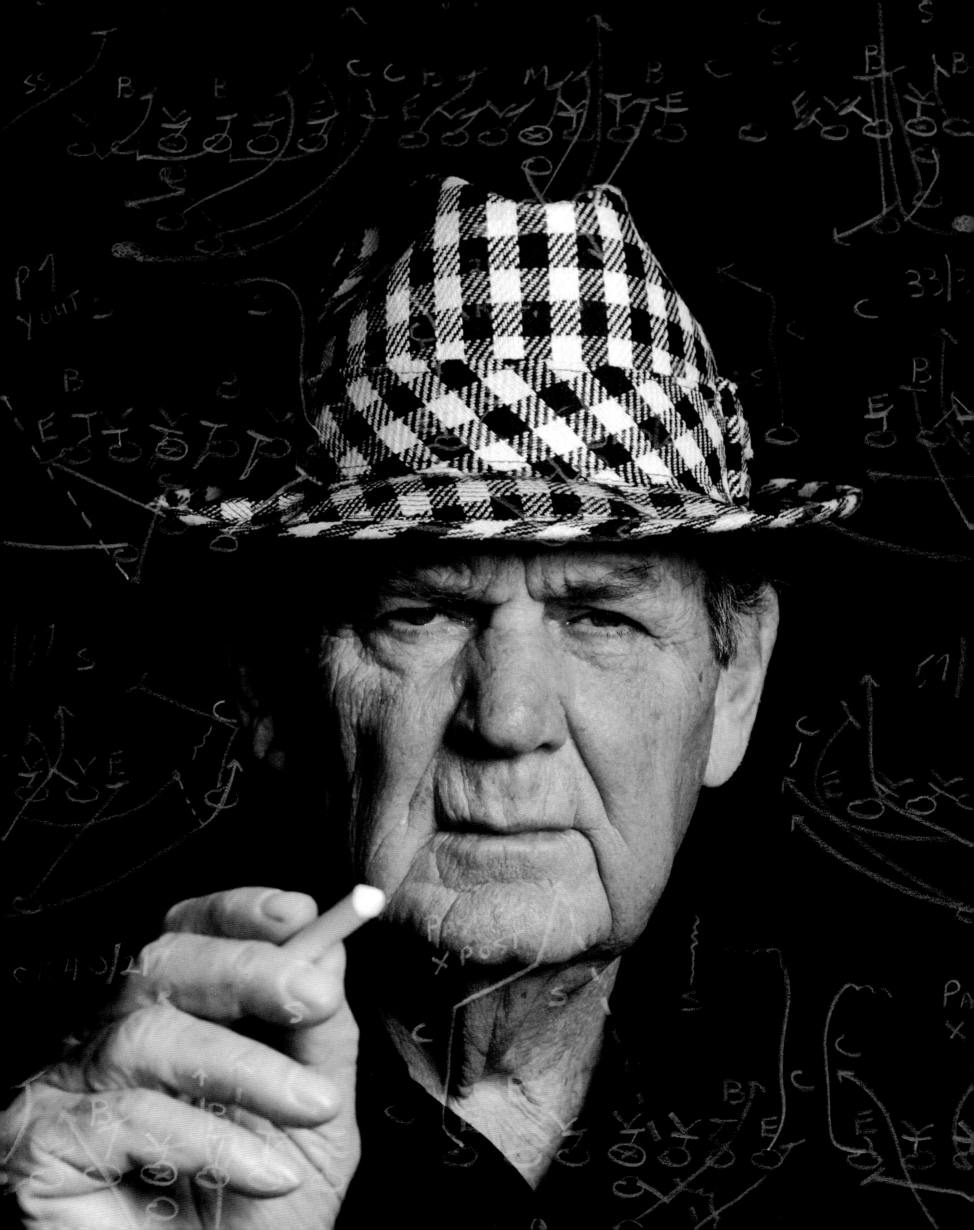

1

PAUL
BRYANT

MARYLAND 1945
KENTUCKY 1946–1953
TEXAS A&M 1954–1957
ALABAMA 1958–1982

" Bryant won six national titles and 15 bowl games. More importantly, he became a larger-than-life folk hero in Alabama and an icon throughout the South. Few coaches have been able to approach his ability to inspire, adapt and win. " —WILLIAM F. REED

▸ 323-85-17 CAREER RECORD
▸ 14 SEC CHAMPIONSHIPS

FOR ALABAMA the Bear is triumph, at last; even more than that, he is justification. The Bear hates all that joking about him being some sort of Dixie Christ (his cardplaying friends back at Indian Hills refer to him as "Old Water-Walker"—behind his back), and he's right to, for whether or not it's sacrilege, it's bad theology. The Bear is very human. That is the point. He is one of their own good old boys who took on the rest of the nation and whipped it. The wisest thing that the Bear never did was to run against George Wallace for governor, not so much because he probably would have lost and that would have burst his balloon of omnipotence, but because he would have forced his fellow Alabamians to choose between their two heroes who didn't pussyfoot around against the Yankees.

—*Frank Deford, SI, November 23, 1981*

Bryant liked to supervise his practices from above.

PHOTOGRAPHS BY NEIL LEIFER (LEFT) AND WALTER IOOSS JR.

2

NICK SABAN

TOLEDO 1990
MICHIGAN STATE 1995–1999
LSU 2000–2004
ALABAMA 2007–PRESENT

" All he does is win—championships. Even with a two-year hiatus to the NFL, Saint Nick has won five national titles at two schools (LSU and Alabama) in 13 years, all while competing in America's premier conference. " —MARK GODICH

▸ FIRST MODERN COACH TO WIN A NATIONAL TITLE AT TWO SCHOOLS
▸ 105–18 RECORD AT ALABAMA

INSTEAD OF TALKING about wins and championships, Saban speaks about the Process. In its most basic form, the Process is Saban's term for concentrating on the steps to success rather than worrying about the end result. Instead of thinking about the scoreboard, think about dominating the man on the opposite side of the line of scrimmage. Instead of thinking about a conference title, think about finishing a ninth rep in the weight room. Instead of thinking about graduating, think about writing a great paper for Intro to Psych. Athletic directors and coaches across the country are trying to replicate his philosophy and results. Call it the Sabanization of college football.

—Andy Staples, SI, August 20, 2012

Saban's teams have dominated the BCS-playoff era.

PHOTOGRAPH BY BOB ROSATO

NOTRE DAME 1918–1930

Rockne had been a Walter Camp All-America at end.

PHOTOGRAPH BY UNIVERSITY OF NOTRE DAME ARCHIVES

3

" The gold standard from the Golden Dome. The Rock perfected the backfield box formation and, most influentially, the pregame and halftime locker room pep talk. During his tenure at Notre Dame his brilliantly drilled teams went 105-12-5. " —DICK FRIEDMAN

ROCKNE BLITHELY confessed that he used a bogus telegram from little Billy to fire up his 1922 team, and that three years later, when Notre Dame trailed Northwestern 10–0 at halftime, he quit as coach in order to goad his players into a 13–10 win. "It was really a great comeback," Rockne observed.

—Coles Phinizy, SI, September 10, 1979

KNUTE ROCKNE

▸ THREE NATIONAL TITLES
▸ FIVE UNDEFEATED TEAMS

4

JOE PATERNO

PENN STATE 1966–2011

" Long hailed as a beacon of rectitude in college sports, Paterno's legacy was altered at the end by scandal. In 46 years as head coach, Paterno's teams won 409 games and two national titles, and gained a reputation as true "student-athletes." However, the 2011 child-abuse scandal involving longtime assistant coach Jerry Sandusky will be forever attached to Paterno's record. " —TIM LAYDEN

▸ NATIONAL COACH OF THE YEAR
  AWARD A RECORD FIVE TIMES
▸ 409-136-3 CAREER RECORD

"JOE'S DIFFERENT from the rest of us," Oklahoma coach Barry Switzer once said, and he's right. How many coaches draw up game plans while listening to opera? How many quote Browning ("A man's reach should exceed his grasp, or what's a heaven for?") to their teams? How many write opinion pieces for *The New York Times* and throw in words like "sophistry," "proselytizing" and "mendacious"? How many gave their seniors the spring off this year so they could get their degrees by December? How many let their best lineman (Mike Reid, 1967) take a year off to star in a theater production? Let their kicker (Chris Bahr, 1973) stay home from a road game at Air Force to play for the soccer team?

—*Rick Reilly, SI, December 22, 1986*

Thick glasses accentuated Paterno's academic bearing.

PHOTOGRAPH BY JAMES DRAKE

5

URBAN MEYER

BOWLING GREEN 2001–2002
UTAH 2003–2004
FLORIDA 2005–2010
OHIO STATE 2012–PRESENT

" Offensive mastermind and maestro of tough love, Meyer became the second coach to win national titles at different schools. His most recent was the most impressive: The 2014 Buckeyes won the title game with their third-string quarterback. " —AUSTIN MURPHY

▸ THREE NATIONAL TITLES
▸ 154–27 CAREER RECORD

BEFORE COACHING one game in the Big Ten, Meyer had trod on toes from Madison to Ann Arbor. To anyone who has watched him turn around programs at Bowling Green, then Utah, then in Gainesville, this comes as zero surprise. Meyer has always operated with a near total absence of regard for what others think of him. While he may be a bit of a loner—his intensity makes him slightly awkward socially—he's very comfortable venturing up to the edge of the rules, but never crossing the line, he insists. In the convocation of Big Ten coaches he is very much the unpolished arriviste. Between that glower and his SEC pedigree, there seems to be something Machiavellian and cutthroat about him. His coaching peers are right to feel threatened.

—Austin Murphy, SI, April 23, 2012

Meyer has a 10–2 postseason record.

FATHER WANTS BEST

Growing up in a household where the demands were great, praise was sparing and quitting was forbidden helped shape Urban Meyer into the coach he would become

BY S.L. PRICE

AT FIRST GLANCE THE premier college football coach in the land grew up in a home so stable that it's a near caricature of normal. His parents, Urban Jr. (known as Bud) and Gisela, were married 38 years and raised their three kids in Ashtabula, Ohio, insulated from the Rust Belt town's economic decline by Bud's job as a chemical engineer and Gisela's as a gourmet chef.

Bud never missed a game Urban played or coached, no matter how far away; when Urban was a lowly football assistant at Illinois State in 1988, he recalls, "we go play Indiana State. There's 500 people in that stadium. My dad and mom drive to Terre Haute, nine hours, watch the game and drive home. How many would do that—to watch you coach?" Gisela's love was unconditional, Bud's cool and flinty. The kids regarded their father with an awe that was growing rare in the Me decade: Bud was God, smarter and more powerful than anyone alive. Such a force, of course, provided a vivid role model for a future coach, old-school division. His dad's expectations were "almost unachievable," Urban says: The kids were to get straight A's, skip grades, be impeccable. Any success was greeted with the barest of praise, and any failure, any transgression, with the command to run hundreds of laps around the house or play fierce games of pepper.

Although Urban (Bud) Meyer Jr. was named, like his father and son, for a pope, and spent three years at seminary and would remain a staunch pre-Vatican II Catholic, he cursed like a stevedore. His idol was Woody Hayes. There's a reason, during games, that Florida players rarely find themselves awash in praise.

When Meyer won his first national title at Florida, after the 2006 season, it was as clear a moment of arrival as football had seen in years. Meyer had grown up worshipping Ohio State, wearing number 45 in honor of Archie Griffin; he had teared up the first time he touched a Buckeyes jersey. Now, on a perfect January night in Phoenix, this son of Ohio had just crushed Woody's old school 41–14. Meyer was 42 years old, in just his sixth year as a head coach. He shook hands with Buckeyes coach Jim Tressel at midfield, walked to the sideline and found his father was waiting. "Well," Bud said. "It's about time you did that."

When Urban was in second grade, his little sister Erika came home crying because two of his classmates had mocked her clothes. Bud told Urban, "Go to school and beat the living crap out of them." Urban rode the morning bus full of dread, "but he did it," Erika says. That night Bud sat his seven-year-old boy at the head of the dinner table and announced, "You became a man today."

That may not have been an exaggeration. "Yeah, it kind of changed him," Erika says, "from the little guy he was then to the man he was in junior high school, this cocky, arrogant guy. He could do no wrong."

His dad, though, wanted results. He'd sit in the stands, taping his thoughts on Urban's at bats and carries into a portable recorder. Sports was Urban's job, and Bud controlled the purse strings: a dollar for home runs, 50 cents for an RBI. Early on he demanded 25 cents back for every strikeout, but by Urban's senior year at St. John High such a refund seemed piddling. So after Urban took one curveball for a called strike three, Bud made him run home. "About eight miles," Urban says.

He was a two-sport king—a fullback and defensive back in the fall, a strong-armed shortstop in the spring. But by his senior year colleges were offering only baseball scholarships. Atlanta selected Urban in the 13th round of the 1982 draft, and a week after graduation he boarded a Pan Am jet for rookie ball in Bradenton, Fla. He was 17 and soon miserable. He was homesick and hitless when a rogue grounder smacked him in the face. One eye swollen shut, he found a pay phone and called Ashtabula in tears. He told his dad that he was through with baseball.

"You're never welcome in this house again," Bud said. "There's no such thing as a quitter in the Meyer household. Do you understand me?" Urban was speechless. "Your mother will want to talk to you," Bud added. "Make sure you give her a call at Christmas."

Urban hung up—and tried harder. But nothing helped. He finished his season of rookie ball hitting .170. When baseball died for him, Meyer enrolled at Cincinnati, planning to salvage his football dreams by walking on. He made the squad as a defensive back, lifted and ran to exhaustion—but failed again. The Bearcats were terrible, though Meyer still wasn't good enough to start. He kept switching majors, but he found his true course of study, when tradition-laden St. Xavier High called in search of a coaching intern.

After graduating from Cincinnati, Meyer spent 1986 and '87 as a graduate assistant at Ohio State, where he weathered his first blast of Earle Bruce. Another two-year stint as an assistant, making about $6,000 at Illinois State, nearly forced the newly wed Meyer into selling insurance, but then he got his break: In 1990 Bruce, by then at Colorado State, had an opening for a receivers coach; he remembered Meyer and gave him the job. But Meyer joined a staff headed for a cliff. Within two years Bruce would be fired, accused by the Colorado State administration of creating "a climate of intimidation and fear" and of having hit at least nine players. Bruce admitted to the physical contact and to having broken NCAA rules against off-season coaching, but he made no apology for the "climate" he created: coats and ties at dinner, no earrings, ironfisted rule by the coach. Meyer fit right in. ∎

6

WOODY HAYES

OHIO STATE 1951–1978

" The domineering Hayes took no prisoners (especially from Ann Arbor) as his Buckeyes routinely pummeled foes into submission. " —DICK FRIEDMAN

▸ FIVE NATIONAL TITLES
▸ 205-60-10 CAREER RECORD

THE ESSENTIAL conflict of Hayes's life was neatly encapsulated in the run-pass dilemma. The one form of attack personified the earth, primal struggle, atavism, simplicity, things that could be controlled; the other embodied air, lightness, modernity, freedom and risk. Hayes was of the earth, an old-fashioned toiler. "I despise gimmicks!" he often roared. A 250-pound fullback was not a gimmick. A pass was. I do not think Woody Hayes was a great football coach. He won a lot, but what does that mean? And yet, having said that, I think it is likely he was a great football man. He had many virtues. He was honest. He affected people. He believed in scholarship. He had no pretenses. He and his wife, Anne, lived for 36 years in the same house, with few possessions. In classes he taught at Ohio State he told his students how Socrates would walk happily through the marketplace saying, "Look at the things I don't need."

—Rick Telander, SI, March 23, 1987

Hayes's teams won 13 Big Ten titles.

Bowden's reign elevated FSU to a powerhouse program.

PHOTOGRAPH BY ROBERT ROGERS

7

BOBBY BOWDEN

WEST VIRGINIA 1970–1975
FLORIDA STATE 1976–2009

"Bowden won the 1993 and '99 national titles, but here's an even more impressive stat: His Seminoles finished in the top four of the final AP poll every year from 1987 to 1999, a feat that will never be duplicated." —ANDY STAPLES

▸ 357-124-4 CAREER RECORD
▸ 28 CONSECUTIVE BOWL APPEARANCES

BOWDEN HAS made Florida State's reputation in part by beating name opponents on the road. He revels in being the short guy in the bar who taps the big guy's chest and says, "Anytime, anywhere." This year the Seminoles will play Florida and Notre Dame—on the road. Why? "Ego, I guess," says Bowden.

—*Austin Murphy, SI, August 30, 1993*

BEST REGULAR-SEASON GAMES

THE 10

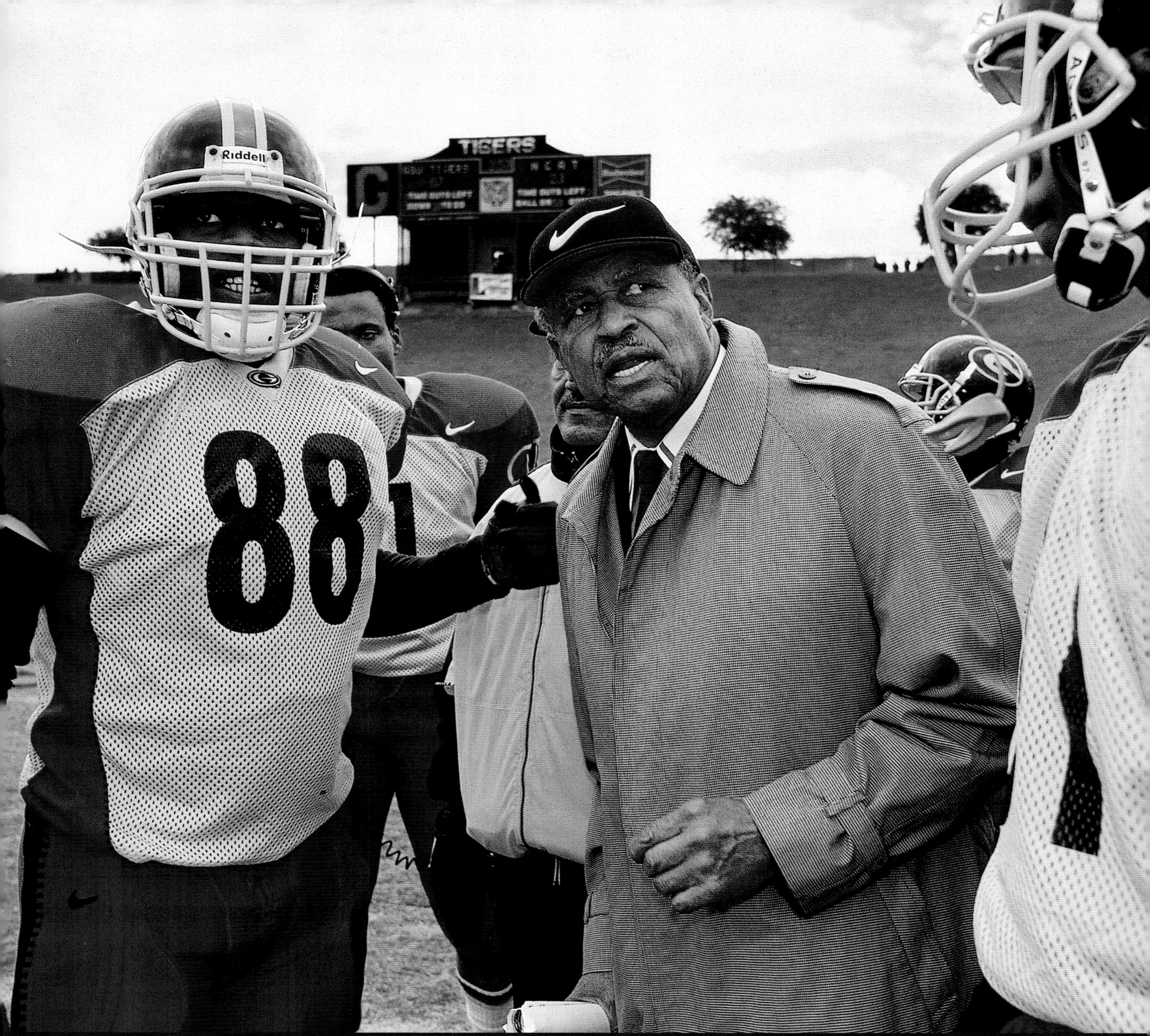

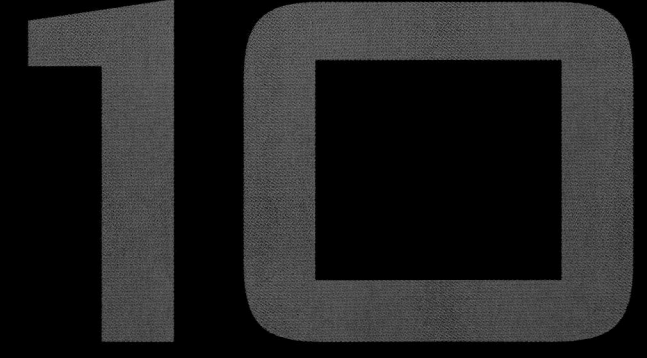

10

EDDIE ROBINSON

GRAMBLING STATE 1941–1997

"The legendary coach at tiny, historically black Grambling State won 408 games, third only to Joe Paterno and Division III coach John Gagliardi. Robinson built Grambling into a nationally recognized name and sent more than 200 players to the NFL." —TIM LAYDEN

- 408-165-15 CAREER RECORD
- 17 SWAC TITLES

From the third grade Robinson wanted to be a coach.

PHOTOGRAPH BY WILLIAM SNYDER

WHEN ROBINSON got to Grambling, La., in 1941, the school was called the Louisiana Negro Normal and Industrial Institute. He was the football, basketball and baseball coach, and he made $63.75 a month. In those days he led the drill team at the half and even wrote the game story for the local newspaper.

—*Richard Hoffer, SI, December 1, 1997*

9

BUD WILKINSON

OKLAHOMA 1947–1963

" For all of Wilkinson's remarkable feats, one mark still stands out most. From 1953 to '57, his Sooners won 47 consecutive games, a record that may never be broken. " —PETE THAMEL

▸ THREE NATIONAL TITLES
▸ 14 BIG 8 CHAMPIONSHIPS, 145-29-4 CARRER RECORD

"THE AVERAGE alumnus looks at the scoreboard and sees that one team won and the other lost—so the team that won was smartly coached, well-conditioned and had outstanding morale. The other team was stupid. That's about the way most of them look at it," Wilkinson says. "In reality what takes place is that both teams are well-conditioned, smartly coached. They're both made up of fine young men. The winning or losing is in that intangible factor of mental toughness. You've got to have that to be a champion . . . where you get it, I don't know, but you've got to have it. If you're going to be a champion, you must be willing to pay a greater price than your opponent will ever pay. There must be the willingness to compete when the chips are down. Some people don't want to pay this price—and I've no objections to them—but I don't want them around because we aren't going to win with them."

—*Joan Flynn Dreyspool, SI, September 12, 1955*

Wilkinson's teams also had a 31-game winning streak.

PHOTOGRAPH BY EARL SHUGARS/AP

8

FRANK LEAHY

"Leahy nurtured and built the mystique of Notre Dame football. A devout Catholic, he saw the program as a sort of holy crusade, endearing him to some and enraging others." —WILLIAM F. REED

▸ FOUR NATIONAL TITLES, SIX UNDEFEATED SEASONS
▸ 107-13-9 CAREER RECORD

"NOTRE DAME is not an ordinary team," Leahy said. "It has a great tradition to live up to. The coach hears the cheers of the thousands present in the stadium, and it all builds up in him until he gets the feeling that it is absolutely unthinkable that the Notre Dame team should go down in defeat."

—*Gerald Holland, SI, October 31, 1955*

Leahy left the Irish for two years to serve in World War II.

PHOTOGRAPH BY HARRY L. HALL/AP

AS RESULTS OF COMPETITIONS GO, THE TIE IS NOT A POPULAR ONE. THE MASTERS OF COLLEGE FOOTBALL THOUGHT SO LITTLE OF TIES THAT THEY OUTLAWED THEM BEGINNING IN THE 1996 SEASON, IN FAVOR OF AN OVERTIME SYSTEM WHICH CAN PRODUCE THE RAPID-FIRE SCORING OF TOUCHDOWNS AND IS GREATLY FAVORED BY ANYONE WHO HAS BET THE OVER.

BUT PERHAPS THE MASTERS OF COLLEGE FOOTBALL HAVE IT WRONG, AND A TIE IS MORE OF A WINNER THAN THEY THINK. OUR PANEL CHOSE THREE TIES TO BE INCLUDED IN OUR LIST OF THE TOP REGULAR-SEASON GAMES EVER.

EACH OF THESE TIES DID HAVE SHOCK VALUE. HARVARD AND YALE TIED IN 1968 AFTER A STUNNING CRIMSON RALLY. THE '66 TIE BETWEEN MICHIGAN STATE AND NOTRE DAME WAS SURPRISING BECAUSE IN THE FINAL MINUTES NOTRE DAME DID NOT PLAY TO WIN. THEN THERE WAS THE '46 ARMY–NOTRE DAME GAME, IN WHICH OFFENSE WAS EXPECTED BUT NONE CAME. THE IRISH CAME CLOSEST TO SCORING WITH A DRIVE THAT STALLED AT ARMY'S THREE-YARD LINE. "LOOK, THE GAME ENDED 0–0," NOTRE DAME QUARTERBACK JOHNNY LUJACK TOLD SI'S PAUL ZIMMERMAN A HALF CENTURY LATER. "IF IT HAD ENDED 7–0, WOULD THEY STILL TALK ABOUT IT?"

1

2013
AUBURN-
ALABAMA

AUBURN 34, ALABAMA 28

"With the score tied and one second remaining in a game that would decide the SEC West title, Alabama coach Nick Saban called for a 57-yard field goal attempt. Believing the attempt might fall short, Auburn coach Gus Malzahn positioned Chris Davis in the end zone. Davis caught the ball and ran it 109 yards for a touchdown." —ANDY STAPLES

▸ ALABAMA WAS UNDEFEATED AND RANKED NO. 1
▸ TIME WAS PUT BACK ON CLOCK FOR THE FINAL PLAY

THOUGH ALABAMA quarterback AJ McCarron had bolstered his chances for a Heisman Trophy with a 99-yard touchdown pass earlier in the quarter, Saban opted against a Hail Mary in a tie game with one second on the clock. He sent out a field goal unit full of jumbo linemen adept at blocking but not athletic enough to cover a kick. The kick came up short. Davis fielded it. He ran it out. Alabama linebacker Adrian Hubbard, perhaps the only Crimson Tide player on the field with a shot to tackle Davis, might have saved his team's chances for a third consecutive national title, but he got sandwiched between two Auburn players and tumbled to the ground.

—Andy Staples, SI, December 9, 2013

Tre Mason (21) watched Davis's run in disbelief.

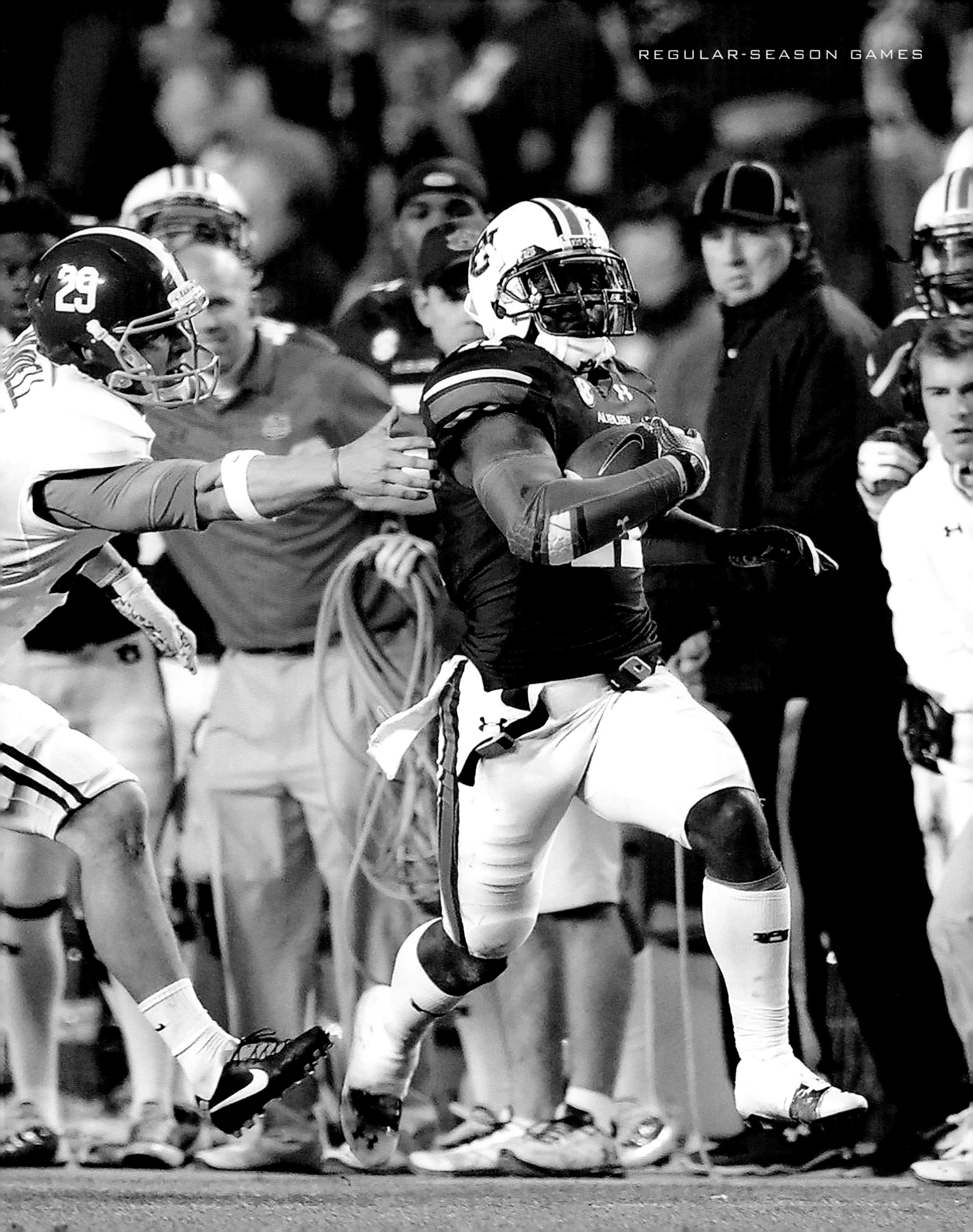

2

1969
TEXAS-
ARKANSAS

" With President Nixon looking on, top-ranked Texas scored all of its points in the fourth quarter. Nixon rankled fans of undefeated Penn State afterward when he proclaimed the Longhorns national champions. "

—MARK GODICH

▸ TEAMS WERE SOUTHWEST CONFERENCE RIVALS
▸ TEXAS MADE TWO-POINT CONVERSION AFTER FIRST TD

IT HAD BEEN quite a football game, but for Fayetteville, Ark., it was merely the climax of a weeklong metamorphosis—from the nation's No. 2 chicken producer to its sports capital. Fayetteville was agog at its first Presidential visit. "Nixon?" said a grinning cab driver. "As far as I'm concerned that's the biggest thing since Johnny Cash came last year."

—*Dan Jenkins, SI, December 15, 1969*

Texas RB Jim Bertelsen scored the decisive TD.

PHOTOGRAPH BY JOHN IACONO

1971
NEBRASKA-
OKLAHOMA

NEBRASKA 35, OKLAHOMA 31

" Nebraska's Thanksgiving-day win started with Johnny Rodgers's 72-yard punt return for a TD and ended with the Cornhuskers driving 74 yards for the winning touchdown. " —TIM LAYDEN

- OKLAHOMA TWICE OVERCAME 11-POINT DEFICITS
- NEBRASKA SCORED WINNING TOUCHDOWN WITH 1:38 LEFT IN FOURTH QUARTER

IN ESSENCE, what won it for Nebraska was a pearl of a punt return in the game's first 3½ minutes. Everything else balances out, more or less, even the precious few mistakes. The two teams swapped touchdowns evenly from scrimmage, four for four, and Oklahoma added a field goal. But always there lingered the one thing they had not traded, that sudden, shocking, punt return by Johnny Rodgers. It was one of those insanely thrilling things in which a single player, seized by the moment, twists, whirls, slips, holds his balance and, sprinting, makes it all the way to the goal line. Rodgers went 72 yards for the touchdown, one which keeps growing larger in the minds of all. And afterward, back on the Nebraska bench, he did what most everybody in Norman, Okla., probably felt like doing: He threw up.

—Dan Jenkins, SI, December 6, 1971

Jeff Kinney ran for four touchdowns against Oklahoma.

PHOTOGRAPH BY RICH CLARKSON/CLARKSON CREATIVE

CAL 25, STANFORD 20

The band's joy, and trombonist, would soon be crushed.

PHOTOGRAPH BY CARL VITI/AP

"On the game's last play, Cal came up with a five-lateral try that concluded when Kevin Moen ran into the Stanford band. Moen hit trombonist Gary Tyrrell, a moment that has been replayed a zillion times over the years." —WILLIAM F. REED

▸ STANFORD KICKED FIELD GOAL WITH :04 REMAINING
▸ STANFORD BAND TOOK FIELD DURING THE RUNBACK

A TROMBONE player became as celebrated afterward as any athlete, and at one point Cal had players named Richard Rodgers and Gilbert and Sullivan on the field at once, only one of them legally. "It appeared to me that the weakest part of the Stanford defense was the woodwinds," said one spectator.

—*Ron Fimrite, SI, September 1, 1983*

1982
CAL-
STANFORD

5

2007
APPALACHIAN STATE-
MICHIGAN

" Somehow, the FCS team ran circles around the sport's winningest program. Trailing 28–17 at halftime, the No. 5 Wolverines clawed back, but lost on a blocked field goal. " —AUSTIN MURPHY

▸ ASU WENT AHEAD ON FIELD GOAL WITH :26 REMAINING
▸ FIRST TIME FCS TEAM BEAT RANKED FBS TEAM

COREY LYNCH, who moments earlier had come slicing off the edge to block Michigan's potential game-winning, 37-yard field goal attempt. stayed on his back "for a couple of minutes," partly because he wanted to bask in the moment. "I was looking around, at 109,000 people, all quiet," he said. "I couldn't believe what I was seeing."

—*Austin Murphy, SI, September 10, 2007*

App State was the two-time defending I-AA champ.

PHOTOGRAPH BY TONY DING/ICON SPORTSWIRE

1984
BOSTON COLLEGE-
MIAMI

BOSTON COLLEGE 47, MIAMI 45

> " The 48-yard Hail Mary from '84 Heisman winner Doug Flutie to Gerard Phelan delivered BC an indelible victory. The game's biggest legacy may be the transformation of the school, as BC's growth from regional to national college was fueled by that moment. In academia, it's known as the "Flutie Effect." " —PETE THAMEL

▸ MIAMI WAS THE DEFENDING NATIONAL CHAMPION
▸ WIDELY SEEN GAME WAS NATIONALLY TELEVISED ON CBS THE DAY AFTER THANKSGIVING

GERALD PHELAN, Flutie's roommate, was one of the three receivers deployed. "You get on the same frequency with Doug," Phelan said, "and somehow things happen." Flutie scrambled and at his own 37 he let fly. Two Miami defenders went up for the ball. Recalled Phelan, "I was falling, and [the ball] came down right here [groin level], and when I rolled over, I could see writing on the ground. Colored writing. I was in the end zone!" Two days later, the Eagles reviewed the films and discovered that Flutie had made a mistake on the play. Tight end Peter Casparriello was wide-open in the end zone. Flutie was awarded the Heisman Trophy anyway.

—*Steve Wulf, SI, October 16, 1991*

Doug Flutie celebrated with teammate brother Darren.

THE ENDING WAS NO FLUKE

The play was called Flood Tip and didn't have much chance of success, but it helped that one Miami corner acted as if Doug Flutie couldn't throw the ball that far

BY JOHN UNDERWOOD

T DOESN'T MATTER IF HE EVER PLAYS A DOWN of pro football, although it would be nice. It doesn't matter if he ever quarterbacks another game for Boston College, although it will be necessary. It doesn't matter, because on one wildly wonderful play, punctuating a wildly wonderful game—if you were there and sat down you couldn't see; if you went out for a hot dog, you missed two touchdowns—Douglas Richard Flutie summed up a wildly wonderful college career last Friday in unsunny Miami. Never mind that he has two more games to play. They can only be anticlimactic.

Of course with Flutie you never know. Forty games into his prolific passing career, you have to think in terms of "anything can happen" and other clichés. But pick your own cliché. With Flutie, they all apply.

"It's not over until the last play"? This was Friday's final play: From the line of scrimmage, a Flutieball arched high into that grieving Miami sky, covering 64 yards from toe to toe, to roommate Gerard Phelan—Flutie pushing off on his right toe and throwing into the gusting wind and rain, Phelan, in the end zone, falling directly behind and beneath the groping hands of two Miami defenders who were doing a stunning impersonation of an open door.

"It's the size of the fight in the man, not the size of the man in the fight"? At 5' 9¾"—if you don't give him the three-fourths, Flutie complains—little Dougie is not much bigger than the Heisman Trophy he will most certainly be awarded this week, deserving as he is of every metallic ounce. Miami was the biggest team on his menu. And on a day better suited for ducks, the Eagles soared with Flutie, his passing alone accounting for 472 yards and three touchdowns, his running for nine yards and another TD. When the computers stopped humming, he had become the first 10,000-yard passer in major-college history. And when he went back outside an hour afterward, still in uniform so a friend could pose him in front of the Orange Bowl scoreboard, the evidence still glistened in the gloaming: Boston College 47, defending national champion Miami 45. Cast it in bronze and put it on the mantel.

There were more than a few touches of improbability in this victory, however, just as Flutie's entire career has seemed so improbable. For in this game of breathtakingly proficient, precision passing—little Flutie and Miami's 6' 5" sophomore phenom Bernie Kosar put the ball up 84 times for 919 yards between them—it was that most imprecise of passes that did the dirty deed. The Hail Mary. The Everybody Go Long. The play you launch on a wing and a prayer when all time is gone and all else has failed. In the BC playbook, it's called Flood Tip, and it works (rarely) the way it sounds.

With six seconds on the clock and Miami ahead 45-41, three BC receivers were deployed far to the right side. At the snap, they were to sprint downfield as fast and as far as they could, in hopes of arriving in the end zone together—flooding it—about the same time Flutie's pass got there. (Fullback Steve Strachan was supposed to block for Flutie, but he, too, ran deep downfield.) If anyone was near the ball but couldn't catch it, his job was to tip it up in the air for somebody who could. On the sideline as the play started, coach Jack Bicknell was "already forming in my mind what I would tell our kids after we lost." That's how much faith he had in Flood Tip.

But such a play works "more often than you would think," says Flutie. "I'd say it's a 50-50." However, he could recall it working exactly one time, against Temple earlier this year. But then, he says, "I've been lucky all my life, so why not?"

Phelan is the best of as sure-handed a group of receivers as any one team has ever had. The Hurricanes tried combination coverages on both sides, with linebackers spraying out to support against the pass and to contain Flutie's scrambling. Miami always seemed just a fingertip away from interceding, but Troy Stradford, Scott Gieselman, Kelvin Martin, et al., made grab after tight-fingered grab of the wet ball.

Among all the others until that final moment, it was Phelan that Flutie had found most often—10 times for 178 yards and a touchdown. Then, on the last play, when Phelan went by Hurricane defensive back Darrell Fullington (alas, a freshman), he was surprised that Fullington let him go. "He must have thought Doug couldn't throw it that far," Phelan said. Phelan was a full step ahead at the Miami 10. Fullington and Reggie Sutton, another of the three Miami defenders in the area, backpedaled like outfielders and still were in good position right in front of the goal line as the fly ball came down.

Upfield, Miami had rushed only two men, but one of them, Jerome Brown, had squeezed through and chased Flutie out of the pocket and to his right. But that was exactly how Flutie wanted it. "The scrambling is important—it gives me the time I need on such a play," he said. (It's oh so matter of fact with Flutie, you understand.) "I knew I could throw it that far, even against the wind. I can throw 75 yards if I have to. Actually, I had to take a little off it to keep it in the end zone." *(See?)*

After Flutie sidestepped Brown, he circled back and around, and was at his 37-yard line when he came forward, planted his left foot and let fly. He said he "really did see Phelan break clear. He was the guy I wanted to get it to, but after I threw the ball, I didn't see anything much until the referee raised his arms. Then, I admit, I couldn't believe it, even when everybody started yelling and picking me up."

Neither could Phelan. Fullington mistimed his leap and was nudged off-balance on the way up by his own man, Sutton, as he also leaped. The ball whistled through their arms.

A fluke? Well, not really. A Flutie. ∎

Pete Varney caught the tying two-point conversion.

PHOTOGRAPH BY JERRY COOKE

1968 HARVARD-YALE

" The Elis led 29–13 with 42 seconds left, but the Crimson tallied two touchdowns and two two-point conversions to close the game. *The Harvard Crimson* headline said it all: HARVARD BEATS YALE, 29–29. " —DICK FRIEDMAN

▸ BOTH TEAMS WERE 8-0
▸ FIRST UNDEFEATED MATCHUP BETWEEN THE RIVALS SINCE 1909

IN THE Yale dressing room, no one spoke. Slowly the team undressed, showered, then dressed. Still no one spoke. Finally an outsider said, "You're still undefeated. You're still the Ivy League co-champions." Bruce Weinstein, a tight end, looked over. "No," he said softly, "when you've done what we just did you've lost."

—*Pat Putnam, SI, December 2, 1968*

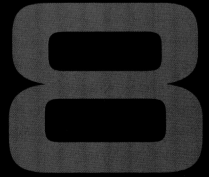

ARMY 0, NOTRE DAME 0

The shutout game featured four Heisman winners.

PHOTOGRAPH BY AL FENN/THE LIFE PICTURE COLLECTION/GETTY IMAGES

"A capacity crowd of 74,121 jammed Yankee Stadium to watch this battle of unbeatens, played when college football was far bigger than the fledgling NFL. They saw two powerhouse offenses be shut down." —TIM LAYDEN

‣ ARMY HAD A 25-GAME WINNING STREAK
‣ NOTRE DAME WAS NAMED 1946 NATIONAL CHAMPION

8

1946 ARMY- NOTRE DAME

NOTRE DAME mounted the most serious threat of the game in the second quarter. But Billy Gompers was stopped on fourth-and-one at the three. "I told [QB Johnny] Lujack, 'Hell, you should have given me the ball,' " John Panelli says. "That was the end zone where my parents were sitting. I'd have scored."

—*Paul Zimmerman, SI, November 24, 1997*

MICHIGAN STATE 10,
NOTRE DAME 10

The defenses dominated this battle of unbeatens.

PHOTOGRAPH BY JAMES DRAKE

" After the Irish decided to settle for a tie instead of going for victory, SI wrote, "Old Notre Dame will tie over all." This twist on the school's fight song led to a magazine bonfire on campus. " —WILLIAM F. REED

EVEN AS the Spartan defenders taunted them and called the timeouts that the Irish should have been calling, Notre Dame ran into the line, the place where the game was hopelessly played all afternoon. No one really expected a verdict in that last desperate moment. But they wanted someone to try.

—Dan Jenkins, SI, November 28, 1966

▸ SCHOOLS WERE RANKED
NO. 1 AND NO. 2
▸ TEAMS FINISHED AS SPLIT
CHAMPIONS IN POLLS

1966
MICHIGAN STATE-
NOTRE DAME

10

NOTRE DAME 31, FLORIDA STATE 24

1993 NOTRE DAME- FLORIDA STATE

"A matchup of the top-ranked Seminoles and second-ranked Fighting Irish came down to a final play. Notre Dame's Shawn Wooden knocked down eventual Heisman winner Charlie Ward's pass near the goal line to seal the win." —ANDY STAPLES

▸ BOTH TEAMS WERE UNBEATEN
▸ SEMINOLES SCORED TD WITH 1:39 TO GO

BEFORE MAKING the trip from Tallahassee, two Seminole players referred to "Rock Knutne." Wide receiver Tamarick Vanover asked, "What's the Gipper?" And quarterback Charlie Ward announced that he wasn't going to South Bend for a history lesson. Instead he became part of one.

—*Austin Murphy, SI, November 22, 1993*

Despite this loss FSU won the '93 national title.

PHOTOGRAPH BY PETER READ MILLER

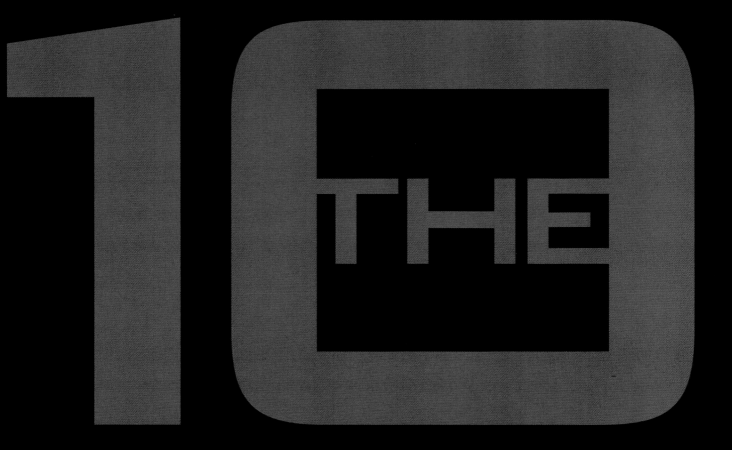

10 THE

BEST BOWL GAMES

SEVEN OF THE BOWL GAMES IN OUR TOP 10 INVOLVED TEAMS THAT WERE PLAYING FOR A NATIONAL CHAMPIONSHIP. IN THE CASE OF THE 1973 SUGAR BOWL, BOTH TEAMS ACTUALLY LEFT THE FIELD WITH A CLAIM TO A TITLE, BECAUSE THE LOSING TEAM, ALABAMA, HAD BEEN AWARDED THE TOP SPOT IN THE COACHES' POLL, WHICH THEN WAS CONDUCTED AT THE END OF THE REGULAR SEASON. THIS WAS THE TIME WHEN BOWLS WERE STILL TRANSITIONING FROM YEAR-END EXHIBITIONS TO THE CULMINATION OF ALL THESE KIDS HAVE WORKED SO HARD FOR.

BUT IF ONLY SEVEN OF OUR TOP 10 GAMES HAD CHAMPIONSHIP STAKES, IT TELLS YOU THAT THE OTHER THREE GAMES WHICH NOSED THEIR WAY ONTO THE LIST HAD TO HAVE A LITTLE SOMETHING EXTRA GOING FOR THEM. TAKE A LOOK AT THEIR STORIES, AND YOU WILL FIND WILD RALLIES, CRAZY PLAYS AND MOMENTS THAT HAVE THE QUALITY OF MYTH.

THE 1979 COTTON BOWL, FOR INSTANCE, FEATURED A COMEBACK LED BY A FLU-RIDDEN QUARTERBACK WHO ATE A BOWL OF CHICKEN SOUP AT HALFTIME, THEN HELPED HIS TEAM OVERCOME A 22-POINT DEFICIT IN THE FOURTH QUARTER. THAT QUARTERBACK WAS NOTRE DAME'S JOE MONTANA. HE DIDN'T WIN A TITLE THAT DAY, BUT HE SURELY SHOWED THAT HE WAS A CHAMPION.

2006 ROSE

TEXAS 41, USC 38

" Vince Young sashayed into the end zone on a fourth-and-five with 19 seconds left to derail the USC dynasty in a breathtaking victory. Trojans fans are still haunted by Pete Carroll's ill-fated gamble on fourth-and-two, a LenDale White run up the gut, that set up the winning Texas drive. " —PETE THAMEL

‣ USC HAD BEEN RANKED NO. 1, TEXAS NO. 2
‣ USC LED BY 12 POINTS WITH 6:42 REMAINING

ALL YOUNG did was outplay a pair of Heisman Trophy winners, amassing 467 yards of total offense. He completed 30 of 40 passes for 267 yards and ran 19 times for 200 yards and three touchdowns. His last carry, on fourth-and-five from the USC eight-yard line with 19 seconds to play, went for the touchdown that clinched the Longhorns' first national title in 35 years. It also terminated the two-time defending champion Trojans' winning streak at 34 games, extending Texas's to 20 and left a loquacious man at a temporary loss for words. "I've been planning this speech for 33 years," Longhorns coach Mack Brown told his players in the winners' locker room, "but right now I don't really know what to say."

—Austin Murphy, SI, January 9, 2006

Young ran for two TDs and a conversion in the final 4:21.

BOWL GAMES

2

1984
ORANGE

MIAMI 31, NEBRASKA 30

"In a game that would announce that the state of Florida was about to dominate the sport, Miami and freshman QB Bernie Kosar led 31–24 when Nebraska scored with 48 seconds to play. Rather than kick the PAT that would probably have locked up the national title, Cornhuskers coach Tom Osborne went for two and was stopped, giving Miami the victory." —TIM LAYDEN

▸ NEBRASKA HAD A 22-GAME WINNING STREAK
▸ KOSAR THREW FOR 300 YARDS, TWO TOUCHDOWNS

ON THE MORNING before he sent his sacrificial lambs out to slaughter the butcher, Miami coach Howard Schnellenberger gazed out a picture window in his hotel suite high above downtown Miami and wondered aloud if Nebraska realized "what a bunch of alley cats they're about to run into." He said he doubted it. He said he doubted a number of things about No. 1–ranked, 12–0 Nebraska, including whether it was as unbeatable as everybody thought. The bookies, for example, had made the Huskers an 11-point favorite. What he didn't doubt was his Hurricanes. "The only thing that worries me," he said, "is that they're so high I have to walk among them like a zombie so they won't get any higher. I mean they are high."

—John Underwood, SI, January 9, 1984

After the upset the 'Canes were voted No. 1.

PHOTOGRAPHS BY RONALD C. MODRA (LEFT) AND MANNY MILLAN

3

2007
FIESTA

BOISE STATE 43, OKLAHOMA 42

" The game ended on Boise State's Statue of Liberty play on a two-point conversion in overtime, but the highlight may be the postgame proposal (accepted!) by Broncos back Ian Johnson to his cheerleader girlfriend. " —DICK FRIEDMAN

▸ OKLAHOMA OVERCAME A 28–10 DEFICIT TO TAKE LATE LEAD
▸ BOISE TIED IN REGULATION ON A HOOK-AND-LATERAL

WAC champs Boise State were 7½ point underdogs.

JOHNSON RAN into the end zone, and Little Boise State had beaten Mighty Oklahoma, and it was the perfect ending to the perfect game. Strangers hugged. First dates kissed. Johnson threw the ball into the crowd hoping it might reach his father—but Ian was too pumped-up and overthrew his family.

—*Joe Posnanski, SI, December 28, 2009*

HOW DID THEY DO THAT?

Boise State's stunning upset of Adrian Peterson's Oklahama team depended on three trick plays, any one of which would stand on its own as jaw-dropper

BY AUSTIN MURPHY

JUST BECAUSE THEY'RE PARTIAL to blue turf and trick plays doesn't mean Boise State always flies in the face of convention. Two weeks and a day after accepting a very public marriage proposal from the team's star running back, Ian Johnson, the head cheerleader was asked if she intended to take his name. "What would you do?" replied the comely Chrissy Popadics.

You may recall the sight of Johnson on bended knee in the moments after the Fiesta Bowl, stunning and delighting not just Popadics but also a national TV audience convinced that the spectacle it had just witnessed could not possibly contain another dramatic turn; could not pack—unless your team was Oklahoma—another iota of joy.

The Broncos mugged the Sooners the moment the Big 12 champions stepped out of the tunnel. Boise State led 14–0 early, 21–10 at the half and 28–10 with 5:16 left in the third quarter. Then an Oklahoma punt took a crazy bounce, caroming off the calf of a Bronco and turning the tide. Twenty-five unanswered points later, the Sooners led 35–28. Facing a fourth-and-18 at midfield with 18 seconds left, Boise State quarterback Jared Zabransky looked to the sideline, where his backup, Taylor Tharp, pantomimed juggling—the signal for a play the Broncos call Circus.

Thus began the most outrageous, implausible conclusion to a college football game since Cal's kickoff-return team lateraled its way through the Stanford band. In truth Boise's win eclipsed even that piece of last-second magic. Circus, after all, was but the first of three acts in an absurdist play.

Circus calls for three receivers to line up to the right, one of whom is speedy senior Jerard Rabb. A fourth—Drisan James, who'd already caught a pair of touchdown passes against the Sooners—is split to the left. He runs a 15-yard square-in and looks for the pass. After making the catch, he turns upfield for a step or two before pivoting and pitching the ball to Rabb, who by this time should be crossing the field behind him, going in the opposite direction. The play is harder to execute than it sounds. Oh, yes—Johnson and Zabransky are charged with pursuing the play, in case more laterals become necessary.

Against Oklahoma, they weren't. That had everything to do with James's gifts as a thespian. He caught Z's pass three yards shy of the first down, tucked the ball and took a step upfield. Five Sooners converged, then gouged out chunks of the turf trying to change direction as Rabb took James's perfect pitch going the other way.

Congratulated on the composure he showed under intense pressure, James shrugs it off. "To be honest," he says, "I didn't realize it was fourth down."

On Oklahoma's first play in the extra session, Adrian Peterson bounced a stretch play to the outside, ran through two tackles like a man pushing through a turnstile and scored on a 25-yard run. "Our D was gassed," says Broncos senior linebacker Korey Hall. By scoring with such ease, Peterson made Boise State coach Chris Petersen's life less complicated. "I decided then and there that if we scored again, we were going for two," the coach says.

The Broncos needed seven plays to grind out the same 25 yards. Facing fourth-and-two from the five, Petersen wanted to run a halfback pass. On Shop to Bunch Right, Q-Out, 18 Crack Halfback Pass, receiver Vinny Perretta takes a direct snap and sweeps right—action identical to a running play Boise used all season. Against the Sooners, he tucked the ball, put his head down and . . . lifted it back up, cocking his arm while looking toward the back of the end zone. The pass was perfect.

Petersen wasn't saving the coolest, deadliest trick in his playbook for last. It just worked out that way. Playcalling at Boise is more democratic than at most other programs. All three of the backup quarterbacks wear headphones and are free to make suggestions. "The whole fourth quarter," says Tharp, "we kept agitating for Statue."

The Statue of Liberty is a hoary sleight-of-hand in which the quarterback fakes a pass, then hands off to a running back. The Boise version features a funky twist, the brainchild of freshman quarterback Nick Lomax (yes, former NFL signal-caller Neil is his dad). During an idle moment in practice this season—such moments are plentiful, Lomax explains, for a fourth-string QB—"this idea popped into my head that we should run this play a different way. You make the same throwing motion, but all the while the ball's in your left hand. I thought it would be even more confusing to defenses."

When Zabransky called Statue Left in the huddle, wideout Legedu Naanee declared, "We just won this game."

Zabransky's throw-fake froze the defense for a full one-Mississippi. During this time, Johnson was loitering behind the quarterback, who then snuck him the ball with his left hand. Left guard Tad Miller stalemated defensive tackle Carl Pendleton. Tackle Ryan Clady looped wide, hinged to his right and took safety Lendy Holmes out of the play. Johnson ran out the side of the end zone and toward the 56 members of his family who were now going bonkers in the nearby stands.

What of the losers? On the quiet ride to the team hotel, Alexander came to terms with the defeat. "I'm sitting on that bus," he recalls, "and my [college] career is over. We'd lost to a team everybody said we were supposed to beat. "But then I started thinking about it. This was a great game—a game people will be talking about 30 years from now. I wish it had gone the other way, but you know something? It was an honor just to play in that game." ∎

4

1973 Sugar

NOTRE DAME 24, ALABAMA 23

"Notre Dame sealed the upset with a late-game, third-and-long, 36-yard pass from Tom Clements to sophomore tight end Robin Weber, who'd never caught a pass from Clements, in practice or a game." —AUSTIN MURPHY

▸ ALABAMA CAME INTO GAME RANKED NO. 1
▸ BAMA MISSED AN EXTRA POINT ON ITS FINAL TD

BEAR BRYANT said that Tom Clements's clinching third-and-eight pass from the end zone was not just a brilliant call but came off a well-executed misdirection play in the backfield that further camouflaged coach Ara Parseghian's intentions. Two scoops for the price of one; surprise on top of surprise. "A great play," said Bryant.

—*John Underwood, SI, January 14, 1974*

Clements's end zone completion doomed Alabama.

PHOTOGRAPH BY RICH CLARKSON

ALABAMA 14, PENN STATE 7

Krauss (77) stuffed Penn State's Guman on fourth down.

PHOTOGRAPH BY WALTER IOOSS JR.

5

"Number 2-ranked Alabama held off No. 1 Penn State thanks to a fourth-quarter goal line stand. With fourth down on the one-foot line, Tide linebacker Barry Krauss stopped Mike Guman's thrust over left tackle." —WILLIAM F. REED

WHEN KRAUSS surged forward to meet Guman they were face-to-face and helmet-to-helmet. Just before the lights went out for Krauss, he recalls, he was staring into Guman's face. When they came back on, Guman and the rest of the Lions were trotting off the field, still a foot from the goal.

—*John Underwood, SI, January 8, 1979*

▸ ALABAMA SACKED QB CHUCK FUSINA FIVE TIMES
▸ PENN STATE FINISHED WITH 19 RUSHING YARDS

1979 SUGAR

NOTRE DAME 35, HOUSTON 34

An ill Montana had to miss part of the third quarter.

PHOTOGRAPH BY BETTMANN/GETTY IMAGES

" Suffering from the flu on an icy day, Irish QB Joe Montana credited chicken soup with healing him. In TIME, Steve Wulf marveled at "an Italian leading the Irish to triumph thanks to a traditional Jewish remedy." " —ANDY STAPLES

▸ HOUSTON LED 34–12 IN FOURTH QUARTER
▸ MONTANA THREW WINNING TD PASS AS TIME EXPIRED

DAVE HUFFMAN, Notre Dame's center, was musing about the Irish mystique. "It's there even when you don't want to believe it," he said. Nobody knows better now than the Cougars. Houston coach Bill Yeoman had tried to convince his team that any such mystique was "garbage." Somewhere, Rockne and Gipp are pounding each other on the back.

—Douglas S. Looney, SI, January 8, 1979

6

1979
Cotton

17

1980 Holiday

BYU 46, SMU 45

" The greatest comeback in bowl history. BYU cashed in after recovering an onside kick and blocking an SMU punt, with Jim McMahon hitting Clay Brown on a 41-yard game winning heave as time expired. " —PETE THAMEL

‣ SMU LED BY 20 POINTS WITH 4:07 REMAINING
‣ MCMAHON THREW FOR 446 YARDS, FOUR TOUCHDOWNS

BEFORE THE game, Jim McMahon, decided to prank coach LaVell Edwards. "Jim went in and said, 'Coach, I goofed up. Sorry. I missed [my] final,' " says Andy Reid, then a BYU tackle. "The next thing I know— *boom!*—he throws [a flowerpot] against the wall. Jim's laughing. 'Coach, I took the test! I got you!' "

—*Peter King, SI, December 1, 2003*

Eric Dickerson scored twice to help build SMU's lead.
PHOTOGRAPH BY AP

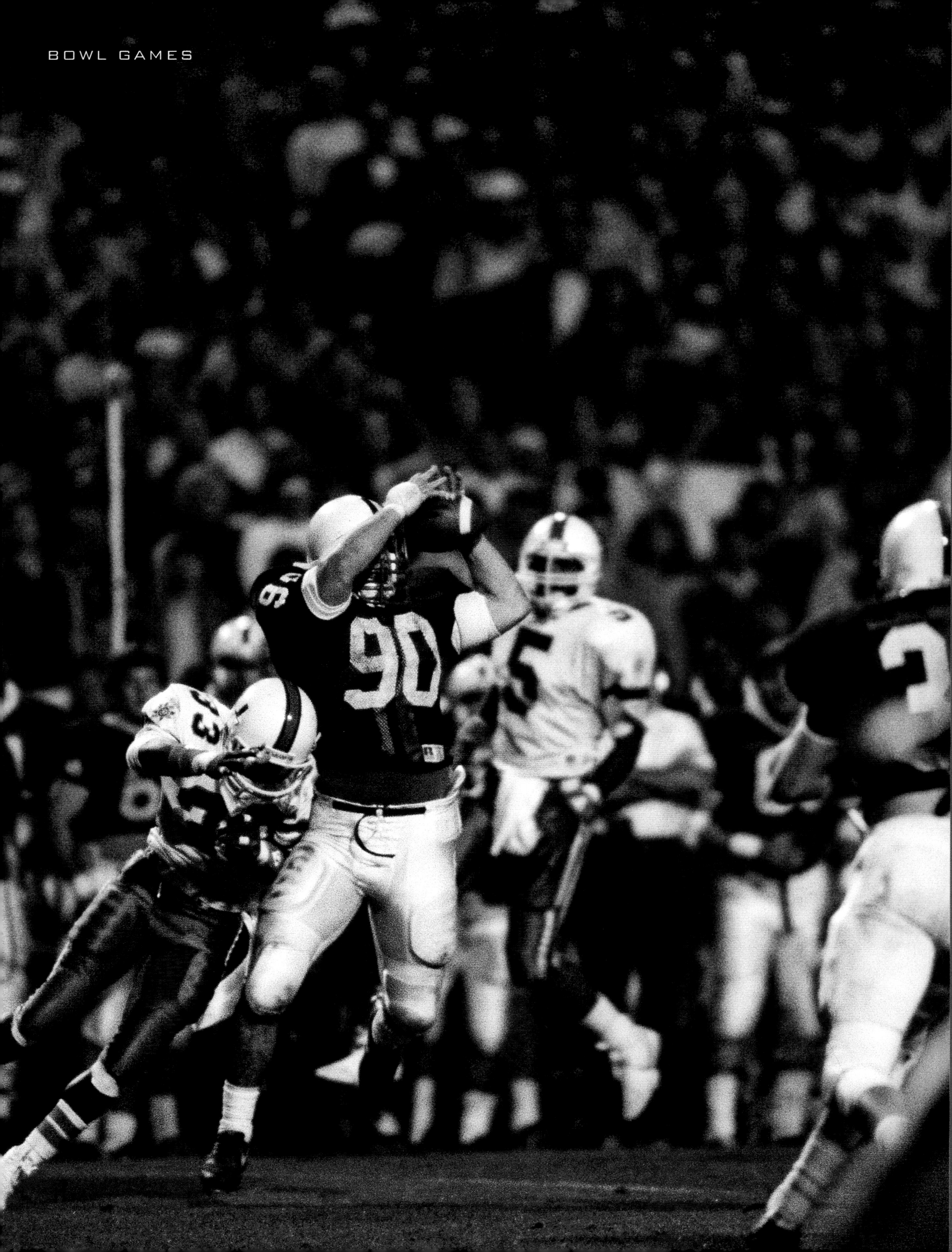
90
5

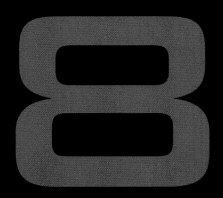

8

1987 FIESTA

PENN STATE 14, MIAMI 10

" The camouflage-favoring, attitude-copping Canes came with half an NFL roster, including Heisman-winning QB Vinny Testaverde. But Testaverde had a terrible night, throwing five interceptions, the last of those to linebacker Pete Giftopoulos. " —AUSTIN MURPHY

▸ TESTAVERDE'S FINAL INTERCEPTION CAME FROM PENN STATE 13-YARD LINE WITH 18 SECONDS TO GO
▸ D.J. DOZIER SCORED ON SIX-YARD RUN FOR GO-AHEAD TD

AFTER THE Nittanies and the Canes finished their skits (at a game-week dinner), several Miami players stood up and removed their shirts to reveal the combat fatigues that they had worn on the flight to Phoenix. Having safely eaten his steak, the Hurricanes' 285-pound All-America defensive tackle and designated orator, Jerome Brown, said, "Did the Japanese sit down and eat with Pearl Harbor before they bombed them? No. We're out of here." And out he marched with all the Canes in tow, leaving the Lions and Fiesta Bowl officials with their molars hanging out. Then Penn State's John Bruno rose. "Hey, wait a minute," he said. "Didn't the Japanese lose that war?" This qualifies as one of the five best lines ever issued by a punter.

—*Rick Reilly, SI, January 12, 1987*

Giftopoulos (left) picked off Testaverde (right).

2003 FIESTA

OHIO STATE 31, MIAMI 24

" This BCS championship game featured two unbeatens, double overtime, 18 future NFL first-rounders and controversy—a late call for pass interference on fourth down in the first OT. " —DICK FRIEDMAN

▸ MIAMI HAD WON 34 CONSECUTIVE GAMES
▸ OHIO STATE BATTED DOWN PASS TO END SECOND OT

Krenzel's sneak tied the game after one overtime.

PHOTOGRAPH BY BILL FRAKES

THE FIRST OT had ended, or so it had seemed, with a failed throw from Craig Krenzel, followed by pyrotechnics, a wave of Hurricanes flowing onto the field and a yellow flag thrown by the back judge, who waited four Mississippis because, he later explained, he wanted to go over the play in his mind.

—Austin Murphy, SI, January 13, 2003

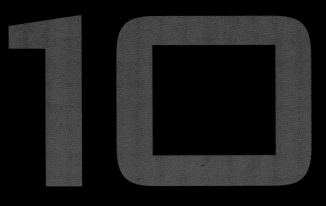

10

1965 ORANGE

TEXAS 21, ALABAMA 17

" In a meeting of two '60s powers and the first night game in bowl history, Texas upset No. 1 Alabama, stopping Joe Namath inches short of the goal line on a fourth-down sneak. " —MARK GODICH

▸ TEXAS FUMBLE SET UP NAMATH'S SNEAK CHANCE
▸ MATCHUP FEATURED THE 1963 AND '64 CHAMPIONS

AT THE LINE of scrimmage on fourth down Namath thought he saw a trace of daylight at right guard. He ignored his knee trouble and disappeared in a cascade of white-and-orange jerseys. "One official said it was a score, but the referee said no," Namath said, and was livid. "I guess you know whose side I was on."

—*John Underwood, SI, January 11, 1965*

Ernie Koy ran for two touchdowns for Texas.
PHOTOGRAPH BY FLIP SCHULKE

10

BEST SINGLE-SEASON TEAMS

WHEN A SCHOOL REGARDS A 10-4 RECORD AS A REASON TO FIRE ITS COACH, IT'S GENERALLY BECAUSE THAT UNIVERSITY HAS A STRONG BASE OF ALUMNI WHO REMEMBER BETTER DAYS. AND IT ISN'T MERE NOSTALGIA, A WISTFUL GRAB AT LOST YOUTH; THEY ARE RECALLING A TIME WHEN THEIR PROGRAMS WERE OBJECTIVELY AND INARGUABLY BETTER.

TAKE NEBRASKA, FOR EXAMPLE. SINCE COACH TOM OSBORNE LEFT THE TEAM AFTER THE 1997 SEASON, THE CORNHUSKERS HAVEN'T WON WITH THE FREQUENCY TO WHICH THEY HAD BECOME ACCUSTOMED. WHILE OSBORNE'S IMMEDIATE SUCCESSOR, FRANK SOLICH, ENJOYED EARLY SUCCESS, THAT FADED AND HE WAS LET GO AFTER THE 2003 SEASON, AND THE THREE FULL-TIME COACHES WHO HAVE FOLLOWED HAVE YET TO SATISFY THOSE FERVENT FANS.

PART OF THE PROBLEM IS THAT NEBRASKA FIELDED, IN THE EYES OF OUR PANEL, THE TWO BEST SINGLE-SEASON TEAMS IN COLLEGE FOOTBALL HISTORY. THE ONLY OTHER SCHOOL TO PLACE TWO TEAMS IN OUR TOP 10 WAS ALABAMA, ANOTHER PROGRAM WITHOUT MUCH PATIENCE. IN THE 24 SEASONS BETWEEN BEAR BRYANT AND NICK SABAN, THE TIDE, DESPITE THE ADVANTAGE OF THE ALABAMA NAME, CYCLED THROUGH SIX COACHES WHO COULDN'T DUPLICATE THE MAGIC. IN PLACES LIKE THAT, IT'S EITHER GO BIG OR GO HOME.

1
1995
NEBRASKA

COACH: TOM OSBORNE

"A veteran team defending its national title, the Cornhuskers were strong, fast and intimidating to the point of fearsome. Nebraska scored at least 49 points eight times and won each game by at least two touchdowns." —TIM LAYDEN

▸ 12–0 RECORD
▸ DEFEATED FLORIDA 62–24 IN FIESTA BOWL

THE CORNHUSKERS program benefits from the convergence of many supporting structures. The Huskers have a smart, stubborn coach with 23 years of experience; unshakable faith in a football system built on the option and the running game and brutal, fast-paced practices. The only major public university in the state, Nebraska has virtually an open admissions policy and low tuition (less than $3,000 for in-state students), which brings in walk-ons by the dozen. (Nebraska had 141 players on its Fiesta Bowl roster, a number reminiscent of Bear Bryant's days at Alabama but unusual in 1996. By contrast, Florida had 94.) Nebraska also willingly accepts athletes who represent academic and/or social risks. Finally, there comes an occasional gift, a once-in-a-generation talent like Tommie Frazier, who arrived in Lincoln from Bradenton, Fla., in 1992.

—*Tim Layden, SI, January 15, 1996*

Ahman Green (left) and Frazier (right) led Nebraska.

PHOTOGRAPHS BY PETER READ MILLER (LEFT) AND BILL FRAKES

2

1971
NEBRASKA

COACH: BOB DEVANEY

"Comprehensively complete, Bob Devaney's undefeated Cornhuskers scored nearly 40 points a game, while giving up just eight. Special teams were the playground of the incandescent Johnny Rodgers, winner of the next year's Heisman." —AUSTIN MURPHY

▸ 13-0 RECORD
▸ DEFEATED ALABAMA 38-6 IN ORANGE BOWL

ONE HAS to look back and wonder what kind of odds a Nebraskan could have gotten from an Alabamian before the opening kickoff if the fellow had said he felt that his Cornhuskers would whip the Crimson Tide worse than Nebraska had whipped Oregon . . . Minnesota . . . Texas A&M . . . Oklahoma State . . . Colorado . . . and Kansas State? Or what if the Nebraskan had said what one of Bob Devaney's associates had whispered that the score would be about 40–7, not knowing that the actual count of 38–6 would be enough to make it the worst loss of Bear Bryant's Alabama career and equal to the worst of his entire life? One thing about The Bear, though. He's always equal to a loss. "We were beaten soundly by a far superior team," he said. "They toyed with us most of the time. They might have been the greatest I've ever seen."

—*Dan Jenkins, SI, January 10, 1972*

Jerry Tagge led the Huskers at quarterback.

PHOTOGRAPH BY RICH CLARKSON/CLARKSON CREATIVE

3

1972 USC

COACH: JOHN MCKAY

"The Trojans had five All-Americas and were held to a single-digit margin of victory only once. They became the first national champion to receive every first-place vote in both the AP and UPI polls." —WILLIAM F. REED

▸ 12-0 RECORD
▸ DEFEATED OHIO STATE 42-17 IN ROSE BOWL

MCKAY ANNOUNCED earlier in the week of that social event known as the UCLA game that all his Trojans intended to do was kick heads and take names. This is exactly what they did, and it was as easy as their other victories this season because the Trojans have so much talent they look like they could play two or three different sports at once.

—*Dan Jenkins, SI, November 27, 1972*

Anthony Davis ran for 17 touchdowns for USC.
PHOTOGRAPH BY LONG PHOTOGRAPHY

COACH: EARL BLAIK

Blanchard and Army topped Michigan 28–7.

4

"Army thumped second-ranked Notre Dame 48–0 at Yankee Stadium; Doc Blanchard won the Heisman Trophy; and the Black Knights finished undefeated and national champions after winning their games by an average score of 46–5." —PETE THAMEL

BLANCHARD WAS extremely fast for a 200-pounder and could generate tremendous explosive hitting power from a standing start. As for [backfield mate] Glenn Davis, he could do just about everything. "He was the most exciting athlete I ever saw at West Point," said Joe Cahill, the Army publicity director.

—*Maury Allen, SI, December 4, 1961*

1945
ARMY

▸ 9–0 RECORD
▸ LED NATION IN SCORING AND FEWEST POINTS ALLOWED

FOOTBALL AT WARTIME

World War II altered the college sports landscape and boosted Army's fortunes as athletes enrolled at military academies as a way of forestalling overseas service

BY CHARLES EINSTEIN

T HE WARTIME COLLEGE GAME was played at two levels, one a kind of enforced deemphasis among the colleges and universities, and the other—far closer to the collegiate game as it had been known up until then—among teams representing various Army, Navy and Marine installations. Some colleges had servicemen on campus, assigned to such military curricula as the V-12 program, who were eligible for football, and a good number of service teams were infused by recent college stars. The NCAA tried to keep the two categories separate in its record, but it was a doomed effort.

For one thing, many college teams played against service teams. For another, the two strongest "service" elevens, Army and Navy, had always been classified as colleges. Besides, individual players who competed in October in college ranks—for, say, Yale—had a way of turning up in November on the El Toro Marines.

Military orders caused other players to switch from college to college. A Duke tackle named Ellis was transferred to North Carolina just in time for the Duke game. Bill Daley, a promising Minnesota fullback, helped the Michigan V-12 team bury the Gophers in 1943. One Big Ten player recalls, "It seemed like no matter who we were playing that Saturday, the coach always gave us the same pregame instructions: 'Watch out for Elroy Hirsch.'"

Some colleges suffered fearfully. From an established football power, Fordham turned almost overnight to a state of puniness, to the point where, at the LSU game in 1942, even the drum major fell down. Other colleges had it even worse. Some went over to six-man football. Others gave up the sport entirely. Georgetown quit the game upon discovering that not a single member of its '42 varsity or freshman squads would be on hand for the '43 season. Nearly 200 colleges in all abandoned the sport in '43. Those that persevered had their troubles too. In the course of one season, Penn State lost 24 varsity players.

In contrast, the service teams could depend on a steady flow of manpower—all of it fit and, perhaps more remarkable for the time, all about the right age. Many pure college teams were fielding aggregations of 16-year-olds, and Utah State, according to an archive in the Helms Hall of Fame, had a 1944 team that included a guard named Anderson who was 35. That may not have been the record. Michigan had two players, both with the same surname, who in the judgment of one suspicious researcher were father and son.

But it was chiefly in the area of recruiting high school talent that the services had all the best of it. There was no such thing as a college deferment from the service, unless it was enrollment in a military

program at a university—one of the V-12 or preflight plans. And so the stories of midnight visitations by recruiters—military recruiters—were legend. One example of this used to be offered by the late Hooks Mylin in the form of an afterdinner talk. Mylin was the coach at Lafayette, in Easton, Pa., in the peacetime season of 1940 and he had his eye on a hot prospect, a senior at the local high school. "Naturally, everybody wanted him to go to Lafayette," Mylin recounted, "but every time a train stopped in town a different coach got off. Frank Thomas of Alabama would arrive on one train, Elmer Layden of Notre Dame on the next. Notre Dame had the inside track because the boy was Catholic."

Undaunted, Mylin called a meeting with the parish priest and the university administration, and it was agreed that to keep the prospect Lafayette would put in a special course of Catholic instruction. The season ended, and Mylin, confident and content, left for a vacation. Shortly afterward he received a frantic call from Easton. Princeton had been to town, had painted the church and taken the boy. They enrolled him in the Peddie School at Hightstown, N.J., for additional finishing, and he was there when the bombs fell on Pearl Harbor. The night afterward there was a rap on the lad's dormitory door. There stood two uniformed emissaries. "Do you want to be drafted or do you want to play for Army?" they inquired. The boy decided to go to West Point.

For Earl (Red) Blaik, the Army coach, the years 1943 to '45 were golden. He had the pick of the nation's collegiate talent, and he made the most of it. Besides Glenn Davis and Doc Blanchard, he had such stars as quarterback Arnold Tucker, end Barney Poole and tackle Tex Coulter. So rich was the West Point crop that Blaik fielded two separate units, and Army fattened up on its former tormentors. In fact, one observer called '44 Army's "year of retribution." Notre Dame, which had not lost to Army since '31 and which had not let Army score a point since '38, was ground under 59–0. Penn, unbeaten in the four previous Army encounters, went down 62–7. Pittsburgh was smashed 69–7 and Villanova 83–0. Navy and Duke, which had a naval program going, were the only opponents to keep the score reasonably close.

Football, of course, was not the only sport that appealed to the jock general officer. Harold Patrick Reiser had a medical history that made it impossible for him to get into the armed forces—until a smart induction officer realized this was Pistol Pete Reiser, the baseball player. Now it was impossible for him to get out. He was sent to Fort Riley, which had 17 major leaguers on its 1944 baseball squad. "I was up for discharge five times," Reiser told writer Bill Heinz after the war, "and each time something happened." Tennis star Bobby Riggs, meanwhile, was stationed with the Navy in Hawaii, and an admiral there assigned him to a special mission. "The mission," Riggs recollected, "was to improve the admiral's backhand." ∎

5

2001
MIAMI

COACH: LARRY COKER

" The undefeated Hurricanes outscored their opponents 512–117. Even Miami's benchwarmers were great; this roster produced 16 first-rounders and 33 overall NFL draft picks. " —ANDY STAPLES

▸ 12–0 RECORD
▸ DEFEATED NEBRASKA 37–14 IN ROSE BOWL

THE TRUTH is, as Division I-A players go, these Hurricanes are downright gentlemanly. They're not like the Miami players who arrived at the 1987 Fiesta Bowl in combat fatigues, and they're unlike those who committed nine personal fouls and unsportsmanlike conduct penalties during a 46–3 Cotton Bowl victory over Texas in '91. The prototypical new Hurricane is soft-spoken middle linebacker Jonathan Vilma. "We have a lot of quiet, easygoing guys like me, who leave it all on the field," he says. "People talk at us, and we listen and say, 'That's nice. Now look at the scoreboard.' " "It's true we haven't had anyone arrested in a while," said Clinton Portis, a twinkle in his eye. "But you know what? Going back to last season, we've had to win 23 games to win this title. It's been a long road. We may get about 30 guys arrested tonight." With that, he disappeared into an orange-and-green-clad crowd and started celebrating.

—*Austin Murphy, SI, January 7, 2002*

Frank Gore ran for 562 yards as a freshman in 2001.

COACH: WOODY HAYES

"Propelled by 10 sophomore starters, Woody Hayes's Buckeyes steamrolled 10 foes, piling up 32.3 points per game while surrendering 15.0. Ohio State clinched the national title by whipping O.J. Simpson and USC in the Rose Bowl 27–16." —DICK FRIEDMAN

▸ 10–0 RECORD
▸ TEAM HAD SIX EVENTUAL NFL FIRST-ROUND PICKS

1968
OHIO STATE

THIS ENTIRE Kiddie Korps had been wound up so tight by Hayes that it was ready to do what a Buckeyes banner in the crowd commanded: KILL. And kill it did [to Michigan], not just in the final score but in terms of what one team can do to another with repetitive hitting and ball-hogging.

—Dan Jenkins, SI, December 2, 1968

7

1956 OKLAHOMA

COACH: BUD WILKINSON

" Winning a second consecutive national championship, the Sooners also had their third-straight unbeaten, untied season. Bud Wilkinson's split T attack, sparked by Tommy McDonald, piled up a 46.6 points a game. " —DICK FRIEDMAN

▸ 10–0 RECORD
▸ LED NATION IN SCORING, SECOND IN FEWEST POINTS ALLOWED

UNDERNEATH THE Sooners' businesslike attitude was a merciless desire to prove themselves. The way to accomplish this was to give the Irish a pasting worse than Michigan State's 47–14 victory of the week before. When Oklahoma scored on the 11th play from scrimmage, Wilkinson remained unthrilled beneath his five-gallon hat.

—*Jack Olsen, SI, November 5, 1956*

The fleet McDonald's teams went 31–0.

PHOTOGRAPH BY JOHN G. ZIMMERMAN

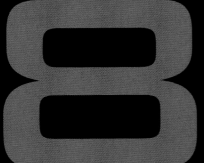

Quarterback Pat Trammell provided senior leadership.

PHOTOGRAPH BY MARVIN E. NEWMAN

" Bryant's first national title team at 'Bama made up for its lack of size with speed, quickness and heart. The Tide shut out its last five regular-season foes and beat Arkansas 10–3 in the Sugar Bowl. " —WILLIAM F. REED

ALABAMA PLAYS defense so well because that is the way Bryant asks his team to play, hitting again and again and again with the viciousness of a pack of sharks. "It'll be easy to pick out the Auburn ballcarrier," boasted an Alabama rooter. "He'll be the one who turns white as soon as they hand him the ball."

—Roy Terrell, SI, December 11, 1961

8

1961
ALABAMA

▸ 11–0 RECORD
▸ DEFENSE ALLOWED JUST 25 TOTAL POINTS FOR THE SEASON

9

1947
MICHIGAN

COACH: FRITZ CRISLER

"The Wolverines, who because of their innovative offense were dubbed the Mad Magicians, were the first team to feature a two-platoon system. They completed an undefeated season by beating USC 49–0 in the Rose Bowl." —MARK GODICH

▸ 10–0 RECORD
▸ OUTSCORED OPPONENTS 394–53

Fullback Jack Weisenburger helped dominate USC.

CRISLER LOOKED at the photograph of his 1947 undefeated Michigan team. "They were a marvelous bunch of kids," he said. "A coach gets a group like that every once in a lifetime. Some never get one. Greatest bunch of ballhandlers I ever saw. The offensive line averaged only 188."

—Gerald Holland, SI, February 3, 1964

10

1979
ALABAMA

COACH: BEAR BRYANT

" This was the only 12–0 team Bear Bryant coached in his tenure at Alabama, and it took a fourth-quarter drive in the Iron Bowl to preserve the record. Quarterback Steadman Shealy, who led the Crimson Tide in rushing and passing that season, scored the game-winner against Auburn. " —ANDY STAPLES

▸ DEFENSE LED NATION WITH 5.6 POINTS ALLOWED
▸ DEFEATED ARKANSAS 24–9 IN SUGAR BOWL

ALABAMA HAS been beset with injuries, including one to its best offensive player, running back Major Ogilvie, who has been out two weeks with a muscle pull in his pelvis. But the Crimson Tide is good and deep. Emory Bellard, the Mississippi State coach, says, "You don't lose much when injuries hit you and you replace a horse with a horse." Tide offensive coordinator Mal Moore admits, "It doesn't seem we have a weakness. Which I can't explain, because we don't have a lot of great players." Junior defensive tackle Byron Braggs says, "If you need a reason for our success, it's coach Bryant." Yup, some things never change. One is that Bryant will mess up pronouncing the names of his players; the other is that he sure gets them to play.

—*Douglas S. Looney, SI, November 12, 1979*

Shealy led Alabama to a 25-18 win in the Iron Bowl.

10 THE

BEST RIVALRIES

THE VERY TOP RIVALRIES IN COLLEGE FOOTBALL HAVE AN IMPORT THAT STRETCHES BEYOND ALUMNI APPEAL. FANS WHO DON'T HARBOR STRONG FEELINGS ABOUT AUBURN AND ALABAMA, FOR EXAMPLE, STILL HAVE REASON TO WATCH THE IRON BOWL MOST YEARS BECAUSE IT WILL INFLUENCE THE NATIONAL TITLE CHASE.

FOR OTHER RIVALRIES, THOUGH, THE GAMES TAKE PLACE IN A BUBBLE. SOMETIMES THE BUBBLE IS HUGE, AS IN THE CASE WITH ARMY AND NAVY. OTHER TIMES IT IS OLD, AS WITH HARVARD AND YALE. THOSE GAMES NO LONGER ROCK THE NATIONAL STANDINGS, BUT STILL ATTRACT FANS WITH HISTORY AND PAGEANTRY AND THE PROMISE THAT TEAMS WILL BE UP FOR THE GAME. WAY UP.

ONE PANELIST'S BALLOT HIGHLIGHTED SEVERAL OF THESE FIERY GEMS, INCLUDING THE LEHIGH-LAFAYETTE RIVALRY. THESE TWO FCS SCHOOLS, SET 17 MILES APART IN EASTERN PENNSYLVANIA, HAVE BEEN PLAYING SINCE 1884, MAKING IT COLLEGE FOOTBALL'S OLDEST CONTINUING RIVALRY. THE TRADITION IS SUCH THAT THE 150TH MEETING BETWEEN THESE SCHOOLS, IN 2014, WAS PLAYED IN YANKEE STADIUM. LEHIGH-LAFAYETTE DID NOT MAKE OUR TOP 10, BUT IF YOU'RE IN THE MIDDLE OF A PARTICULAR RIVALRY, YOU MAY HAVE YOUR OWN IDEAS ABOUT WHICH IS NUMBER 1.

1

ALABAMA-
AUBURN

FIRST MEETING: 1893

"The Iron Bowl is the most heated
in-state rivalry in sports. The schools
hated each other so much that they
stopped playing until a legislative threat
to withhold state funding got the series
reinstated in 1948. The Run in the Mud,
Wrong Way Bo, the Camback and the
Kick Six followed, bringing cheers
and tears across the Yellowhammer
State." —ANDY STAPLES

▸ ALABAMA LEADS 44-35-1

BRUISED FEELINGS run deep
at Auburn. Unquestionably,
it's the jokes that offend War
Eagles fans even more than the
scores. And it's the wisecracks
by Alabama coach Bear Bryant
that offend the most. This year
Bryant outdid himself, observing
that if his team couldn't beat
Auburn, he'd just as soon stay
home and plow as go to a bowl.
That incensed the War Eagles,
who took it as another slur on
their agricultural heritage. Said
Bear in extenuation, "Plowing's
not too bad. There's a lot of
old folks plowing. There's more
plowing than coaching. When
you plow, you work hard, then
come in for a cool lemonade.
There's not much worrying
involved. All you need is a good
mule." Auburn was not mollified.

—Douglas S. Looney, SI, December 10, 1979

Alabama swarmed James Bostic in a 1992 win.

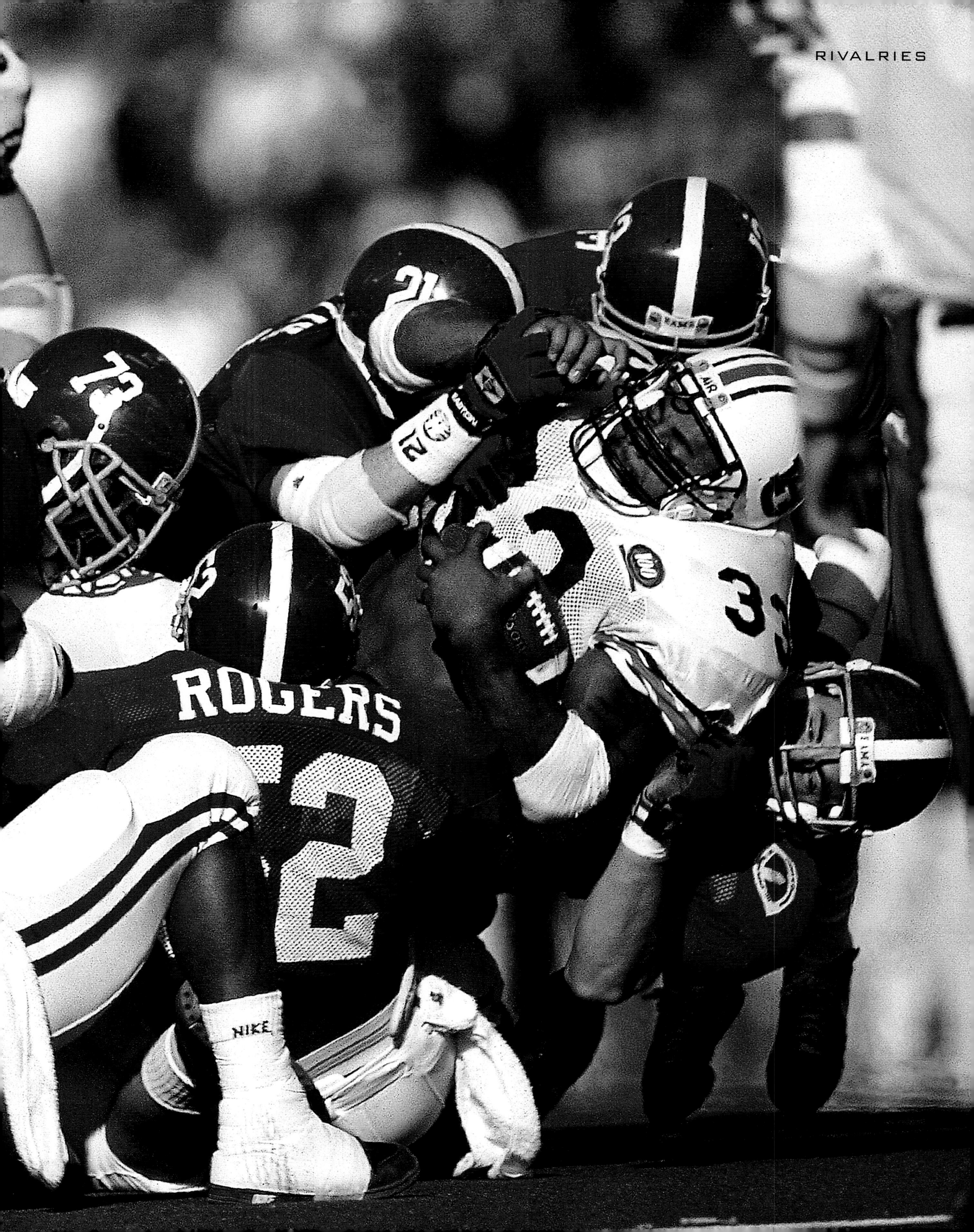
ROGERS
52
NIKE

MICHIGAN-OHIO STATE

FIRST MEETING: 1897

The game's winner has been national champ 19 times.

❝ This series didn't become truly special until 1969, when Bo Schembechler's first Michigan team ended Ohio State's 22-game winning streak, 24–12, in Ann Arbor. For the next decade, Schembechler and his former boss at Ohio State, Woody Hayes, engaged in an epic battle of egos and wits. ❞ —WILLIAM F. REED

► MICHIGAN LEADS 58-48-6

THIS ONE is not played for an ax, or a bucket or a jug. These two teams don't need to play for a relic, because when they knock heads something bigger is usually at stake. If the Big Game is where the Big Ten championship is often determined, it is also where grand ambitions go to die.

—*Austin Murphy, SI, December 1, 2003*

3

OKLAHOMA-
TEXAS

" The annual bloodbath between these preeminent programs is played at the Cotton Bowl, 200 miles from each campus, in the middle of the Texas State Fair. You want a spectacle? Typically, more than 200,000 are on the grounds when the rivals square off each October. " —MARK GODICH

▸ TEXAS LEADS 61-44-5

FRIDAY NIGHT before a Texas–OU game is the biggest gut check of all for the fans. Dallas comes under siege of drunks, wanderers, rooters, shouters, musicmakers and pranksters. They jam side streets, thoroughfares, hotel lobbies, restaurants and bars and try to see if they can break the NCAA record for arrests.

—*Dan Jenkins, SI, October 20, 1969*

At the Red River Showdown, only the site is neutral.

PHOTOGRAPH BY PETER READ MILLER

4

ARMY-NAVY

" The consummate American sports rivalry hasn't lost its gravitas even as the programs have faded from the national conversation in recent decades. Navy now leads, thanks to a 14-game win streak. The series regularly features Presidential attendance, sold-out stadiums and guaranteed chills. " —PETE THAMEL

▸ NAVY LEADS 60-49-7

GIVEN RECENT events, did this game mean more? Or did it mean less? "You can look at it both ways," Navy's Ed Malinowski said. "More, because the American people get a chance to see what kinds of leaders they'll have. Less, because in the back of your head you're thinking, Guys are risking their lives, getting shot at, so we can play this game."

—*Alexander Wolff, SI, December 10, 2001*

QB Ronald Klemick led Navy to a 13–7 win in 1961.

PHOTOGRAPH BY NEIL LEIFER

FIRST MEETING: 1892

Kodi Whitfield delivered a hit in a 2015 Stanford win.

5

CAL-STANFORD

▸ STANFORD LEADS 61-46-11

" The oldest rivalry in the West—future president Herbert Hoover was a Stanford student manager at the first Big Game— this is a sublime clash of Bay Area schools, one public, one private. In 1982, it gave us the coolest finish—featuring five laterals and one pretzeled trombone—ever. " —AUSTIN MURPHY

THE CARDINAL, despite a 1–9 record, had emotional advantages. It bristled at Cal's gloating over [last year's] victory. And ironically, Dwight Garner, who Cardinal fans insist was stopped before he made the third of The Play's five laterals, received the opening kickoff. This time he was brought down after a 12-yard return.

—Ron Fimrite, SI, November 28, 1983

Bush (5) gave Leinart a winning nudge in 2005.

PHOTOGRAPH BY BILL FRAKES

6

NOTRE DAME-

"The rivalry began when Notre Dame coach Knute Rockne took his team to Los Angeles to build Notre Dame's reputation as a national program, appease alums on the West Coast and receive a big paycheck. Since then, it has evolved into perhaps the game's greatest intersectional matchup." —WILLIAM F. REED

UNKNOWN TO all but a few intimates, coach Dan Devine had ordered green jerseys for the wearin' on Saturday—the first time the Fighting Irish had donned such shirts since 1963. When Notre Dame came onto the field, the crowd erupted and Southern Cal started checking to see if it was in the right stadium.

GOTTA LOVE THAT SHOVE

An illegal push by Reggie Bush propelled Matt Leinart across the goal line, gave undefeated USC a victory and elevated this historic series to even greater heights

BY AUSTIN MURPHY

THIS IS WHY WE PUT UP WITH it—the interminable halftimes and incessant stoppages of play, the frat boys with megaphones telling us when and what to yell. We put up with it because once in a great while college football delivers a day like last Saturday, when you needed a satellite dish and a bank of TVs to keep track of the outrageous, heart-stopping finishes. No denouement was more cardiac-arresting than the one in South Bend.

USC's 27-game winning streak was history. The scoreboard showed a 31–28 Notre Dame lead and zeros on the clock. The game had ended with a valiant goal line stand by the Irish: Trojans quarterback Matt Leinart had scrambled to his left, only to be walloped a foot shy of the end zone by middle linebacker Corey Mays—who, looking back on it, may have done his job too well. So hard did Mays hit Leinart that the ball flew out-of-bounds.

While the line judge clearly waved his arms for time to stop, the game clock continued to bleed seconds until none remained, and a wave of delirious Notre Dame fans breached the yellow line of ushers and stormed the field. Then the zebras convened. The Golden Domers were shooed off the grass. Seven seconds were put on the clock, and USC was given the ball inside the one-yard line. The Trojans had no timeouts, but they were not without experience in such situations. Once a week USC's offense practices this precise goal line play. "I have a two-way go," Leinart later explained. "I can spike it or sneak it."

While coach Pete Carroll and some of his assistants motioned for Leinart to spike the ball—to stop the clock and give them time to think about what play to run or whether to kick a tying field goal—those gesticulations turned out to be so much play-acting. Carroll, who as coach of the New York Jets in 1994 had been burned on a last-minute fake spike by the Miami Dolphins' Dan Marino, had made it clear to Leinart that he wanted him to go for it while officials discussed how much time to put on the clock.

Leinart's resolve was stiffened by tailback Reggie Bush, who asked the quarterback before he stepped under center, "You going to go for it?" Standing at his locker afterward, Bush recalled Leinart's reply: "You think I should?"

"Man, just do it," replied Bush.

Trying to run over left guard, Leinart was repelled on his first effort, but, displaying a sprightliness befitting an undergraduate enrolled in ballroom dancing class, he spun to his left. Thrusting the ball in the air and twisting backward as Bush provided a forbidden shove, Leinart fell forward and broke the plane—and an untold number of Domers' hearts.

While the quarterback and several of his teammates wept for joy over their 34–31 victory, some of their opponents merely wept.

This depth of emotion is college football's greatest advantage over the pro game. In college there is no sliding into the postseason with a .500 record. There is a dire need to win throughout September and October. In the NFL there are no triple overtimes, just as there are no pep rallies that draw 45,000, like the one last Friday night at Notre Dame Stadium, where a leprechaun emerged from the belly of a plywood Trojan horse. First-year Irish coach Charlie Weis reminded the congregation of what he had told the Irish faithful at a basketball game last February, "On Oct. 15, when that team from California comes in here, I hope they're undefeated."

"Well," he said on Friday, "they are."

That the Trojans remain so is no fault of Weis's. Controlling the clock, battering Leinart, torching USC's overmatched cornerbacks and making game-changing plays on special teams, Weis and his ninth-ranked Irish inked in every box on the HOW TO BEAT THE TROJANS checklist.

Except one. Most of the day it was as if Reggie Bush had a big S on his chest. He netted 160 yards and three touchdowns on 15 carries, and added another 105 yards on pass receptions and kick returns.

Emotionally and physically drained after the game, Leinart lamented over and over that he "wasn't on" and that he'd "missed some easy throws," both of which were true. But with the season and the streak on the line, Leinart showed what he was made of. On fourth-and-nine at the USC 26, with 1:32 left, Leinart surveyed the defense and—this is the stuff of national champions—checked out of the play he had called. Instead, he lofted a pass 24 yards down the left sideline, just beyond the reach of Notre Dame cornerback Ambrose Wooden and into the waiting hands of wideout Dwayne Jarrett, who'd injured his right eye while diving for a ball earlier in the quarter and whose vision was still blurred.

"We had the perfect defense [called]," said Weis. "They threw a fade route into our Two Tampa [scheme]. It's complete by an inch. I mean, you don't throw fade routes into Two Tampa, but this guy did."

A squinting Jarrett was brought down after a 61-yard gain, at the Irish 13. Four snaps after that, Leinart fumbled the ball out-of-bounds. If he holds on to the rock, the streak is over. If he fumbles anywhere but out-of-bounds, the streak is over.

But the streak lives. Afterward, in a display of sportsmanship that characterizes what is undoubtedly the coolest intersectional rivalry in the country, Weis entered the visitors' dressing room. "I just want to wish you guys luck the rest of the way," he told the Trojans. "That was a friggin' hard-fought battle. I hope you win out."

Of course he hopes the Trojans win out. Just as he hopes that, when the Irish travel to California next year, USC is still undefeated. ■

7

FLORIDA STATE- MIAMI

"Beginning in the '80s, this Sunshine State hatefest often has had national title implications. Few series have provided more kicks. Sadly for the Seminoles, many were memorably wide— wide right, in '91, '92, 2000 and '04; and left, in '02." —DICK FRIEDMAN

▸ MIAMI LEADS 31-29-0

AFTER DAN MOWREY had driven his last-second field goal attempt wide to the right, allowing Miami to carjack Florida State's national championship hopes for the fourth time in five years, he gamely met the press in the dressing room. At one point he looked down and mumbled, "Why did it have to be wide right?"

—*Austin Murphy, SI, October 12, 1992*

Matt Munyon (86) joined the wide-right club in 2000.

PHOTOGRAPH BY AMY E. CONN/AP

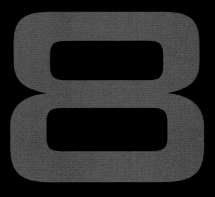

8

HARVARD-YALE

FIRST MEETING: 1875

"It has been more than a century since Harvard and Yale played a game with national championship implications, but that has done nothing to diminish the fervor of their rivalry. The outcome of the game confers bragging rights upon alumni in boardrooms across America." —TIM LAYDEN

▸ YALE LEADS 65-59-8

WHENEVER THE GAME is played at Harvard, representatives of the New Haven tailoring establishments entrain for Cambridge to see what the young gentlemen are wearing. By custom they do not speak to one another. Following tradition, Paul Press stands his Cambridge branch employees to a buffet luncheon of cream soda and hot pastrami.

—*Robert H. Boyle, SI, December 17, 1962*

The Game is college football's second-oldest rivalry.

PHOTOGRAPH BY CHUCK SOLOMON

9

KANSAS-MISSOURI

FIRST MEETING: 1891

❝ The Border War was the oldest rivalry west of the Mississippi until the teams stopped playing after 2011. And talk about bad blood—it was also the only rivalry in which men went from trying to kill each during and after the Civil War to watching their descendants face off on the football field. ❞ —MARK GODICH

▸ MISSOURI LEADS 57-54-9

THE RIVALRY has stood out less for the quality of the football than for the two states' shared history, and the depth and provenance of the ill will. In the early 1860s the infamous William Quantrill staged raids along the Missouri-Kansas border and eventually became a captain in the Confederacy. (Kansas was part of the Union.) In 1863 the then Missouri-based Quantrill and 450 of his Raiders attacked Lawrence, slaughtering scores of unarmed citizens and torching parts of the city. Recounting the atrocity, coach Don Fambrough prefers to garnish it with this small fiction: He tells the players, after the massacre "they found out . . . [Quantrill] was a Missouri alum!" When an overly credulous football player included that falsehood on a history exam, the professor phoned Fambrough. "I'll let you coach football," he said, "if you'll let me teach history."

—*Austin Murphy, SI, November 26, 2007*

In the 2007 meeting each team ranked in the top three.

PHOTOGRAPH BY JAMIE SQUIRE/GETTY IMAGES

FIRST MEETING: 1915

Fans meet in the middle each year in Jacksonville.

PHOTOGRAPH BY GARY BOGDON

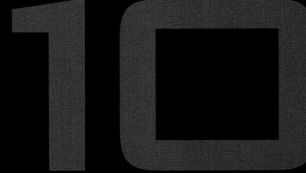

10

FLORIDA-
GEORGIA

▸ GEORGIA LEADS 49-42-2

" The World's Largest Outdoor Cocktail Party. In 1966, after Georgia's 27–10 upset, Bulldogs defensive tackle Bill Stanfill exulted, "Holding pigs for my dad to castrate was quite a challenge. I can't say that helped prepare me for football, but it sure did remind me an awful lot of sacking Steve Spurrier." " —DICK FRIEDMAN

SEVENTY GEORGIA players stormed the field to celebrate the team's first touchdown. The officials ran out of things to throw. Georgia coach Mark Richt's explanation, short version: He ordered his players to draw an excessive celebration penalty, but he never imagined the whole team would charge the field.

—Andy Staples, SI.com, October 30, 2008

10 THE

Best Programs

THE LIST OF PROGRAMS IS PRESENTED AS A TOP 10 BECAUSE THAT IS OUR FORMAT, BUT THE WAY THE VOTE BROKE DOWN, IT COULD BE ARGUED THAT IT WOULD HAVE MADE MORE SENSE AS A SMALLER GROUP. THE TOP SIX OF THESE PROGRAMS WERE NAMED ON ALL SEVEN OF OUR PANELISTS' BALLOTS. THE NEXT TWO WERE NAMED ON NEARLY ALL THE BALLOTS. AFTER THAT, A SECOND GROUPING OF FIVE SCHOOLS WAS LEFT IN A TIGHT SCRAP FOR THOSE LAST TWO SPOTS.

IF WE HAD FOLLOWED SOMETHING AKIN TO THE PROCESS THE ACADEMY AWARDS USE FOR BEST PICTURE, IN WHICH BETWEEN FIVE AND 10 FILMS CAN BE NOMINATED DEPENDING ON HOW MANY ACHIEVE A CERTAIN DEGREE OF CONSENSUS, THE LAST TWO PROGRAMS WOULD HAVE BEEN LEFT ON THE CUTTING ROOM FLOOR. BUT LEAVING OUT ANY OF THESE PROGRAMS, LET ALONE ALL FIVE OF THEM, WOULDN'T FEEL RIGHT, BECAUSE EVEN THE SCHOOLS THAT FINISHED JUST OUTSIDE THE TOP 10 CONTAIN SO MUCH THAT IS ESSENTIAL TO COLLEGE FOOTBALL HISTORY.

THESE ARE SCHOOLS THAT HAVE WON NATIONAL CHAMPIONSHIPS, THAT HAVE HAVE BEEN LED BY LEGENDARY COACHES, THAT IN SOME CASES HAVE TOP 10 GAME-DAY EXPERIENCES. THAT THEY DIDN'T MAKE THE LIST IS REALLY A TESTAMENT TO THE RICHNESS OF THE COLLEGE FOOTBALL LANDSCAPE.

1

ALABAMA

SINCE 1892

"The Crimson Tide are as enduringly great as they are worshipped by their faithful. Alabama rose to power in the '20s and '30s under Wallace Wade and Frank Thomas and remain there under Nick Saban, with the towering figure of Bear Bryant in between. They have won eight undisputed national titles and parts of eight others, and their rabid fans can recite chapter and verse on every one." —TIM LAYDEN

▸ 864-326-43 RECORD
▸ 29 CONFERENCE TITLES

WHEN ALABAMA was picked to play in the 1926 Rose Bowl against mighty Washington, it was considered by many to be the worst mismatch in the game's history. Alabama had a good enough record but experts all knew that Southern football was barely on a level with JV play in the rest of the country. As it turned out, Alabama won and no one ever again sneered at Southern football. Southern teams played in 13 of the next 20 Rose Bowl games, and today teams from the South dominate the big business of bowl games across the nation . . . . The crowd in 1926 was an estimated 45,000. "That 45,000 was close to capacity," says former Crimson Tide player Johnny Mack Brown, "because the Rose Bowl wasn't really a bowl; it was more of a horseshoe. One end wasn't closed. Alabama closed it for them."

—*Dave Anderson, SI, December 24, 1962*

Mark Ingram in 2010 (left) and '16 fans celebrate titles.

SINCE 1887

Leahy (in hat) led the Irish to post-World War II success.

PHOTOGRAPH BY BETTMANN/CORBIS

NOTRE DAME

"Immigrant Catholic families from coast to coach, known as the "subway alumni," gave Notre Dame a national following in the early 20th century, and legendary coaches Knute Rockne, Frank Leahy, Ara Parseghian and Lou Holtz capitalized on that passion." —WILLIAM F. REED

▸ 892-313-42 RECORD
▸ 11 NATIONAL TITLES

AT THE dining hall Raghib Ismail listens as players revisit those stirring days when they were big fish in small high school ponds. Then they talk about reality—how they came to South Bend and discovered how ordinary they were in the context of one another and the history of Notre Dame football.

—Ralph Wiley, SI, September 25, 1989

3

Ohio State

" Eight national titles, 10 undefeated seasons, Woody Hayes, the Horseshoe, and a list of great players including Howard Cassady, Archie Griffin, Orlando Pace and, more recently, Ezekiel Elliott. All that and The Best Damn Band in the Land. " —AUSTIN MURPHY

▸ 875-320-53 RECORD
▸ 38 CONFERENCE TITLES

OHIO STATE is tough, baby. Buckeyes fans want to know what kind of leadership and pizzazz a coach is going to provide while he piles up the W's. Because the wins are a given. Ask anybody in the state. What the Ohio State football coach must be is a demigod, a man of mythic proportions, his shield flashing in the sun, a hero. Like Woody.

—*Rick Telander, SI, August 22, 1988*

Craig Krenzel (16) celebrated a win over Michigan.
PHOTOGRAPH BY DAVID BERGMAN

Coach Schembechler led his team into the Big House.

4

MICHIGAN

" The Wolverines have more wins than any team in college football history. At the turn of the century, Fielding Yost helped shape how the game was played and how conferences were formed. Tom Harmon and Desmond Howard helped carry on the tradition. " —ANDY STAPLES

▸ 925-331-36 RECORD
▸ 11 NATIONAL TITLES,
42 CONFERENCE TITLES

ONE HOUSE caught Jim Harbaugh's eye. He called his wife, Sarah, and said, "I think I found our house." Sarah flew to Michigan and agreed. They bought it. There are more than 1,000 streets in Ann Arbor. Only later did Jim tell Sarah they would live on the one where Bo Schembechler had lived.

—Michael Rosenberg, SI, May 18, 2015

THE BO AND WOODY SHOW

Before Bo Schembechler became Michigan's coach and later its athletic director, he learned from a temperamental soulmate who would become his fiercest rival

BY DOUGLAS S. LOONEY

HIO STATE AND MICHIGAN are always linked because for years they've been the only schools in the conference that have played superior football. Further, the Woody-Bo Show made that annual confrontation bigger than life. Perhaps too big, because the players were so on edge that their performances weren't always splendid. Only now, with Woody three years out of coaching, is Bo emerging as his own man after a near lifetime of being linked with Hayes.

It all traces back to Miami of Ohio, where Bo played for Woody. At a reunion of Miami players last summer, Hayes recalled a 28–0 victory he coached over Cincinnati in 1950. "We scored four touchdowns," he said, "and would have had five if a certain overeager tackle hadn't been offside." That tackle was Schembechler. But once you have played for a coach, he's always the coach and you're always the player. At this same reunion, Hayes was organizing things—surprise—and suddenly looked over at Bo standing across the way. "Bo," he said, "you sit right here." Bo sat. And one suspects that if Woody had said, "Bo, run through that wall," Schembechler would have done that too, without question.

Bo was an assistant under Hayes at Ohio State in 1951 and then again from '58 to '62. They were, although both vigorously deny it, two damn peas in a damn pod. In football meeting rooms, they even threw chairs at each other.

"No, no," says Hayes when asked about the flying furniture. "We just argued to beat hell."

But you didn't throw chairs at each other?

"No, no. We just got damn mad."

But you didn't throw chairs at each other?

"Oh, well, sometimes we threw chairs . . . but not at each other."

Just sort of a case in which the two of you were in the same room when chairs were thrown?

"Yeah, that's right."

So what's the big deal? Of course they threw chairs at each other. Why wouldn't they? Don't bulls lock horns in the field? Since his days as an assistant Bo's been called "Little Woody." And there were distressing signs that the nickname fit. In fact, Dick Larkins, the former Ohio State athletic director, once advised Donald Canham, Michigan's athletic director, "Don't hire Schembechler. You'll end up with him just like we have with Woody. You'll never be comfortable with him." But Woody would tear up yard markers; Bo didn't. Woody hit a TV cameraman; Bo didn't. Woody hit an opposing player; Bo didn't. A

Bo watcher says, "I think he was learning something all along. He thought, and thinks, that Woody was a great coach, but he was telling himself not to copy some of the old man's mannerisms."

To this day, Schembechler speaks of Hayes with reverence. "I'm a Woody Hayes man," he says. Indeed, after Hayes's slugging of the Clemson player in the Gator Bowl, Bo arranged a meeting with his mentor/rival at a midway point between Columbus and Ann Arbor. He hoped to get Hayes to apologize publicly. Sadly, Bo couldn't get Woody to say those two little words that would have made all the difference: "I'm sorry." Subsequently, Woody admitted to the conversation, but snorted, "Bo isn't always right."

Hayes and Schembechler were, then, the greatest of friends and the bitterest of rivals. They loved each other and they hated each other. They were a study in contradictions. "We respected one another so damn much," says Hayes. "Now that doesn't mean I didn't get so mad at him that I wanted to kick him in the, uh, groin." And for his part, Schembechler says, "You beat Woody and you beat the best. It's always best to beat the coach you have the most respect for."

The fact is, Schembechler is emerging now as King of the Mountain only because Woody is gone. Never mind that in the 10 games in which the two faced each other, Bo's teams won five. Hayes' four, and they tied once. Bo was Little Woody, got it? But that was yesterday.

Former players often drop by to see Bo, and he makes time for each of them. "All the players embellish the hell out of the stories," says Schembechler. "They say I was the toughest, meanest bastard that ever lived. I know that isn't true."

Yet Bo inspires extravagant tales because he can be so outrageous and because he is sooooooo competitive. Former linebacker Mel Owens, No. 1 draft pick of the L.A. Rams, says, "Every day Bo is fired up, every day. He's feisty and he goes after it." Once, on a quiet social outing, Bo and two other guys climbed on bikes for a peaceful ride through the countryside. No sooner was everybody rolling than Bo said, "Let's race." Another time, on Canham's boat for a pleasure cruise on Lake Erie, everybody was relaxed except Bo, who was trying to make sure the boat was exactly on course. Never mind that nobody had a course planned.

And Bo can now laugh at himself, which he does, recalling the night before the 1975 Northwestern game. Northwestern is a college football power on the order of most any high school you'd care to name. Sitting in his hotel room looking at films, Bo suddenly bolted upright. "Goddam, Northwestern is good and we aren't ready," he said. "I am sitting on an upset." Whereupon he raged through the hotel, clicking off TVs, screaming, berating, threatening, kicking ass and taking names. He finally returned to his hotel room, spent. Next day, Michigan won 69–0. ∎

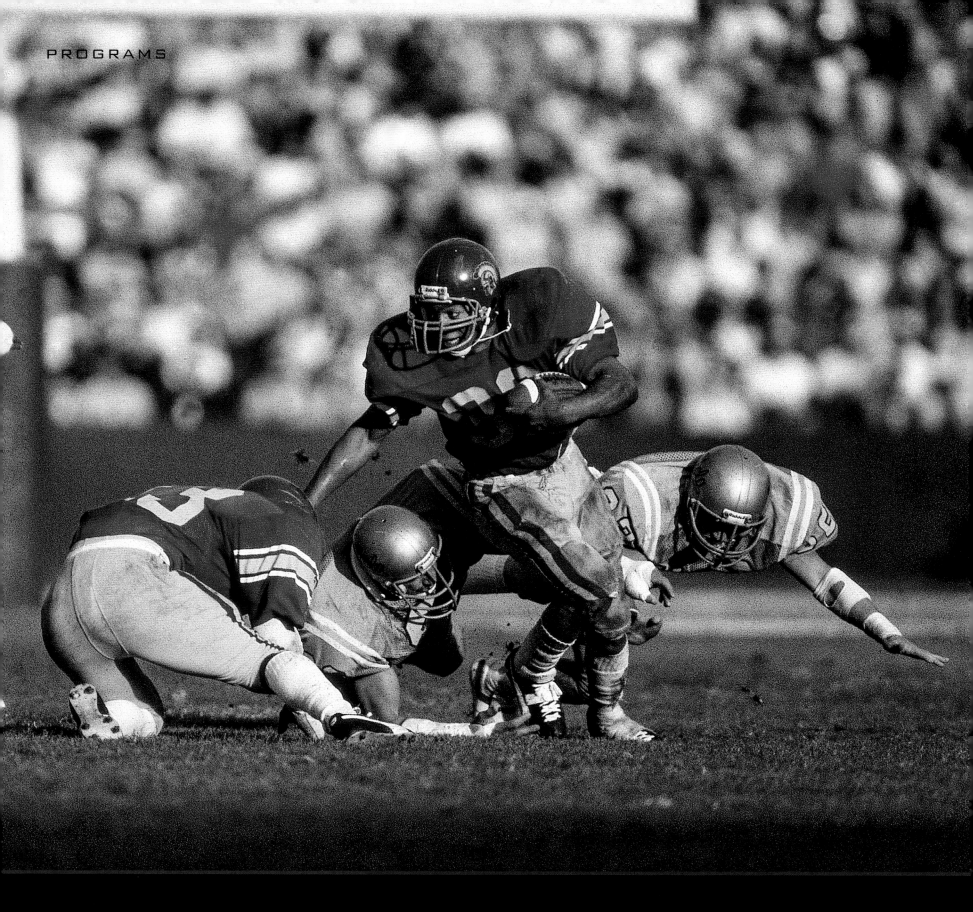

Marcus Allen helped forge USC's status as Tailback U.

PHOTOGRAPH BY MANNY MILLAN

" USC's seven Heisman Trophy winners tie it with Notre Dame and Ohio State for most of all time, and the Football Writers Association of America credits the Trojans with having the most All-Americans in the past 75 years. " —PETE THAMEL

USC

▸ 813-333-54 RECORD
▸ 11 NATIONAL TITLES,
38 CONFERENCE TITLES

BY COMMITTING to USC, defensive lineman Shaun Cody became a pioneer of sorts: the first big-name recruit to sign with Pete Carroll, to take that leap of faith [with a down program]. "Look at us now," Cody said before the 2005 Orange Bowl. "I feel so fortunate to have made that choice."

—Austin Murphy, SI, January 10, 2005

OKLAHOMA

SINCE 1903

"Boomer Sooner first climbed to the top with consecutive national titles in 1955–56 under coach Bud Wilkinson's T formation, won three more with Barry Switzer's wildfire Wishbone formation in the '70s and '80s and returned to the top under defensive guru Bob Stoops in 2000." —TIM LAYDEN

▸ 861-319-53 RECORD
▸ SEVEN NATIONAL TITLES, 44 CONFERENCE TITLES

ALMOST AS if the first strains of the fight song were wafting through the pines, coach Barry Switzer leaned forward, stuck out his jaw for emphasis and said, "I mean, man, when you take a team down that ramp to play Texas, you damn well feel the emotion . . . . *Boomer Sooner, Boomer Sooner . . . .* When you hit the floor of that Cotton Bowl, there's electricity . . . . *I'm a Sooner born and a Sooner bred . . . .* You watch those young guys going in there for the first time and right away they know they're somewhere special. Whoomp! Whoomp! They hear that hitting, those sounds like two pickup trucks running together out there and their eyes start rolling . . . . *And when I die, I'll be a Sooner dead . . . .* And when you win, boy, that's the best part. Sixteen of us in that pool there at 3 a.m. whooping and hollering . . . *Rah Oklahoma! Rah Oklahoma! . . .* Boy, that's fun!"

—Ray Kennedy, SI, August 9, 1976

The Schooner's ponies are named Boomer and Sooner.

SINCE 1900

Osborne led the Cornhuskers from 1973 to '97.

PHOTOGRAPH BY JOHN W. MCDONOUGH

" From 1962 through '97 under coaches Bob Devaney and Tom Osborne, the Cornhuskers literally ran roughshod. In Osborne's final five seasons, the Big Red was 60-3—which happens to be the best five-year run in major college football history. " —DICK FRIEDMAN

WHEN GOD went to work creating Nebraska, He thought, "O.K., I keep giving other areas of this country mountains, beaches, stuff like that. Everywhere I look, beauty. I need a change." What resulted is a landscape of wall-to-wall dust. To try to make up, God later gave Nebraska football.

—Douglas S. Looney, SI, November 10, 1975

NEBRASKA

▸ 880-368-40 RECORD
▸ FIVE NATIONAL TITLES, 46 CONFERENCE TITLES

TEXAS

▸ 885-353-33 RECORD
▸ 31 CONFERENCE CHAMPIONSHIPS

No question about it: Longhorns fans are hooked.

PHOTOGRAPH BY JIM COWSERT/ICON SPORTSWIRE

9

FLORIDA

" Florida's history includes three Heisman Trophy winners—Steve Spurrier, Danny Wuerffel and Tim Tebow. As coach Spurrier ushered in a new era of football in the 1990s with the Fun-n-Gun, much like Urban Meyer did with the spread offense in the 2000s. " —PETE THAMEL

▸ 701-404-40 RECORD
▸ THREE NATIONAL TITLES

DOWN THERE in back-biting country, amid the mud-choked rivers and crawling vines, the Florida Gators are untouched by reason. What good is reason, anyway, in 100° heat? The Gators prefer the feverish gesticulating of Steve Spurrier, who orders up touchdowns with a wave of his hand and incites victories with a toss of his visor.

—Sally Jenkins, SI, September 27, 1993

Fans at the Swamp love their chomp.

PHOTOGRAPH BY BILL FRAKES

Warrick Dunn is Florida State's career rushing leader.

PHOTOGRAPH BY DAMIAN STROHMEYER

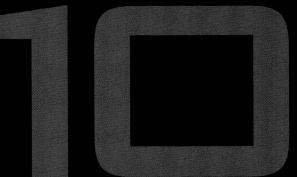

10
FLORIDA STATE

"The original road warrior—his early Seminoles squads would play anyone, anywhere—Bobby Bowden built Florida State into a juggernaut with 14 straight Top 5 finishes in the AP poll and a pair of Heisman winners." —AUSTIN MURPHY

▸ 522-241-17 RECORD
▸ THREE NATIONAL TITLES, 18 CONFERENCE TITLES

FOUR OF Bowden's 20 grandchildren sat in his office while a small television set showed highlights of the Game of the Year, in which a Florida field goal attempt that would have tied the game drifted just outside the right upright. "Look at that," said Bowden. "We finally got one of those wide rights."

—Tim Layden, SI, December 9, 1996

10 THE

BEST GAME-DAY EXPERIENCES

THE ARGUMENT AS TO WHICH IS MORE ENJOYABLE, COLLEGE FOOTBALL OR THE PRO GAME, IS NOT ONE THAT CRIES OUT FOR RESOLUTION—IT'S NOT LIKE THE NCAA AND NFL RUN THEIR MAIN SLATES ON THE SAME DAY. THE DISCUSSION IS ONE PEOPLE LIKE TO HAVE. IF YOU WERE TO MAKE THE CASE FOR THE SUPERIORITY OF THE COLLEGE GAME, YOU WOULD DO WELL TO DRAW ON THE STORIES IN THIS SECTION.

THIS IS BECAUSE COLLEGE FOOTBALL, MORE THAN THE PROS, IS ABOUT THE TRADITIONS ENJOYED BY THE FANS AT THE GAMES. THESE ARE JOYS THAT TRANSCEND PARTISAN LOYALTIES. YOU MIGHT NOT HAVE EVER SET FOOT IN COLUMBUS AND STILL GET A KICK OUT OF SEEING THE A SOUSAPHONE PLAYER DOT THE *I* DURING THE HALFTIME PERFORMANCE OF SCRIPT *OHIO*. THE RED SEA OF BOUNCING STUDENTS IN CAMP RANDALL STADIUM CAPTURES THE IMAGINATIONS OF MANY OUTSIDE THE STATE OF WISCONSIN. NO MATTER HOW MUCH YOU LOVE YOUR ALMA MATER, THE SIGHT OF STUDENTS TAILGATING IN THE GROVE IN COCKTAIL ATTIRE FORCES DAYDREAMS ABOUT WHAT IT WOULD HAVE BEEN LIKE TO SPEND YOUR COLLEGE YEARS AT OLE MISS.

THESE ARE TRADITIONS THAT ARE ENJOYED BY STUDENTS, AND MAYBE MORE SO, BY ALUMNI, WHO HAVE MEMORIES OF A TIME AND A PLACE THAT, EVERY FALL SATURDAY, KEEPS 'EM COMING BACK.

1

NOTRE DAME

SOUTH BEND, IND.

" Cue the goose bumps from all corners of campus. The Golden Dome glistening in the autumn sun. Touchdown Jesus looming above in his wishful pose. Notre Dame makes every game feel like a walk back through time, including a Friday pep rally and on-campus Glee Club performances. " —PETE THAMEL

▸ UNDERGRADUATE STUDENT ENROLLMENT: 8,448
▸ STADIUM CAPACITY: 80,795

THERE WAS that night-before concession Notre Dame makes to hysterics, the pep rally. Since coach Parseghian came to launch what is advertised on lapel pins as THE NEW ARA [sic] IN NOTRE DAME FOOTBALL, Notre Dame pep rallies have become happenings. Parseghian clears his throat and 6,000 people cheer. Human pyramids are built and often collapse spectacularly, as the last man up rips open his shirt to reveal a huge green tattoo on his chest: IRISH. They shout, "Ara, Ara, Ara," and when Ara gets up to talk they cheer every fragmentary sentence: "We're going to—" "Ruhaaaaa!" "We'll get Griese just like we—" "Grreaaaaah!" It is believed around South Bend that at these charged moments Parseghian could tell the students to go soak their heads and they would cheer him wildly.

—*John Underwood, SI, October 3, 1966*

Students enjoy high times at Notre Dame Stadium.

PHOTOGRAPH BY JOHN BIEVER

LOUISIANA STATE

BATON ROUGE, LA.

" Before entering "Death Valley," opposing players must walk past an actual caged tiger (a Bengal-Siberian mix named Mike). Big cats and perennially stacked rosters aside, LSU's most formidable weapon is sunset. In his first 11 seasons in Baton Rouge, coach Les Miles was 49–5 in night games at home. " —AUSTIN MURPHY

▸ UNDERGRADUATE STUDENT ENROLLMENT: 25,572
▸ STADIUM CAPACITY: 102,321

FAMILIES LIVING near Tiger Stadium ran from their homes in fear when a giant roar arose on Halloween night 1959. There was no emergency—Billy Cannon had just returned a punt 89 yards for a touchdown against Ole Miss. The noise emanating from Death Valley has only grown louder through the decades: The din unleashed by a game-winning touchdown over Auburn in '88 jiggled the needle on a seismograph in LSU's geology department. Before night games, rather than squander daylight hours, many LSU fans spend them ingesting adult beverages. The result, according to everydayshouldbesaturday. com, is a game-day experience "peerless in terms of demonstrated intensity, lunacy, commitment, flair and menace."

—Austin Murphy, SI, August 22, 2011

The first Mike came to LSU in 1936.

33
MISSISSIPPI

" The Grove, a 10-acre, oak-shaded plot tucked in the middle of the Ole Miss campus, features the finest in tailgating. Expect to see exquisite spreads, replete with fine china and sparkling candelabras. " —MARK GODICH

▸ UNDERGRADUATE STUDENT ENROLLMENT: 18,101
▸ STADIUM CAPACITY: 64,038

OXFORD IS the town that William Faulkner famously called home, where the men don bow ties and the women wear heels to games. Football games are the social events of the season at other SEC schools, but no one creates an atmosphere quite so romantically as Rebs fans, who throw a debutante ball with porta-potties.

—Andy Staples, SI, October 13, 2014

In the Grove, cheerleaders herald a player processional.
PHOTOGRAPH BY THOMAS GRANING/AP

4

MICHIGAN

ANN ARBOR, MICH.

" Think big! Big Ten, Big House (Michigan Stadium is the nation's largest), big victory total (925, the most for any college football program). Add in a big (406-member) marching band playing arguably the best fight song, "The Victors," and you have a big day. " —DICK FRIEDMAN

▸ UNDERGRADUATE STUDENT ENROLLMENT: 28,395
▸ STADIUM CAPACITY: 107,601

AMONG THE 4,287 ways college football beats the living beaver snot out of pro football, the best is fight songs. As they say in Texas, a good fight song'll give you chill bumps. Your star and your coach may leave, but your fight song never will. Even at 96, on her death bed, with the pastor reading from the Good Book, a true college fan, upon hearing her fight song played on the horn of a passing Winnebago, will leap up and bellow from the bottom of her bellower. Most people begrudgingly concede that either Notre Dame's or Wisconsin's fight song stirs something deep within them. Me, I like Michigan's.

Hail! to the victors valiant
Hail! to the conqu'ring heroes
Hail! Hail! to Michigan
The champions of the West!

Problem is, that's pretty much the whole song, repeated over and over. What do you want from the state that gave you the K-Car?

—Rick Reilly, SI, August 14, 2000

Attendance often exceeds the Big House's capacity.

COLUMBUS, OHIO

" At "The Horseshoe," fans roar not only for Ohio State touchdowns, but when the band dots the "i" in script Ohio at halftime and when the victory bell is rung at the finish of the game. The experience is part football, part revival, all Buckeyes. " —TIM LAYDEN

▸ UNDERGRADUATE STUDENT ENROLLMENT: 44,741
▸ STADIUM CAPACITY: 104,944

Ohio's football passion has deep roots.

PHOTOGRAPH BY JASON MOWRY/ICON SPORTSWIRE

INCENSED ONE day [in 1914], an Ohio State rooter leaped from the stands, doused the goalposts with kerosene and set fire to the whole thing. Should one question what the fellow was doing with a can of kerosene in the stands, Ohioans merely shrug and suggest that all sections of the country have their idiosyncrasies.

—*Roy Terrell, SI, October 6, 1958*

5

OHIO
STATE

6

WISCONSIN

MADISON, WIS.

" From the pregame tailgates in the historic neighborhoods that abut Camp Randall Stadium to the student "Jump Around" between the third and fourth quarters to the band's fifth-quarter on-field performance, the Badgers have it all. " —MARK GODICH

▸ UNDERGRADUATE STUDENT ENROLLMENT: 31,289
▸ STADIUM CAPACITY: 80,321

WIN OR LOSE, the marching band takes the field after every game, playing such numbers as "On Wisconsin" and "You've Said It All" (the Budweiser song). [After a win over Ohio State], however, the band was unable to march onto the field, it being occupied for the next hour or so by the student body and the football team. No one seemed to mind much.

—*Austin Murphy, SI, October 25, 2010*

Students have been jumping on cue since 1998.

PHOTOGRAPH BY JOHN BIEVER

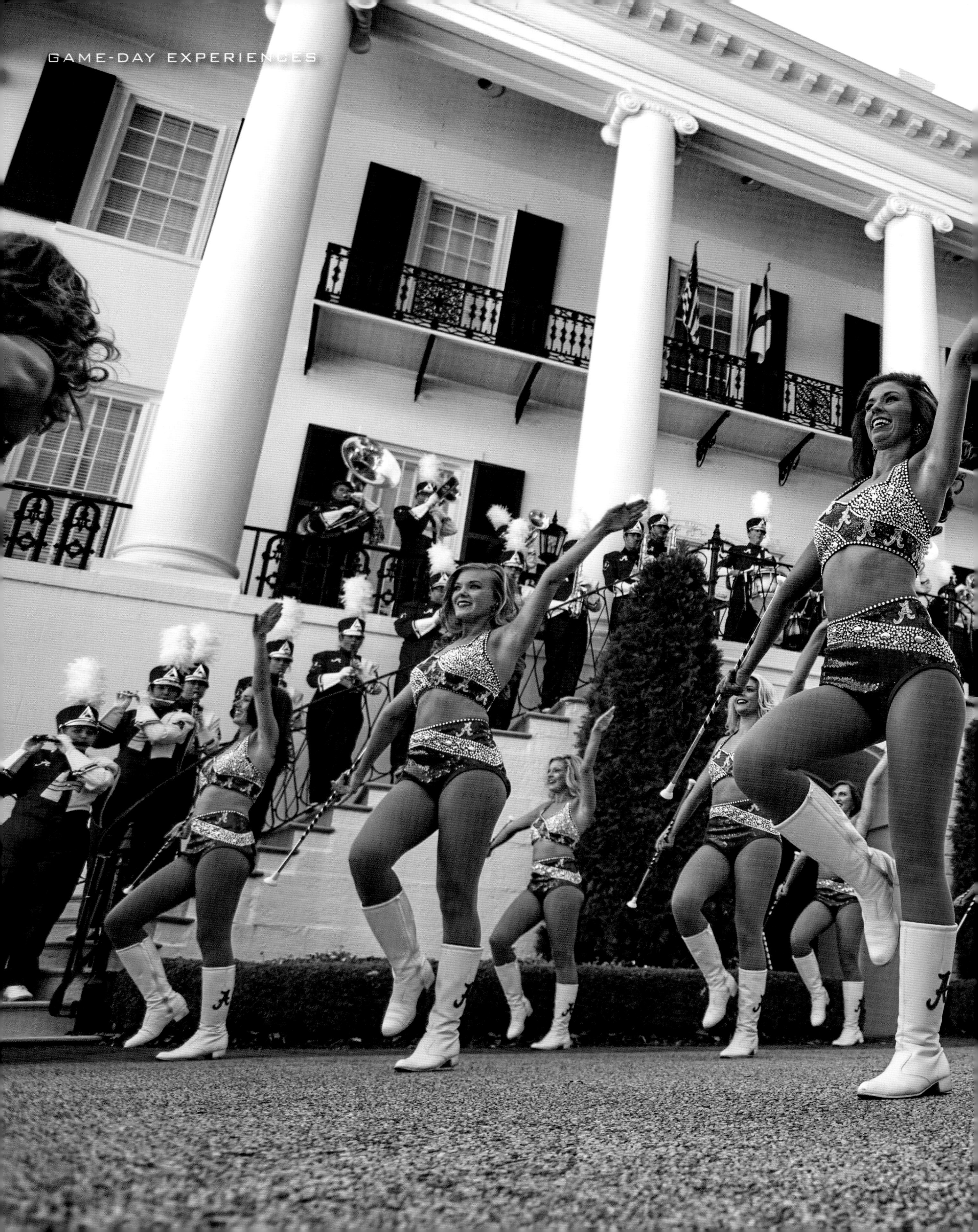

7

ALABAMA

TUSCALOOSA, ALA.

" Before kickoff, stop on the steps of the Gorgas Library for the Million Dollar Band's "Elephant Stomp." A few hours later, the sound of fans singing "Rammer Jammer Yellow Hammer" means victory is secure. " —AUSTIN MURPHY

▸ UNDERGRADUATE STUDENT ENROLLMENT: 30,752
▸ STADIUM CAPACITY: 101,821

HANK WILLIAMS once said he could throw his cowboy hat onto the stage of the Grand Ole Opry after he finished "Lovesick Blues" and it would get at least one curtain call. It has been that way for decades in Tuscaloosa, except the hat is houndstooth. Will Nevin, a first-year law student, places an offering the night before every game at the feet of Bear Bryant's statue in front of the football stadium. He and his friends leave a bag of Golden Flake potato chips and an old-fashioned glass bottle of Coca-Cola, the sponsors of Bryant's old TV show. Nevin, 21, never saw the show, never saw Bryant on the sideline. But the image of the Bear is alive in his mind's eye. He just knows how it must have been, like hearing someone tell you how sweet an old Mustang used to run, before it was put up on blocks in the barn and covered with a tarp. The most you can do is run your hand over the paint and imagine.

—*Rick Bragg, SI, August 27, 2007*

The elephant joined Bama's parade in 1979.

PHOTOGRAPH BY JASON PARKHURST

CLEMSON, S.C.

Players make an ebullient descent into Death Valley.

PHOTOGRAPH BY SIMON BRUTY

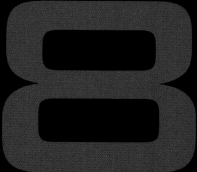

8

CLEMSON

" No entrance in college football can surpass Clemson players' taking a one-block bus ride, rubbing Howard's Rock and sprinting down a steep hill through a throng of fans as balloons fly into the sky. " —ANDY STAPLES

▸ UNDERGRADUATE STUDENT ENROLLMENT: 17,260

▸ STADIUM CAPACITY: 81,500

WITH THE BAND, the cheerleaders, the dance team and the majorettes, there are almost three uniformed supporters for every uniformed player, and that's not counting the dozens of male fans wearing nothing but purple and orange body paint north of their navels, with Tiger paws painted on their nipples.

Michael Bamberger, SI, October 31, 2011

THE MAN ON THE ROCK

When you do as much for a program and for a town as Frank Howard did for Clemson, you earn a gesture of respect from every player who takes the field

BY CURRY KIRKPATRICK

T WAS WAY BACK THERE IN THE STATE OF ALABAMA, when ol' Frank Howard was coaching baseball at the insane asylum which was right next door to the university in Tuscaloosa, that one of the patients—it may have been his centerfielder—came galloping by on a broomstick. Giddyap. Giddyap. This guy said he was Jesus Christ hisself, but another ol' boy told Frank not to worry about it.

"That ol' boy is crazy," he said.

"How can you tell, buddy?" ol' Frank said.

"'Cause ever'body knows there's only but one Jesus," that other ol' boy said. "And *I'm* him."

The thing about it is, there isn't much difference between Alabama, where ol' Frank played even before his lifetime friend, ol' Bear Bryant, got to school there, and Clemson, where ol' Frank went on to be an honest-to-golleee coach in 1931 and stayed until . . . until. . . .

Well, he's still there, by gawd, chewin' and spittin' and snarlin' nearly six decades later about how Bear wanted to come be his assistant coach back in the early '40s. "Smartest thing I ever did, buddy, not hirin' that sweet ol' Bear," says ol' Frank. "He would have done grabbed my whiskey hisself, took my woman, cut my throat, drunk my blood and had us on probation for life, that's all."

Actually, the difference between Tuscaloosa and the foothills of South Carolina was this: At Alabama the coaches were always playing for the national championship. At Clemson they were trying to whip teams like Erskine and The Citadel and Wofford and Newberry. When Clemson lost to Wofford 14–13 in 1933, ol' Frank, then an assistant to Jess Neely, had had just about enough. Along with Neely and some Clemson alumni, he started a fund-raising organization to build up the football program—even though nobody around Clemson had what you might call funds to be raised. All the same, when ol' Frank and his friends came up with their club called IPTAY—I Pay Ten A Year—the cotton farmer and the truck driver, the grocery clerk and the gas jockey, the preacher and the housewife all responded.

If ever a college, a town, an environment was set in time, made, stamped and fingerprinted by one man, it's Frank Howard's Clemson. The everyday population is about 8,000—approximately 7,000 of whom have been known to dress up in orange hats and orange suspenders or orange pantyhose and to paint orange Tiger paws on their noses. On autumn Wednesdays, however, the orange begins to spread; caravans of RVs and campers and pickups start trickling into town and parking in the vast fields and blacktop lots lining the highways to Clemson Memorial Stadium, otherwise known as Frank Howard Field, otherwise known as Death Valley. By Thursday night, traffic is backed up on all thoroughfares.

Suddenly this thimble of a rural burg, where 72 hours earlier there was barely a sign of life, has become a raging ocean of orange humanity, more than 80,000 people strong, that comes downright close to being the second-largest city in the state and, decibel-wise, one of the loudest in creation.

"Where al these people come from is still a mystery to me, buddy," says Danny Ford, 41, the current Clemson head coach. "We don't have but about 50,000 living alumni. I guess you could say the biggest thing IPTAY did was get a whole bunch of other folks involved with Clemson."

The charm of Clemson is that both town and gown and the country folk around know full well who and what they are. They're not only fightin' proud of their Southern sticks heritage; they can make fun of it as well as any ol' Yankee. A T-shirt prominent in Clemson these days shows the cartoon faces of the wizened ol' Bartles and Jaymes wine cooler codgers with the words: CLEM AND SON: THANK YU FOR YOUR SUPPORT.

All Clemson humor, of course, traces back to that rotund, cow-pie-kickin', tractor-pedalin' clown-cum-sage, ol' Frank hisself, 80 years young last March and somehow getting younger. Wondrous stories, apocryphal or not, have grown up around him like moss. Football fans throughout the South refer to him simply as the Legend. There's ol' Frank driving comedian Bob Hope through Clemson. "Frank, I thought you were going to show me the town," says Hope. "Buddy, you want me to back up and show you again?" says Howard.

Did Rockne or Wilkinson or Parseghian or Schembechler ever make a straight man out of Bob Hope?

Clemson's first football coach, Walter Riggs, became the school's sixth president. Riggs hired John Heisman—yes, *that* Heisman—to coach football. The human trophy-to-be wound up winning 19 games in four seasons (1900–03) while establishing a philosophy. "At Clemson we have a style of football play radically different from anything on earth," wrote Heisman, no Humble Johnny, he, in '03. "All colleges should have fixed athletic traditions and should be loyal to them as to the institution itself."

When ol' Frank bowed out as coach, Clemson's marketing people greeted the new age with a more benign look in Tiger paraphernalia, namely cute, cuddly footprints that would appeal to children of all ages. Ol' Frank, cursing progress, referred to them as Men-o-paws. But the Greek element at Clemson responded as if the school administration had ordered up free love, and soon fraternities and sororities made it one of the pledges' annual duties to paint huge orange Tiger paws on every roadway and parking lot in five counties.

In retrospect, the paw was—and is—the perfect embodiment of the total Clemson experience. ∎

9

TENNESSEE

" You can see boatloads of fans—literally—when the Volunteer Navy arrives from the nearby Tennessee River. The checkerboard end zone is the game's most distinctive, and beloved mascot Smokey the coonhound cavorts on the sideline. " —DICK FRIEDMAN

▸ UNDERGRADUATE STUDENT
ENROLLMENT: 21,863
▸ STADIUM CAPACITY: 102,455

HE HAD on an orange shirt and hat. His wife had on an orange dress and was carrying an orange purse. His little boy had on an orange hat, shirt and bow tie. They were on their way into Neyland Stadium, and they were surrounded by enough orange shirts, hats, purses, dresses, ties and trousers to subdue the Irish Republican Army.

—*Roy Blount Jr., SI, September 25, 1972*

Players make the game-day march to Neyland Stadium.

PHOTOGRAPH BY JIM BROWN/USA TODAY SPORTS

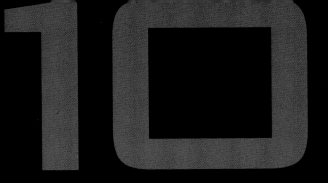

10

GEORGIA

" Every time Georgia plays at home, a white English bulldog clad in a red sweater reigns supreme " 'tween the hedges." The current "damn good dog" is Uga X. His predecessors are buried on an incline at the southwest end of the stadium. " —WILLIAM F. REED

AT THE VARSITY—a chain of throwback drive-ins—patrons have been known to forgo mustard lest the color be mistaken for fealty to Georgia Tech. This is a state where not long ago a couple named their son David Alexander William Gibbs, enabling him to buy monogrammed apparel off the rack anywhere from Dahlonega to Valdosta.

—*L. Jon Wertheim, SI, December 23, 2002*

▸ UNDERGRADUATE STUDENT ENROLLMENT: 26,882
▸ STADIUM CAPACITY: 92,746

After wins, the excitement spills across the hedges.

PHOTOGRAPH BY JEFFREY VEST/ICON SPORTSWIRE

10 THE

BEST MASCOTS, BACKFIELDS, TWO-SPORT STARS, MOVIES, BLACK-COLLEGE PLAYERS, WALK-ON PLAYERS, OVERTIME GAMES AND THE FULL RESULTS

IN THIS SECTION, THE MEMBERS OF OUR PANEL GO OFF IN THEIR OWN DIRECTION. INSTEAD OF POLLING THEM AND ARRIVING AT A CONSENSUS AS WE DID IN OTHER CATEGORIES, PANELISTS HERE WERE ASKED TO CHOOSE A TOPIC AND THEN POPULATE ITS TOP 10 ENTIRELY ON THEIR OWN. LET SUBJECTIVITY RUN AMOK.

MANY OF THE TOPICS THAT OUR PANELISTS CHOSE TOUCH ON ASPECTS OF FOOTBALL THAT ARE UNIQUE TO THE COLLEGE VERSION OF THE GAME. ONE LIST RANKS PLAYERS FROM HISTORICALLY BLACK COLLEGES, WHILE ANOTHER RANKS THE TOP GAMES PLAYED UNDER THE MODERN GO-GO OVERTIME RULES. OTHERS PAY HEED TO TWO OF THE MOST COLLEGIATE OF CHARACTERS, THE WALK-ON AND THE MULTISPORT ATHLETE.

ALSO RANKED ARE MASCOTS, A TRADITION THAT IS THE VERY EMBODIMENT OF THE COLLEGE GAME. IN A UNIVERSE THAT HAS PLAYERS AND SOMETIMES COACHES FLASH THOUGH CAMPUS IN A FEW QUICK YEARS, MASCOTS ARE AMONG THE GAME'S FEW BREATHING CONSTANTS. AT NOTRE DAME, QUARTERBACKS FROM JOE MONTANA TO TONY RICE TO RON POWLUS TO JIMMY CLAUSEN WILL PASS THROUGH THE BUILDING, COACHES SUCH AS LOU HOLTZ, TYRONE WILLINGHAM AND CHARLIE WEIS WILL COME AND GO, BUT THAT LEPRECHAUN IS THERE TO STAY. COLLEGE FOOTBALL IS ONE COURT IN WHICH THE JESTER HAS AN ENVIABLE STAYING POWER.

10 THE

BEST MASCOTS

SI senior writer AUSTIN MURPHY names the most adorable, intimidating and spirit-raising creatures to roam college stadiums

UGA THE BULLDOG GEORGIA

1 The spike-collared, red-jerseyed canine resides in an air-conditioned doghouse at Sanford Stadium. Several Ugas have been retired in pregame "passing of the collar" ceremonies during which students chant, "Damn good dog!

2 | **RALPHIE THE BUFFALO** COLORADO
Held in an undisclosed location to avoid a reprise of its 1970 kidnapping by Air Force Academy cadets, the bison requires five "handlers" for its traditional loops across Folsom Field.

3 | **BEVO THE STEER** TEXAS
The 15 Bevos have included such obstreperous long-horns as Bevo III (escaped from his pen and ran amok on campus for 48 hours) and Bevo V (escaped its handlers and scattered the Baylor band).

4 | **THE LEPRECHAUN** NOTRE DAME
Detained by police at Michigan State in 2006, (the offense: crowd surfing) the feisty welterweight could not produce an ID, explaining to the authorities, "These knickers don't have any pockets."

5 | **MIKE THE TIGER** LSU
Generous donors raised money to build Mike a $3 million "habitat," hard by Tiger Stadium, where the Bengal-Siberian mix lolls in luxury, behind plexi-glass, between games.

BUCKY THE BADGER WISCONSIN

The resilient icon survived 1973 attempt to replace him with Henrietta Holstein, "a lovable cow." Cited for crowd surfing in '96, he was asked by police to spell his name. "Badger," he began. "B-A-D-G . . ."

7 SEBASTIAN THE IBIS MIAMI

The plucky native marsh bird once brought a fire extinguisher to a Florida State game to douse Chief Osceola's flaming spear. Alas, the spear remained aflame, and Sebastian was roughed up by police.

8 SPARTY MICHIGAN STATE

A perma-scowl and a hypertrophied physique help the nation's most buff mascot project masculinity, despite the fact that he performs his duties in a skimpy skirt.

9 RAMBLIN' WRECK GEORGIA TECH

One of the more charming vignettes in college football is the sight of the gold and white, oogha-ing Ramblin' Wreck—a 1930 Ford Cabriolet Sport Coupe—making its pregame dash across the field.

10 MASKED RIDER TEXAS TECH

Long before there was a Traveler (Southern Cal) or a Renegade (Florida State), a masked, caped student in a gaucho hat on horseback led the Red Raiders onto the field.

BEST BACKFIELDS

In college football a strong pair can be a winning hand, and SI senior editor MARK GODICH identifies the top duos of them all

1. FELIX (DOC) BLANCHARD AND GLENN DAVIS, ARMY

From 1944 to '46, Mr. Inside (Blanchard) and Mr. Outside (Davis) led the Cadets to a 27-0-1 record. The most celebrated tandem in the history of the game combined for 97 touchdowns, and in '45 Blanchard became the first junior to win the Heisman. The next year Davis, who averaged a record 8.3 yards a carry for his career, won the award too.

2. ERIC DICKERSON AND CRAIG JAMES, SMU

From 1979 to '82 the Pony Express combined for 8,705 rushing yards and 79 total touchdowns while alternating at tailback. In Dickerson's senior season he ran for 1,617 yards, averaging 7.0 yards a carry and finished third in the 1982 Heisman race behind Herschel Walker and John Elway. James, who doubled as SMU's punter in his last two seasons, had a career 3,742 rushing yards.

3. DARREN MCFADDEN AND FELIX JONES, ARKANSAS

The duo combined for 7,546 rushing yards and 61 touchdowns from 2005 to '07, and in their final two seasons they each topped 1,000 yards rushing both years. In his senior year, McFadden, a two-time Heisman runner-up, regularly took direct snaps out of the Wild Hog formation, keeping the ball or throwing it when he wasn't handing off to his sidekick (or to the third member of the backfield, future pro Peyton Hillis). As a junior Jones averaged 8.7 yards a carry.

4. LENDALE WHITE AND REGGIE BUSH, USC

Thunder and Lightning. White was the punishing inside runner, while Bush could score in the blink of an eye. From 2003 to '05, they combined for 99 touchdowns. Their numbers in '05 were staggering: 3,042 rushing yards and 45 total TDs. Bush, who ran for 1,740 yards that season on only 200 carries and was just as dangerous as a receiver and return man, would win the Heisman, only to be stripped of it years later for accepting impermissible benefits.

5. GREG PRUITT AND JACK MILDREN, OKLAHOMA

We know—Mildren wasn't a running back, but how do you leave out the best quarterback of the wishbone era? As a senior in 1971, Mildren ran for 1,289 yards and 20 touchdowns. When he wasn't keeping the ball, he was often pitching it to the electrifying Pruitt, who ran for 1,760 yards, averaged 9.0 yards a carry and scored 18 TDs. Pruitt finished third in the '71 Heisman race; Mildren, sixth.

6. LAURENCE MARONEY AND MARION BARBER III, MINNESOTA

The first pair of teammates to run for 1,000 yards in consecutive seasons, Maroney and Barber combined for 4,934 rushing yards and 50 TDs in 2003 and '04. Not coincidentally, the Golden Gophers enjoyed one of their betters stretches, going 17–8 over the two seasons.

7. BARRY SANDERS AND THURMAN THOMAS, OKLAHOMA STATE

In 1987 Thomas rushed for 1,613 yards and finish seventh in the Heisman vote, while understudy Barry Sanders ran for 603 yards. After Thomas became a Buffalo Bill, Sanders really showed what he could do, running for a record 2,628 yards and scoring 37 touchdowns while winning the '88 Heisman.

8. FLOYD LITTLE AND LARRY CSONKA, SYRACUSE

For two seasons Little and Csonka formed a feared inside-outside threat, combining for 3,683 rushing yards and 37 touchdowns. Little finished fifth in both the 1965 and '66 Heisman vote, and the year after he left, Csonka was fourth.

9. MIKE ROZIER AND ROGER CRAIG, NEBRASKA

After rushing for 1,060 yards on 173 carries as a junior in 1981, Craig was asked to move to fullback so the Cornhuskers could feature Rozier more prominently. The next season Rozier set a school record for rushing with 1,689 yards, while the selfless Craig chipped in 586 rushing yards on a mere 119 carries for the Cornhuskers, who finished 12–1 and ranked third in the country.

10. MARK INGRAM AND TRENT RICHARDSON, ALABAMA

The two-headed monster helped lead the Crimson Tide to the national championship in 2009. Ingram, the first 'Bama player to win the Heisman, was the workhorse, running for 1,658 yards and 17 touchdowns. Richardson chipped in with 751 yards and eight TDs. The pair also combined for 48 catches, 460 receiving yards and three scores.

Davis (left) and Blanchard each brought a Heisman to Army.

James (left) and Dickerson defined SMU's peak of football success.

1. BO JACKSON, AUBURN

An outstanding baseball player for the Tigers, Jackson became a Southern icon in football, winning the 1985 Heisman Trophy. He played both sports professionally, and was an all-star in each, for the Royals and Raiders. He was known for his tape-measure homers in baseball and his elusive and powerful running in football.

2. DEION SANDERS, FLORIDA STATE

The Seminole was a Hall of Fame cornerback in the NFL and played major league baseball for the Braves and three other teams. The only athlete ever to appear in both a World Series and a Super Bowl, his biggest asset in both sports was his speed.

3. CHARLIE WARD, FLORIDA STATE

In 1993, Ward was a point guard on a team that advanced to the Elite Eight, and then quarterbacked the Seminoles to their first national football title while winning the Heisman Trophy. One of the few Heisman winners to go undrafted by the NFL—at 6'2" he was considered too short to play quarterback in the pros—Ward played in the NBA for the Knicks, Spurs and Rockets. He also was drafted twice by major league baseball, even though he didn't play the sport in college.

4. HALE IRWIN, COLORADO

A two-time all-conference cornerback and an academic All-American (as well as the 1967 NCAA golf champion), Irwin went on to a stellar career on the PGA Tour. He won the U.S. Open three times and is one of four golfers to win an official tournament on all six continents where pro golf is played.

5. JIM BROWN, SYRACUSE

He is primarily remembered as an All-America running back in the sport in which he had such great professional success, but Brown also lettered in basketball and track at Syracuse and was an All-America in lacrosse. As a senior midfielder, he scored 43 goals (in 10 games), the second-best total in the country for that season.

6. FRANK THOMAS, AUBURN

Although he went to college on a football scholarship and was an accomplished tight end, Thomas focused on baseball after suffering a serious ankle injury before his sophomore football season. Good choice. Thomas played in the major leagues from 1990 through 2008 and is now enshrined in the National Baseball Hall of Fame.

7. JAKE GIBBS, MISSISSIPPI

After quarterbacking the Rebels to shares of the national championship in 1959 and '60, Gibbs was drafted by both the Cleveland Browns of the NFL and the Houston Oilers of the AFL. However he signed a baseball contract with the Yankees and, after several call-ups, stuck on the roster as a catcher from '65 until his retirement in '71.

8. TONY GONZALEZ, CALIFORNIA

As a Golden Bear, Gonzalez drew raves as both a tight end in football and a power forward in basketball. As a junior in 1997, Gonzalez's team made it to the Sweet Sixteen of the NCAA tournament. He opted, however, to play football professionally and retired in 2013 with the second-most receptions in NFL history.

9. WALLACE (WAH WAH) JONES, KENTUCKY

The only Wildcats player to have his jersey (number 27) retired in both football and basketball, Jones played end for Bear Bryant and power forward for Adolph Rupp, making all-conference in both sports. He won a gold medal in basketball at the 1948 Olympics, and played three seasons for the Indianapolis Olympians of the NBA.

10. TERRY BAKER, OREGON STATE

As a senior in 1962–63, the quarterback/point guard became the first (and only) player to win the Heisman Trophy and play in the NCAA Final Four in basketball. He was SI's Sportsman of the Year for 1962.

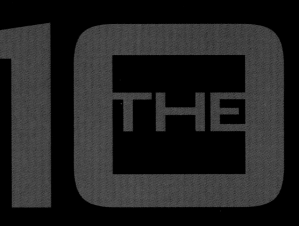

THE 10 BEST TWO-SPORT STARS

The players on this list by former SI senior writer WILLIAM F. REED did more than hit the weight room when winter and spring rolled around

Irwin went from nailing receivers to sticking putts.

Ward's passing skills translated from the field to the court.

249

10 THE

BEST MOVIES

Hollywood's greatest have mined college football for laughs and tears, and former SI senior editor DICK FRIEDMAN gives his gridiron Oscars

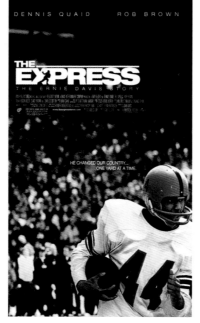

1. RUDY (1993)

The fact-based saga of undersized walk-on Daniel (Rudy) Ruettiger, whose quest to take the field for the Fighting Irish—if only for one play!—demonstrates college football's magnetic hold. Sean Astin is well-cast as the wide-eyed, plucky title character. Best supporting figure is Irish coach Dan Devine, who for purposes of drama allowed himself to be portrayed as being against letting Rudy even dress for the game; in fact, Devine was on board with the dream.

2. EVERYBODY'S ALL-AMERICAN (1988)

Dennis Quaid has the right moves as Gavin Grey, a golden-boy halfback at a Southern school thrown for a loss by postcollege life. In the gridiron sequences (some shot at LSU's Tiger Stadium), director Taylor Hackford captures the big-game vibe and on-field crunch. John Goodman is entertaining as Grey's blasphemous blocking buddy.

3. KNUTE ROCKNE ALL AMERICAN (1940)

Hokey, hoary—and an American film classic, thanks largely to Pat O'Brien's hammy portrayal of the Rock. The coach's pep talk has become football's most memorable oration; the tearjerking deathbed request of George Gipp (Ronald Reagan) to "win one for the Gipper" also helped elect a president four decades later.

4. THE EXPRESS (2008)

This biopic about Syracuse's 1961 Heisman winner Ernie Davis hurtles along excitingly, thanks to Rob Brown's performance as the doomed (by leukemia) Davis and to a crackerjack turn by Dennis Quaid as Ben Schwartzwalder, the Orangemen's hardass coach with a soft heart.

5. THE BLIND SIDE (2009)

Sandra Bullock works hard in her Oscar-winning portrayal of Leigh Anne Tuohy, who kick-starts gentle giant Michael Oher (Quinton Aaron) on the road to becoming an All-America offensive lineman at Ole Miss. But the scene stealers are the salivating SEC coaches (especially Nick Saban) making their recruiting pitches to Big Mike.

6. THE PROGRAM (1993)

Recruiting excesses, academic scandals, even steroids are among the ills credibly trotted out by writer-director David S. Ward. Would rank higher if a charisma-challenged James Caan (as the beleaguered coach) and Craig Sheffer (as the star quarterback) weren't so hard to root for.

7. HARVARD BEATS YALE 29-29 (2008)

Kevin Rafferty's documentary revisits The Game of 1968, in which the Crimson earned a draw by scoring 16 points in the last 42 seconds (thus prompting the *Harvard Crimson* headline that Rafferty uses as his title). Providing comic relief is Yale linebacker Mike Bouscaren, who impishly recounts his desire to put a hurt on the Harvards.

8. JIM THORPE—ALL-AMERICAN (1951)

The modern viewer must get past having a Caucasian (a buff Burt Lancaster) playing a Native American. Once we do, we can appreciate football action that is well-staged (by legendary Michael Curtiz, director of *Casablanca*) and gives us a sense of how the game looked in the smashmouth days of the early 20th century.

9. HORSE FEATHERS (1932)

The Marx Brothers take on King Football. Is there any doubt who would win? Along the way to the gridiron triumph of Huxley College over archival Darwin, the boys unfurl some of the most deathless lines in film comedy. (Groucho as President Wagstaff, addressing the Huxley faculty: "And I say to you gentlemen that this college is a failure. The trouble is we're neglecting football for education.")

10. THE FRESHMAN (1925)

Harold Lloyd's silent comedy makes brilliant use of its star's elastic athleticism in its football scenes, including one in which his hapless character is used as a practice tackling dummy. The big-game finale is startling for its vision of the capacity crowd at Cal's newly opened Memorial Stadium.

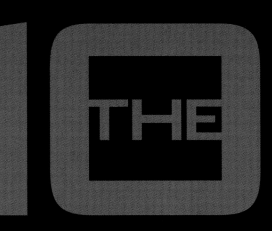

THE 10

BEST BLACK-COLLEGE PLAYERS

SI senior writer TIM LAYDEN identifies the greatest performers from historically black colleges and universities

1. JERRY RICE, MISSISSIPPI VALLEY STATE (1981–1984)

During his career, which included three years paired with dynamic quarterback Willie Totten, Rice caught more than 300 passes for nearly 5,000 yards and 51 touchdowns, towering statistics that predate the evolution of the passing game in college football. As a senior in 1984, Rice was the only Division I-AA player to make the major-college consensus All-America list and finished ninth in the voting for the Heisman Trophy.

2. WALTER PAYTON, JACKSON STATE (1971–1974)

Payton, largely ignored by major colleges during recruiting, initially committed to Kansas State but then switched to Jackson State to play with his brother. For the Tigers he averaged more than six yards per carry, scored 66 touchdowns, and picked up the nickname "Sweetness," which would follow him into the NFL and beyond.

3. STEVE MCNAIR, ALCORN STATE (1991–1994)

Despite playing outside Division I-A, McNair's passing and running abilities created enough of a sensation that he made a serious run at the 1994 Heisman Trophy before finishing third. As a senior he accumulated a then NCAA record of 5,799 yards in total offense, including nearly 1,000 on ground, and threw 44 touchdown passes.

4. WILLIE LANIER, MORGAN STATE (1963–1966)

At 6' 1", 245 pounds, Lanier was a powerhouse at middle linebacker for legendary coach Earl Banks. Lanier was twice named a small college All-America and was drafted in the second round by the Chiefs in 1967, where he became the first African-American to star at middle linebacker in the pros.

5. PAUL (TANK) YOUNGER, GRAMBLING (1945–1948)

The first NFL player to come from a predominantly black college, the 6' 3", 225-pound Younger was moved by coach Eddie Robinson (who was Younger's high school coach) from defensive tackle to running back and linebacker, and acquired his bruising nickname after bowling over would-be tacklers. Younger scored 60 touchdowns at Grambling, a remarkable number in an era when scoring was far lower.

6. JACKIE SLATER, JACKSON STATE (1972–1975)

Slater was a 277-pound tackle who cleared the path for much of Payton's yardage and later developed into a skilled pass blocker in the NFL. After his senior year, he was selected to play in the last College All-Star Football Classic, a preseason game which matched the best college players against the defending NFL champion.

7. DOUG WILLIAMS, GRAMBLING (1974–1977)

Before he became the first African-American quarterback to win a Super Bowl (in 1988, with the Redskins), Williams used his powerful right arm to pass for 8,411 yards and 93 touchdowns for the Tigers. He finished fourth in the voting for the 1977 Heisman Trophy.

8. ED (TOO TALL) JONES, TENNESSEE STATE (1970–1973)

Jones went to Tennessee State in 1970 with designs on a basketball career, but it was on the football field that he developed into a fearsome player. His teams lost only two games in three years, and in the 1974 the Cowboys made the 6' 9" Jones the first—and still the only—player from a historically black college to be selected first overall in the NFL draft.

9. BUCK BUCHANAN, GRAMBLING (1959–1962)

Despite growing up in Birmingham, Buchanan, like so many players at historically black colleges, wasn't given a chance by the football powerhouses of the Southeastern Conference. Instead the 6' 7", 270-pound Buchanan signed with Grambling and became an NAIA All-America on the defensive line.

10. JOHNNY SAMPLE, MARYLAND STATE (1954–1957)

Sample rushed for 37 touchdowns as his teams went 28-1-1, and the running back was the first player from a historically black school selected to the College All-Star game. Later as a defensive back in the NFL, he was known as a fierce and intimidating hitter.

The versatile McNair was a surprise Heisman candidate for the Braves.

THE 10 BEST WALK-ONS

SI senior writer ANDY STAPLES names the top players who, without a scholarship offer, were able to make the team—and their mark

1. J.J. WATT, DE, WISCONSIN
Watt began his college career as a scholarship tight end at Central Michigan, but when the Chippewas wanted to move him to offensive tackle after his freshman year, Watt transferred to Wisconsin as a walk-on defensive end. As a junior, Watt had 21 tackles for loss, nine pass deflections and was named first-team All–Big Ten before going pro.

2. AENEAS WILLIAMS, CB, SOUTHERN
The accounting major spent two years as a student before he decided to walk on to the football team. Five games in, Williams was a starter. He tied for the NCAA lead in interceptions with 11 as a senior in 1990, and then went on to a Hall of Fame career in the NFL.

3. BRANDON BURLSWORTH, G, ARKANSAS
Burlsworth, unmistakable because he wore horn-rimmed glasses while playing, walked on in 1994 and won a starting job as a redshirt sophomore in '96. He was named to All-SEC teams as a junior and senior. Burlsworth died in a car crash driving home from his first minicamp after being drafted in the third round of the '99 draft by the Indianapolis Colts. An award bearing his name is given annually to the nation's best player who began hias career as a walk-on.

4. JIMMY WILLIAMS, DE, NEBRASKA
The best player to emerge from the nation's top walk-on program, Williams was named a first-team Walter Camp All-America as a senior in 1981 after leading the Cornhuskers with 10 sacks. To make ends meet in Lincoln, he and his brother (also a walk-on) worked on farms and in a slaughterhouse.

5. LOUIS OLIVER, S, FLORIDA
Oliver was lightly recruited out of Belle Glade, Fla., but the safety knew he was good enough to play at college football's highest level. He walked on at Florida in 1984, redshirted, earned a starting spot in '86 and was a consensus All-America as a senior in '88.

6. JORDY NELSON, WR, KANSAS STATE
Nelson was a high school quarterback and defensive back in Riley, Kans., who walked on in Manhattan as a safety, and blossomed after moving to wide receiver before his redshirt sophomore season. As a senior in 2007, Nelson caught 122 passes for 1,606 yards and 11 touchdowns.

7. COLT BRENNAN, QB, HAWAII
Brennan walked on at Colorado and Hawaii, but it was in paradise that he found success. In three seasons as Hawaii's starter, Brennan threw for 14,193 yards and 131 touchdowns. He still holds the major-college record for TD passes in one season, with 56 in 2006.

8. ANDRE WADSWORTH, DL, FLORIDA STATE
Wadsworth walked on in Tallahassee in 1993, and he found his way onto the field in '95 as a defensive tackle. Wadsworth moved to defensive end as a senior, piled up 16 sacks and earned first-team All-America honors in 1996.

9. SCOTT FUJITA, LB, CAL
Fujita left high school as a tweener—too small to play linebacker and too slow to play safety. The walk-on bulked up and found a home at linebacker. After a neck surgery following the 1999 season to eliminate painful stingers, Fujita's play soared. As a senior in 2001, he wound up a great player on a terrible (1–10, 0–8 Pac-10) team.

10. DARREN WOODSON, LB, ARIZONA STATE
Though Woodson knew greater fame as a safety for the Dallas Cowboys, he found his way onto the field in Tempe as an undersized linebacker. He walked on in 1987 and won a starting job in '89. Woodson led the Sun Devils in tackles with 122 that season.

Nelson, a high school quarterback, proved himself as a Kansas State receiver.

Watt skipped the scholarship to jump from Central Michigan to Wisconsin.

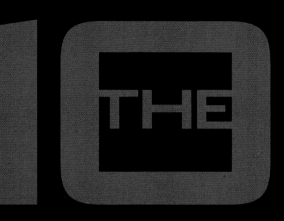

1. BOISE STATE 43, OKLAHOMA 42 (OT), 2007 FIESTA BOWL

Boise State squandered an 18-point second-half lead, tied the game on a fourth-and-18 hook and lateral with seven seconds left and won it in overtime on Ian Johnson's Statue of Liberty two-point conversion. Lost in the madness? The Broncos held the Sooners' Adrian Peterson to 77 yards on 20 carries.

2. OHIO STATE 31, MIAMI 24 (2OT), 2003 FIESTA BOWL

The Hurricanes thought they won in the first overtime when a Craig Krenzel fourth-down pass fell incomplete in the end zone. But a controversial pass interference call gave Ohio State new life. The Buckeyes sealed the game on a Maurice Clarett five-yard run.

3. ARKANSAS 58, MISSISSIPPI 56 (7OT), 2001

The game included eight ties, five lead changes and set seven SEC or NCAA records. The teams combined for 988 yards of offense until Arkansas's Jermaine Petty foiled Eli Manning's two-point conversion completion to Doug Zeigler, stopping him a yard short of the end zone.

4. TEXAS A&M 36, KANSAS STATE 33 (2OT), 1998

The Aggies' stunning victory in the Big 12 championship game handed Kansas State its first loss of the season and prevented the Wildcats from playing for the national title. A&M came back from a 27–12 fourth-quarter deficit, and Sirr Parker scored the game-winner for the Aggies on a 32-yard catch on third-and-17.

5. ARKANSAS 71, KENTUCKY 63 (7OT), 2003

With the game tied at 24 at the end of regulation, quarterback Matt Jones led the Razorbacks to an NCAA-record 47 points after regulation. The Matt Jones–led Razorbacks won after a fumble by Kentucky's Jared Lorenzen on fourth-and-three at the five-yard line.

6. WASHINGTON 29, WASHINGTON STATE 26 (3OT), 2002

The most controversial finish in Apple Cup history ended with the No. 3 Cougars knocked out of the national title race. Backup Washington State quarterback Matt Kegel's batted-down screen pass was ruled a backward pass, which Huskies defensive end Kai Ellis pounced on, ending the game. Angry Washington State fans tossed bottles on the field in protest.

7. WAKE FOREST 6, VIRGINIA TECH 3 (2OT), 2014

The teams played the first scoreless FBS regulation game in nine years, a contest immortalized by the screen shot of Hokies' coach Frank Beamer celebrating with arms raised above a 0–0 score graphic. Wake Forest's Mike Weaver won the game on a 39-yard field goal in double overtime after missing three in regulation.

8. CAL 34, USC 31 (3OT), 2003

A 38-yard field goal by Tyler Fredrickson in the third overtime ended an 11-game USC win streak and gave Cal its first home victory over a Top 5 team since 1975. The victory proved to be one of the defining victories of Jeff Tedford's time at Cal, as Reggie Robertson relieved Aaron Rodgers and outdueled Matt Leinart.

9. ARKANSAS 53, MISSISSIPPI 52 (OT), 2015

Yes, Arkansas again. The Razorbacks are tied for the NCAA record with 17 overtime games. A wild lateral play on fourth-and-25 kept the game alive for Arkansas in overtime. Tight end Hunter Henry flung the ball backwards to Alex Collins, who snaked 31 yards for the first down. Arkansas went for two in the first overtime and won on a Brandon Allen keeper. The Ole Miss loss helped Alabama to win the SEC West and secure a spot in the College Football Playoff.

10. IOWA STATE 37, OKLAHOMA STATE 31 (2OT), 2011

Iowa State overcame a 24–7 deficit to upset the No. 2 Cowboys and knock them out of national title contention. Iowa State entered the game as 27-point underdogs, and the victory is considered the biggest Big 12 win in school history. Iowa State entered the game 0-56-2 against teams ranked No. 6 or higher.

BEST OVERTIME GAMES

SI senior writer PETE THAMEL names the most exciting games from the regular season and postseason that went into extra frames

Arkansas and Kentucky went seven extra periods in 2003.

Iowa State's win upended Oklahoma State's title aspirations.

The Full Results

IF THEY WERE LISTED ON A PANELIST'S BALLOT, THEY MAKE IT HERE TOO, IN THIS FULL RANKING OF EVERYONE WHO RECEIVED A VOTE IN EVERY CATEGORY

QUARTERBACK

1. TIM TEBOW
2. ROGER STAUBACH
3. TOMMIE FRAZIER
4. DANNY WUERFFEL
5. VINCE YOUNG
6. PEYTON MANNING
7. SAMMY BAUGH
8. DOUG FLUTIE
9. MATT LEINART
10. JOE NAMATH
11. JIM PLUNKETT
12. ARCHIE MANNING
13. CAM NEWTON
14. JOHN ELWAY
15. MARCUS MARIOTA
16. STEVE SPURRIER
17. SAM BRADFORD
18. TY DETMER
19. DAVEY O'BRIEN
20. CHARLIE WARD
21. DAN MARINO
22. TIM COUCH
23. OTTO GRAHAM
24. JACK MILDREN

RUNNING BACK

1. HERSCHEL WALKER
2. ARCHIE GRIFFIN
3. BO JACKSON
4. EARL CAMPBELL
5. O.J. SIMPSON
6. BARRY SANDERS
7. TONY DORSETT
8. JIM BROWN
9. DOAK WALKER
10. RED GRANGE
11. MARCUS ALLEN
12. BILLY CANNON
13. GALE SAYERS
14. REGGIE BUSH
15. ADRIAN PETERSON
16. BILLY SIMS
17. ERNIE DAVIS
18. TOM HARMON
19. JIM THORPE
20. LADAINIAN TOMLINSON
21. JEROME BETTIS
22. EMMITT SMITH
23. CHARLES WHITE

WIDE RECEIVER

1. LARRY FITZGERALD
2. RANDY MOSS
3. TIM BROWN
4. JERRY RICE
5. JOHNNY RODGERS
6. ANTHONY CARTER
7. FRED BILETNIKOFF
8. DESMOND HOWARD
9. CALVIN JOHNSON
10. MICHAEL CRABTREE
11. LYNN SWANN
12. HOWARD TWILLEY
13. CRIS CARTER
14. CRIS COLLINSWORTH
15. DON HUTSON
16. LANCE ALWORTH
17. RYAN BROYLES
18. MICHAEL IRVIN
19. TROY EDWARDS
20. BOB HAYES
21. CARLOS ALVAREZ
22. TREVOR INSLEY
23. PETER WARRICK

TIGHT END

1. KEITH JACKSON
2. MIKE DITKA
3. KELLEN WINSLOW
4. TONY GONZALEZ
5. JOHN MACKEY
6. OZZIE NEWSOME
7. CHARLES YOUNG
8. DAVE CASPER
9. JASON WITTEN
10. GORDON HUDSON
11. JIM MANDICH
12. TED KWALICK
13. CHASE COFFMAN
14. AARON HERNANDEZ
15. TODD CHRISTENSEN
16. ROB GRONKOWSKI
17. LEON HART
18. JERMAINE GRESHAM
19. GREG OLSEN
20. MARK BAVARO
21. KEN MCAFEE
22. JEREMY SHOCKEY
23. RON KRAMER
24. JAMES WHALEN

OFFENSIVE LINE

1. JOHN HANNAH
2. ORLANDO PACE
3. ANTHONY MUÑOZ
4. DAVE RIMINGTON
5. BILL FRALIC
6. JONATHAN OGDEN
7. RON YARY
8. JOE THOMAS
9. JIM PARKER
10. CHUCK BEDNARIK
11. WILLIE ROAF
12. BRYANT MCKINNIE
13. BARRETT JONES
14. WILL SHIELDS
15. DAN DIERDORF
16. BOB GAIN
17. JAKE LONG
18. JERRY SISEMORE
19. CALVIN JONES
20. BRUCE MATTHEWS
21. ALAN FANECA
22. WILLIAM HEFFELFINGER
23. DEAN STEINKUHLER
24. STEVE WISNIEWSKI

DEFENSIVE LINE

1. LEE ROY SELMON
2. HUGH GREEN
3. BUBBA SMITH
4. REGGIE WHITE
5. BRUCE SMITH
6. NDAMUKONG SUH
7. TED HENDRICKS
8. LEON HART
9. RANDY WHITE
10. MERLIN OLSEN
11. JACK YOUNGBLOOD
12. WARREN SAPP
13. BRONKO NAGURSKI
14. JULIUS PEPPERS
15. TERRELL SUGGS
16. J.J. WATT
17. JADEVEON CLOWNEY
18. ALAN PAGE
19. DAVID POLLACK
20. JOE GREENE
21. LOU MICHAELS
22. TONY CASILLAS
23. ROSS BROWNER
24. STEVE EMTMAN
25. MIKE REID

LINEBACKER

1. DICK BUTKUS
2. BRIAN BOSWORTH
3. TOMMY NOBIS
4. DERRICK THOMAS
5. JACK HAM
6. LAWRENCE TAYLOR
7. MIKE SINGLETARY
8. CHRIS SPIELMAN
9. LEE ROY JORDAN
10. LUKE KUECHLY
11. GEORGE WEBSTER
12. KEN NORTON JR.
13. PATRICK WILLIS
14. PAUL POSLUSZNY
15. BOBBY BELL
16. RAY LEWIS
17. LAVAR ARRINGTON
18. CORNELIUS BENNETT
19. BRONKO NAGURSKI
20. CHUCK BEDNARIK
21. TEDY BRUSCHI
22. WILLIE LANIER
23. PERCY SNOW
24. MARVIN JONES
25. D.D. LEWIS
26. ANDY KATZENMOYER
27. WILBER MARSHALL

DEFENSIVE BACK

1. CHARLES WOODSON
2. DEION SANDERS
3. RONNIE LOTT
4. JACK TATUM
5. KENNY EASLEY
6. CHAMP BAILEY
7. JERRY GRAY
8. ED REED

9. ROD WOODSON
10. TROY POLAMALU
11. JIM THORPE
12. BENNIE BLADES
13. DRE BLY
14. ROY WILLIAMS
15. TERRELL BUCKLEY
16. ERIC BERRY
17. SAMMY BAUGH
18. PATRICK PETERSON
19. CHARLEY TRIPPI
20. SEAN TAYLOR
21. JOHNNY LUJACK
22. TOMMY CASANOVA
23. DARRELL GREEN
24. JAKE SCOTT
25. JERRY STOVALL

COACH

1. PAUL BRYANT
2. NICK SABAN
3. KNUTE ROCKNE
4. JOE PATERNO
5. URBAN MEYER
6. WOODY HAYES
7. BOBBY BOWDEN
8. FRANK LEAHY
9. BUD WILKINSON
10. EDDIE ROBINSON
11. TOM OSBORNE
12. BARRY SWITZER
13. ARA PARSEGHIAN
14. BO SCHEMBECHLER
15. DARRELL ROYAL
16. JIMMY JOHNSON
17. PETE CARROLL
18. POP WARNER
19. BERNIE BIERMAN
20. ROBERT NEYLAND

REGULAR-SEASON GAME

1. 2013 AUBURN-ALABAMA
2. 1969 TEXAS-ARKANSAS
3. 1971 NEBRASKA-OKLAHOMA
4. 1982 CAL-STANFORD
5. 2007 APPALACHIAN STATE-MICHIGAN
6. 1984 BOSTON COLLEGE-MIAMI
7. 1968 HARVARD-YALE
8. 1946 ARMY-NOTRE DAME
9. 1966 MICHIGAN STATE-NOTRE DAME
10. 1993 NOTRE DAME-FLORIDA STATE
11. 1969 MICHIGAN-OHIO STATE
12. 2005 USC-NOTRE DAME

13. 1967 USC-UCLA
14. 1970 USC-ALABAMA
15. 1991 MIAMI-FLORIDA STATE
16. 1869 RUTGERS-PRINCETON
17. 1959 LSU-MISSISSIPPI
18. 1997 WILLIAMS-AMHERST
19. 2007 MISSOURI-KANSAS
20. 2006 OHIO STATE-MICHIGAN
21. 1994 COLORADO-MICHIGAN
22. 1996 FLORIDA STATE-FLORIDA
23. 1913 NOTRE DAME-ARMY
24. 1994 FLORIDA-FLORIDA STATE
25. 2010 AUBURN-ALABAMA
26. 2014 BAYLOR-TCU

BOWL GAME

1. 2006 ROSE BOWL (TEXAS-USC)
2. 1984 ORANGE BOWL (MIAMI-NEBRASKA)
3. 2007 FIESTA BOWL (BOISE STATE-OKLAHOMA)
4. 1973 SUGAR BOWL (NOTRE DAME-ALABAMA)
5. 1979 SUGAR BOWL (ALABAMA-PENN STATE)
6. 1979 COTTON BOWL (NOTRE DAME-HOUSTON)
7. 1980 HOLIDAY BOWL (BYU-SMU)
8. 1987 FIESTA BOWL (PENN STATE-MIAMI)
9. 2003 FIESTA BOWL (OHIO STATE-MIAMI)
10. 1965 ORANGE BOWL (TEXAS-ALABAMA)
11. 2014 BCS TITLE GAME (FLORIDA STATE-AUBURN)
12. 1951 SUGAR BOWL (KENTUCKY-OKLAHOMA)
13. 1963 ROSE BOWL (USC-WISCONSIN)
14. 1971 ROSE BOWL (STANFORD-OHIO STATE)
15. 1934 ROSE BOWL (COLUMBIA-STANFORD)
16. 1993 ORANGE BOWL (FLORIDA STATE-NEBRASKA
17. 1980 ROSE BOWL (USC-OHIO STATE)
18. 2001 GMAC BOWL (MARSHALL-EAST CAROLINA)
19. 1970 COTTON BOWL (TEXAS-NOTRE DAME)

20. 1997 ROSE BOWL (OHIO STATE-ARIZONA STATE)
21. 2005 ROSE BOWL (TEXAS-MICHIGAN)
22. 1960 COTTON BOWL (SYRACUSE-TEXAS)
23. 2006 INSIGHT BOWL (TEXAS TECH-MINNESOTA)
24. 1965 COTTON BOWL (ARKANSAS-NEBRASKA)
25. 2014 BAHAMAS BOWL (WESTERN KENTUCKY-CENTRAL MICHIGAN)
26. 2000 INDEPENDENCE BOWL (MISSISSIPPI STATE-TEXAS A&M)

SINGLE-SEASON TEAM

1. 1995 NEBRASKA
2. 1971 NEBRASKA
3. 1972 USC
4. 1945 ARMY
5. 2001 MIAMI
6. 1968 OHIO STATE
7. 1956 OKLAHOMA
8. 1961 ALABAMA
9. 1947 MICHIGAN
10. 1979 ALABAMA
11. 1947 NOTRE DAME
12. 1932 USC
13. 1946 NOTRE DAME
14. 1978 ALABAMA
15. 1999 FLORIDA STATE
16. 1958 LSU
17. 1969 TEXAS
18. 1987 MIAMI
19. 2009 ALABAMA
20. 1966 MICHIGAN STATE
21. 1974 OKLAHOMA
22. 1934 MINNESOTA
23. 1949 NOTRE DAME
24. 1944 ARMY
25. 1946 ARMY
26. 1988 NOTRE DAME
27. 1994 PENN STATE
28. 1909 YALE

RIVALRY

1. ALABAMA-AUBURN
2. MICHIGAN-OHIO STATE
3. OKLAHOMA-TEXAS
4. ARMY-NAVY
5. CAL-STANFORD
6. NOTRE DAME-USC
7. MIAMI-FLORIDA STATE
8. HARVARD-YALE
9. KANSAS-MISSOURI
10. FLORIDA-GEORGIA
11. OREGON-OREGON STATE
12. NEBRASKA-OKLAHOMA

13. CLEMSON-SOUTH CAROLINA
14. ALABAMA-LSU
15. AMHERST-WILLIAMS
16. BYU-UTAH
17. FLORIDA-FLORIDA STATE
18. MICHIGAN-NOTRE DAME
19. TEXAS-TEXAS A&M
20. UCLA-USC
21. LAFAYETTE-LEHIGH
22. OKLAHOMA-OKLAHOMA STATE
23. ARIZONA-ARIZONA STATE

PROGRAM

1. ALABAMA
2. NOTRE DAME
3. OHIO STATE
4. MICHIGAN
5. USC
6. OKLAHOMA
7. NEBRASKA
8. TEXAS
9. FLORIDA
10. FLORIDA STATE
11. PENN STATE
12. TENNESSEE
13. LSU
14. AUBURN
15. GEORGIA
16. MIAMI
17. VIRGINIA TECH
18. ARMY

GAME-DAY EXPERIENCE

1. NOTRE DAME
2. LSU
3. MISSISSIPPI
4. MICHIGAN
5. OHIO STATE
6. WISCONSIN
7. ALABAMA
8. CLEMSON
9. TENNESSEE
10. GEORGIA
11. OREGON
12. NEBRASKA
13. TEXAS A&M
14. AUBURN
15. PENN STATE
16. OKLAHOMA
17. VIRGINIA TECH
18. RED RIVER SHOWDOWN
19. WASHINGTON
20. COLORADO
21. UCLA
22. ARMY

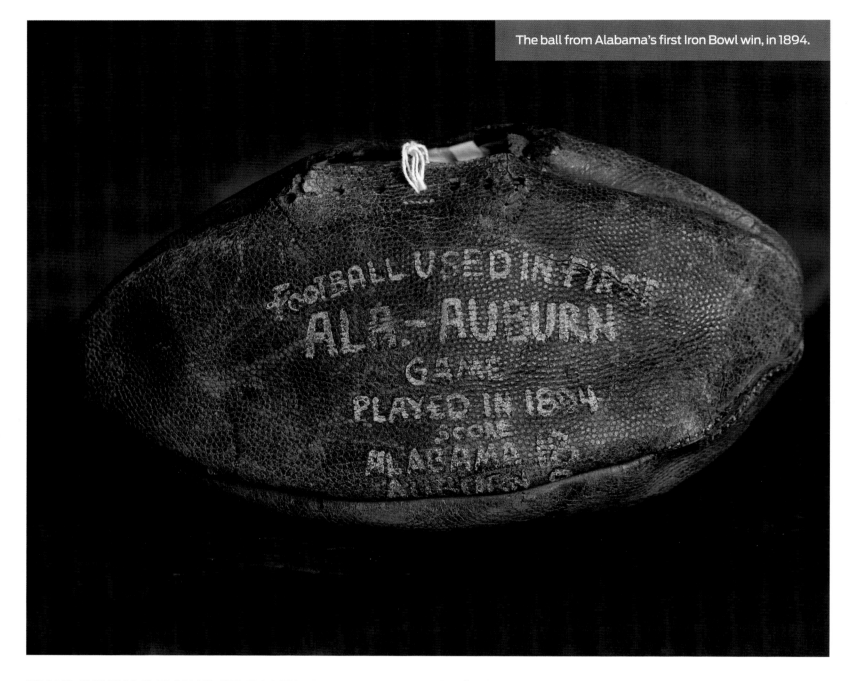

The ball from Alabama's first Iron Bowl win, in 1894.

THIS BOOK DRAWS FROM THE EFFORTS of a legion of SPORTS ILLUSTRATED writers, editors, reporters and photographers who have covered the sport of college football since the magazine's inception in 1954; COLLEGE FOOTBALL'S GREATEST would not have been possible without them. Special thanks also goes to Karen Carpenter, Prem Kalliat, George Amores, Will Welt, Stephen Skalocky and Ed Truscio for their generous help; and to Dan Larkin and the rest of the Time Inc. Premedia Group for their tireless work on this project.

PHOTO CREDITS

COVER: FRONT (left to right, from top): Chuck Solomon, John Iacono, Damian Strohmeyer, John Biever, Manny Rubio/USA Today Sports, Walter Iooss Jr., Malcolm Emmons/USA Today Sports, Neil Leifer, Damian Strohmeyer, Heinz Kluetmeier, Damian Strohmeyer, Neil Leifer. **BACK** (left to right, from top): James Drake, Bill Frakes, Neil Leifer, David Bergman, Heinz Kluetmeier, Mike Longo/AP, Robert Beck, Tony Tomsic, Simon Bruty, Bill Luster, Bill Frakes. **BACK FLAP:** Mark Kauffman.

SECTION OPENERS: Page 22: John W. McDonough; Page 38: Doug Hoke; Page 54: Joe Robbins; Page 68: Jamie Squire/Getty Images; Page 82: Al Tielemans; Page 96: Bill Frakes; Page 110: John Iacono; Page 124: Al Tielemans; Page 138: Simon Bruty; Page 154: Troy Tuttle/Appalachian State University; Page 168: Robert Beck; Page 184: Bill Frakes; Page 198: John Biever; Page 212: Richard Mackson; Page 226: Marvin Gentry/USA Today Sports; Page 242: Jed Jacobsohn/Getty Images.

ADDITIONAL CREDITS: Page 244: Gary Bogdon; Page 245 (left to right, from top): David E. Klutho, Darren Carroll, John Biever, Doug Benc/Getty Images; Page 246: John Biever; Page 247 (left to right, from top): Bill Frakes, Jeff Haynes, Stanley Leary/Georgia Tech/AP, Tony Gutierrez/AP; Page 248: AP (2); Page 249 (left to right, from top): Courtesy of University of Colorado, John Iacono, Al Tielemans, Manny Millan; Page 250 (left to right, from top): Universal History Archive/UIG/Getty Images, Tristar Pictures/The Everett Collection, Warner Bros. Pictures/The Everett Collection, Universal/The Everett Collection; Page 251: Bill Frakes; Page 252 (from left): Peter F. Aiken/Getty Images, John Biever; Page 253 (from top): Garry L. Jones/AP Beth Hall/USA Today Sports. Page 256: Bill Frakes.

ENDPAPERS: David E. Klutho (front spread), John W. McDonough (2), Bill Frakes (back spread).